★ ★ ★ ★ ★

"Henry 'Hap' Arnold was a critical architect of the U.S. Air Force and a key player in World War II. Bill Yenne writes a primer on this oft-neglected figure, and along the way provides a good introduction not only to the air war but to the roots of the modern American Air Force. His overview of Arnold's life and career will appeal to anyone interested in aviation history or World War II in general."

—**JIM DeFELICE**, author of *American Sniper* and *Omar Bradley: General at War*

★ ★ ★ ★ ★

"Bill Yenne's *Hap Arnold: Inventing the Air Force* takes a complex and wide-ranging subject and makes it a well-written, engaging, and compelling read. This book provides the reader with detail and historical context in a solid account of the rise of American airpower and my grandfather's role at the center of it starting in 1911 and his continuing influence today. Bill Yenne keeps the story moving at a crisp pace and at the same time recounts many of the Arnold family's legendary stories.

But this book is not just focused on Hap. The author brings others, including George Marshall, Franklin D. Roosevelt, General Eisenhower, Winston Churchill, Billy Mitchell, Jimmy Doolittle, and Donald Douglas, into precise focus. This book lays out how U.S. military aviation did not arrive victorious in 1945 by accident or inevitability. The U.S. Army Air Force's amazing rise from a just a few planes and pilots in 1941 to the largest and most powerful air force the world will ever know depended on Hap Arnold's singular ability to engage, persuade, and educate American and world leaders about it. In addition, he had to gain their support to execute his plans at a time of great peril.

This is not simply an 'airplane book.' It shows how winning World War II in the air required a team effort with General Hap Arnold in the left seat, at the controls of U.S. airpower."

—**ROBERT ARNOLD**, author, proprietor of Chandelle Winery in Sonoma, California, and the grandson of both Hap Arnold and Donald Douglas

HAP ARNOLD

HAP ARNOLD

★ ★ ★ ★ ★

INVENTING THE AIR FORCE

BILL YENNE

REGNERY
HISTORY

ISBN 978-1-62157-081-3 (hard cover)
This paperback edition published in 2014, ISBN 978-1-62157-300-5

Library of Congress Cataloging-in-Publication Data

Yenne, Bill, 1949-
  Hap Arnold : inventing the Air Force / Bill Yenne.
    pages cm
  Includes bibliographical references and index.
  ISBN 978-1-62157-300-5 (pbk. : alk. paper)
  1. Arnold, Henry Harley, 1886-1950. 2. United States. Air Force--Officers--Biography. 3. Generals--United States--Biography. 4. Aeronautics, Military--United States--History--20th century. I. Title.
  UG626.2.A76Y46 2014
  358.40092--dc23
  [B]
                                    2014029638

Published in the United States by
Regnery History
An imprint of Regnery Publishing
300 New Jersey Avenue NW
Washington, DC 20001
www.RegneryHistory.com

Manufactured in the United States of America

10 9 8 7 6 5 4 3 2 1

Books are available in quantity for promotional or premium use. For information on discounts and terms, please visit our website: www.Regnery.com.

Distributed to the trade by
Perseus Distribution
250 West 57th Street
New York, NY 10107

CONTENTS

INTRODUCTION

I t is axiomatic that history's great generals and great admirals are usually controversial. For decisions they have made, or for the paths they've followed professionally, most have their detractors, often within their own services. All of the greats, from Grant to Patton, from Bradley to MacArthur, have their critics. However, it is hard to find anyone—at least since the days of George Washington and John Paul Jones—who is more universally admired, even revered, within their own service than Henry Harley Arnold is within the U.S. Air Force.

Having been taught to fly by Wilbur and Orville Wright, Arnold was one of America's first military aviators. He grew up with U.S. Army aviation, and ultimately he became its leader. In 1938, when he became chief of the U.S. Army Air Corps, the air arm was pigeonholed into a minor role within the Army in terms of funding, prestige, and tactical doctrine. Within three years, he had turned it into the autonomous U.S. Army Air Forces, and within the next three, he turned the USAAF into the largest air force in history. At its peak in 1944, Arnold's USAAF had nearly eighty thousand aircraft and 2.4 million men and women in uniform. He, and his personally chosen staff, successfully managed, trained, and deployed this enormous force over six continents. Yet, beyond the mere size of the USAAF, there is the singular vision of a man who could imagine how airpower was the key to victory: the one force that could crush the industrial economies of Germany and Japan and provide the battlefield support that guaranteed victory on the ground. It was no accident but rather Arnold's leadership that ensured the United States achieved air supremacy in 1944—and has held it in every battle America has fought ever since. Logistically, the USAAF Air Transport Command, which was Arnold's brainchild, grew into a global "airline" with more routes than any air service up to that time.

After the war, Arnold became the founding father of the modern United States Air Force. No American general or admiral of the Second World War had such a lasting impact on his branch of the armed services as Arnold had on the Air Force. He organized the Air Force, provided its doctrine of "global vigilance, reach, and power," and gave it his example of dedicated, visionary leadership, all of which have made him one of the greatest—if underappreciated—generals in American history. This book is his story.

CHAPTER 1

EARLY DAYS

When he thought of this being his first and possibly his only airplane ride, he wished that they still had the full two hours to remain in the air. Hoxey held up his hand and opened it twice. Bill then looked at the watch and saw that they had to stay up only ten minutes more to complete the two hours. There seemed to be no reason why they shouldn't stay up even longer, for the engine was running perfectly and, as far as he was concerned, all danger of his sliding off the plane was gone. He hoped that they would stay up for three hours. They flew across the aviation field and Bill saw the upturned faces of the mechanics as they stood in front of the tents. During the first part of their flight other planes had been in the air.

Now and again a plane would come close to theirs and the occupants would wave to them, but now it was getting late and the other planes had landed. Some had already been taken into their tents, others he could see being rolled in. How small they all looked! He could hardly realize that the miniature planes on the ground were in reality as large as the one in which he was riding and the mechanics handling them were truly life-sized men.

Bill figured that with two more turns of the field they would have broken the record. He wondered if Hoxey would land at once or stay up longer. This was by far the most pleasant method of traveling that he had ever experienced. It was better than motorcycling in every way. In the air they were not tied down to roads. They could follow any route which their fancy dictated. No wonder that the birds seemed to enjoy themselves so much when soaring overhead. Hills, trees, villages, fences and rivers were all alike when flying. It was possible to go over them or pass around them, whichever the pilot preferred. How different it was from earthbound travel!

—HENRY HARLEY ARNOLD describing his protagonist's first airplane flight in his novel *Bill Bruce and the Pioneer Aviators*

The birth of the twentieth century, like that of the twenty-first, was accompanied by a simmering sense of excitement that a new form of technology was on the threshold of taking us to a place that most people had never been before. At the turn of the twenty-first century, that place was cyberspace. At the turn of the twentieth, it was the sky.

In each case, that simmering sense of excitement was nurtured among those of a younger generation unencumbered with preconceptions—people who saw a future of possibilities, people whose eyes were focused on human potential, not on impediments to human progress.

Henry Harley Arnold was part of that younger generation. He was not an aviation pioneer, nor was he part of that first generation who clustered around the earliest pioneers, but once bitten by the aviation bug, few young men burned with a greater fever. He would definitely make up for lost time. Despite joining later than most the race to embrace the new technology, it is evident in his Bill Bruce novels that he wished he *had been* among that first generation. That is to say, Henry Harley Arnold wished he had been Bill Bruce, and he lived his life as Bill would have.

Henry Harley Arnold was born on June 25, 1886, on a farm near Merion Square, a town in Montgomery County on Pennsylvania's well-to-do Main Line. When he was five, the town was renamed Gladwyne, the name that appears in most accounts, including his own, as that of his birthplace. Still included in the top ten richest zip codes in America, the Main Line was a fashionable strip of wealthy suburbs stretching northwest of Philadelphia and running parallel to the old, eighteenth-century Lancaster Turnpike (later known as Lancaster Avenue) and the original main line of the Pennsylvania Railroad.

The Arnolds, as well as the Harleys, his mother's family, had been in the area for generations. Though not among the wealthiest strata of Main Line society, the family was comfortably upper-middle class. Henry's father, Dr. Herbert Alonzo Arnold, known later as "Daddy Doc" to his grandchildren, was a country doctor—a general practitioner who made as many house calls to the farms and rural communities of Montgomery County as he did to families on the Main Line. His great-grandfather, Peter Arnold, had emigrated from Germany and had fought in the Revolutionary War.

Henry's mother was Ann Louise Harley Arnold, usually called Louise, known as "Lou" to her husband and later as "Gangy" to her grandchildren. She had four ancestors who had fought in the Revolution, among them Pennsylvania militiaman Henry Harley, her son's namesake.

As a boy, Henry Harley Arnold was known as "Harley," although his mother always called him "Sunny." His eventual nickname, "Hap," came later. The middle of five children, Harley grew up being called "the doctor's second boy." His older siblings were Thomas Herbert and Sophie Elizabeth—called "Betty"—who were born at opposite ends of 1884. The younger boys were Clifford and Price, born in 1888 and 1894, respectively.

Arnold did not write much about his boyhood—though it would seem the basics were fairly typical of boys living in semi-rural, late nineteenth-century America: walking to school, learning to ride and to shoot, attending services at the Baptist church on Sundays. He relates just one childhood anecdote in his memoirs, and that was to illustrate an early interest in science. At the age of three, he tried to float a horseshoe in a rain barrel. When the inevitable happened, he went into the water after the horseshoe and was rescued from drowning by his five-year-old brother, Tom.

During the Civil War, Dr. Arnold's father, Thomas Griffith Arnold, a Montgomery County nailmaker, served briefly with Company I of the 43rd Regiment of the Pennsylvania Militia during the Civil War. He was mustered in on July 6, 1863, in the immediate aftermath of the Battle of Gettysburg, which was fought in Pennsylvania. He was discharged as a sergeant five weeks later. In 1898, when Harley was eleven, the United States went to war with Spain, and his father suspended his rural practice to volunteer for service as a U.S. Army surgeon with the Pennsylvania Volunteer Cavalry, which saw action in Puerto Rico. Dr. Arnold was on active duty for only a few months, but he remained in the Pennsylvania National Guard, eventually attaining the rank of lieutenant colonel. It was that experience, Hap Arnold later surmised, that led Dr. Arnold to plan on a military career for his eldest son Tom, while Hap (or Harley as he then was) would be destined for the clergy.

Tom, however, had other ideas. He announced that he wanted to attend Pennsylvania State to study electrical engineering. With Tom intractable, Dr. Arnold decided that Harley would go to West Point. Although his academic career to date had been less than stellar, Harley placed second among Pennsylvania candidates taking the West Point entrance exam. The problem was there was only one slot available. But when it was determined that the front-runner was secretly married, something that the academy forbade of its cadets, Henry Harley Arnold entered West Point as a plebe in July of 1903.

At West Point, Arnold fell into a routine that he later observed to be "strikingly" unchanged since Ulysses S. Grant had attended as a member of the class of 1843. The one notable change was the introduction of football in 1890.

Arnold went out for football himself, playing substitute fullback, and he was a shot-putter in intramural track and field. A horseman all his life, he was part of the polo squad, rode whenever possible, and imagined a career in the cavalry. Academically, he was middling, placing eighty-third out of 136 cadets during his first year and graduating sixty-sixth out of a class of 111 on June 14, 1907.

"After I had once learned how to study in my Plebe Year, in 1903, I skated along without too much effort in a spot just below the middle of the Class," he wrote in his memoirs. His diary noted he was "scanty in regard to my military progress. (I never even made Cadet Corporal.)" He stayed busy in other ways, including courting a banker's daughter, Eleanor Alexander Pool (her father was a patient of Dr. Arnold), and becoming a member of the Black Hand Society, an organization of pranksters that kept him in trouble. The climax of his membership in the Black Hand was a spectacular, unauthorized midnight fireworks display on New Year's Eve 1907. As punishment, he was kept confined to his room on visitors' day.

Through it all, Arnold had his sights set on the cavalry. For many cadets, the cavalry spelled glory. As Arnold wrote, "The thing that dominated the cadet lives of one little group of us at least was—the cavalry! That was why we were here! It was what we lived for—our whole future! The Horse Cavalry! It was the last romantic thing left on earth. The galloping charge! Indian fighting!"

For four years Arnold assumed that when he graduated in 1907 as a second lieutenant, he *would be* commissioned into the cavalry. When his paperwork arrived, he tossed it aside, sure that his hopes had been rewarded. His mother had to break the news to him. Second Lieutenant Henry Harley Arnold, U.S. Army, had been assigned to the *infantry*! It was his academic standing that had cursed him. Those at the top of the class had a choice and were usually groomed for the Corps of Engineers. The bottom of the class was rewarded with the infantry.

Lieutenant Arnold grumbled, and his father, the former Pennsylvania cavalry officer, complained to longtime Pennsylvania senator Boies Penrose, who complained to the U.S. Army adjutant general, Major General Fred Ainsworth. "Orders are orders," Ainsworth told Penrose when Boies and the Arnolds came to meet with him. "The only person who could possibly make a change is the Secretary of War." That was not going to happen if for no other reason than that the secretary of war, William Howard Taft, was on an inspection tour of the Philippines.

Arnold *was* offered a choice of duty station, but his mind drew a blank. For four years, it had fixated only upon the *cavalry* posts in the American West—Fort Apache, Fort Crook, Fort Custer, Fort Wingate, and Fort Riley. Then he seized inspiration. If the secretary of war was in the Philippines, Arnold would go after him and maybe get the assignment he wanted: "I blurted out that I would like to go to the Philippines."

The adjutant general said he thought that could be arranged.

After a cross-country train trip and a few weeks in San Francisco, Lieutenant Arnold departed on November 7, 1907, aboard a steamer bound for Manila, where Taft had opened the First Philippine Assembly three weeks earlier. As might have been anticipated, the young officer and the future president never crossed paths in Manila.

Arnold's youthful naiveté was further underscored by his decision to postpone the purchase of a tropical weight uniform until he arrived in the Philippines, where it would be cheaper—not anticipating that the journey *to* Manila would take him through the sticky heat of the tropics. The only clothing he had with him was his heavy wool uniform, which became a fetid, sweat-soaked torture.

Shipping out from San Francisco, Arnold was assigned to guard a large quantity of currency destined for the Philippine colonial government. When he disembarked in Manila on December 6, he supervised the loading of the currency boxes onto two carts. The cart drivers then shot off in opposite directions; Arnold tried to pursue one of the carts but lost it in traffic. By the end of the day, however, he learned that both consignments had been delivered to the correct destination, and a receipt was waiting for him.

Lieutenant Henry Harley Arnold reported for duty with the 29th Infantry Regiment at Fort William McKinley, located immediately south of Manila on the Pasig River. The 29th Infantry had seen plenty of combat from 1902 to 1904, during the Philippine Insurrection, but had spent the last three years on garrison duty in Utah and Arizona and had returned for equally mundane garrison duty in the now-pacified Philippines. Looking for something more exciting, Arnold volunteered for temporary duty with the 20th Infantry Regiment, which was assisting the Corps of Engineers with mapping projects. Arnold's survey team was based in Mabalacat, in the mountains due north of Manila Bay.

Already, in 1908, there were fears of Japanese expansion into the Philippines. Arnold later recalled,

> We really expected Japan to invade the Philippines at any minute. We were ready to hike to Baguio and make a last stand. Men slept with two hundred rounds of ammunition at the foot of their beds. This feeling was not the hysteria of greenhorns or recruits (many of the soldiers who felt it had grown brown in the Philippine service), nor was it whipped up by any propaganda trend. The Japanese, methodically and almost openly, were making war preparations all around us.

His team of men helping the engineers with their topographical maps of Luzon was constantly running into Japanese photographers, itinerant Japanese "peddlers," and Japanese "botanists." He described the latter as being "solemnly absorbed by the flora of the island, whose best specimens always happened to be growing just where we had set up our instruments."

After the Luzon project was finished, Arnold was assigned to help map the island of Corregidor in Manila Bay, which became America's last-stand fortress against the invading Japanese in 1942.

Arnold's tour of duty in the Philippines, which he later described as "unexpectedly exciting," came to an end in June 1909 as the 29th Infantry was reassigned to Fort Jay on Governors Island in New York Harbor. But with money in his pocket—living in the Philippines was cheap—and with no urgency in his getting to New York, he decided to spend some time and money seeing a little more of the world. He chose to return to the United States, not sailing eastward back across the Pacific, but westward—around the world.

He set sail on a commercial ship from Manila to Hong Kong, and then from Singapore to the Suez Canal. His fellow passengers, he recalled, ranged from "friendly British officers coming home on leave from India and Burma, to the British career diplomat returning from thirty years' service in the Far East, and to the cocky German officers bringing their battalion of infantry home from Tientsin … [to] American school teachers, each with her Baedeker, [and] the Dutch father who had guarded his twenty-four-year-old son so anxiously ever since the two red-light 'ladies' had come aboard at Singapore." He recalled in his memoirs that dinner conversation often turned to the confidence expressed by the British officers that the English Channel effectively isolated Britain from the tribulations of continental Europe—something that would be proved wrong in only five years' time.

CHAPTER 2

A YOUNG AIRMAN TAKES TO THE AIR

As Lieutenant Henry Harley Arnold sailed toward the Suez Canal, several well-known aviators announced that they were going to compete for a prize offered by London's *Daily Mail*: £1,000 to anyone who could fly across the English Channel. One of the competitors was Louis Blériot, a dashing pilot, aeronautical engineer, aircraft builder, and the inventor of first practical automobile headlight.

At sunrise on July 25, 1909, Blériot entered the cockpit of his monoplane and took off from a field near Calais. After a thirty-six-minute flight, he circled Dover Castle twice and then touched down at nearby Northfall Meadow. Blériot collected his £1,000 check and returned to Paris a hero. His Type XI monoplane, meanwhile, was put on display, suspended above a street near the Place de l'Opéra.

Among the thousands of pedestrians who passed by and saw this airplane was a young American lieutenant on his way home from the Far East.

"I was walking along, taking in the sights and sounds and smells of Paris, and, all of a sudden, there it was, a queer contraption hanging overhead," Lieutenant Arnold wrote in his memoirs. Using his "best West Point French," he deduced that this was the famous Blériot flying machine.

It was the first airplane that he had ever seen.

A manned hot air balloon, also French by coincidence, had put in an appearance at West Point, but Henry Harley Arnold had never before laid eyes on a heavier-than-air craft. He later wrote in retrospect that he should have been impressed, that this moment should have been some sort of epiphany in his life, but instead, that which he described in his memoirs as a "frail, heroic freak" of a monoplane would take on importance only in retrospect.

"I'll confess I hadn't any blinding vision of the future of Airpower at this moment," Arnold remembered,

> but one thought I did have was probably as good as anybody else's who looked at Blériot plane that summer. I thought: "If one man could do it once, what if a lot of men did it together at the same time? What happens then to England's Splendid Isolation?" That was no clairvoyant vision, either. If Blériot's flight hadn't happened to be across the English Channel I probably wouldn't have thought even that much about his flying machine. But the Channel, and England's isolation, had been the refrain of my whole trip from Hong Kong to Genoa, night after night.

At the time, he could not yet comprehend that the airplane would one day end America's own "splendid isolation," its heretofore secure separation from the rest of the world by two great oceans.

He added that it was only after the start of World War II that the "heroic freak" could at last be seen for what it was, "the forerunner of a human instrument that, for good or evil, in war and peace, was to change the face of the earth."

Two weeks after his seeing the Blériot Type XI suspended above a Parisian street, he reported for duty at Governors Island where, he wrote, "My worst fears were immediately realized. Governors Island was so flat that it wasn't even fun to ride a horse on it, when a second lieutenant could get one, and the life there was flatter than the terrain."

Riding a horse might not have been fun there, but the flat terrain of the 172-acre island made it ideal for aviation. During the first week of October 1909, the island was the site of New York City's first air show. The occasion was the Hudson-Fulton Celebration, commemorating the three hundredth anniversary of Henry Hudson's sailing into New York and the centennial of Robert Fulton's bringing the first successful commercial steamship into New York Harbor.

Two of the founding fathers of American aviation, Wilbur Wright and Glenn Curtiss, arrived for demonstration flights. Among the spectators was young Lieutenant Henry Harley Arnold. He spoke with Wright, Curtiss, and several other pilots, and later fictionalized this experience in his novel *Bill Bruce and the Pioneer Aviators*.

In the six years since Wilbur Wright and his brother Orville had made their first powered flights at Kill Devil Hills in North Carolina, aviation had moved from being a curiosity, to something of a sport, to something more, including something with possible military applications. The British government, for instance, contacted the Wright brothers soon after their first flights became public, asking to buy their flying machine. The Wrights declined, hoping instead to interest officials in Washington.

The War Department, however, reacted with skepticism and ambivalence. Government officials in Washington were still smarting from the Smithsonian Institution's failed attempt to sponsor the first powered flight. The recipient of their largess had been Samuel Pierpont Langley, whose last spectacular failure, on December 8, 1903, had occurred just nine days before the Wrights—a pair of self-financed bicycle mechanics from Dayton, Ohio—had succeeded spectacularly.

It was not until the Aero Club of America went directly to President Theodore Roosevelt that the War Department was prodded to act, establishing the Aeronautical Division of the Signal Corps in 1907 to oversee matters pertaining to the military application of "ballooning, air machines and all kindred subjects."

In September 1908, Lieutenant Frank Lahm became the first U.S. Army officer to fly in an airplane, and Lieutenant Thomas Selfridge became the first U.S. Army officer to die in a crash. Both had been passengers in aircraft flown by and owned by Orville Wright, who survived the crash that killed Selfridge.

The Army finally bought a plane of its own, a single Wright Military Flyer, and in the fall of 1909, Wilbur trained Lieutenant Lahm, Lieutenant Frederic Humphreys, and Lieutenant Benjamin "Benny" Foulois to fly the Military Flyer at a field in College Park, Maryland. On November 5, Lahm and Humphreys, both with about three hours of flying time, crashed. The plane was totaled, the men survived, and Lahm and Humphreys, who had only been on temporary duty with the Aeronautical Division, were recalled to their regular assignments.

The Navy actually seemed more interested in aviation than the Army. In 1909 Eugene Ely, a civilian, became the first man to land on the deck of a warship, and in January of 1911, Lieutenant Theodore

"Spuds" Ellyson reported for duty as the U.S. Navy's first aviator. Taught to fly by Glenn Curtiss at Hammondsport, New York, Ellyson executed both a takeoff and a landing from the deck of a battleship. This feat sparked a bit more interest in the Army, which did not want to get left behind, and Curtiss did his part. His winter flying school at North Island in San Diego, founded in 1910, offered free instruction to both Army and Navy officers. He naturally hoped that this would result in the services buying Curtiss airplanes.

Arnold was not yet among the thirty men from the U.S. Army who volunteered for the flight school. At the time, his ambition was not to fly but rather the more practical desire of earning a promotion to first lieutenant. Promotion in the peacetime Army was slow; officers often languished in the same grade for years. But Arnold had a plan.

He applied for a transfer to the Ordnance Department, where, he heard, the *lowest* rank was first lieutenant. While waiting to hear back, he received a letter from the War Department. It was an invitation from the Signal Corps to volunteer for flight training. Arnold's commanding officer cautioned him that it was an invitation to commit suicide. But for a twenty-four-year-old second lieutenant, it promised an escape from the monotony of Governors Island.

Second Lieutenant Henry Harley Arnold, late of the 29th Infantry, left New York's Penn Station with a copy of War Department Special Order 95 tucked into his pocket. Dated April 21, 1911, it officially assigned him, as well as Second Lieutenant Thomas "Tommy" Milling, late of the 15th Cavalry, to "aeronautical duty with the Signal Corps," and ordered them to proceed to Dayton, Ohio, "for the purpose of undergoing a course of instruction in operating the Wright airplane." It was a simple scrap of paper that would change the course of American military aviation.

Who to contact when they reached Dayton?

Wilbur and Orville Wright.

★   ★   ★   ★   ★

It was when he arrived at the Wright factory in Dayton—with its smell of oil and gasoline, the sounds of sputtering engines, the sight of brilliant mechanics and brave pilots, the great men of aviation, about whom he had read, standing around in coveralls—that Henry Harley Arnold finally realized that aviation was his future. Here was a new romance to displace his old longing for the cavalry.

In addition to their factory in Dayton, the Wrights owned "the Field." It was a former cow pasture, nine miles from town, and fenced to keep the cattle from reclaiming it. It was at a place then called Simms Station, later known as Huffman Field or Huffman Prairie after the family that owned most of the land in the area.

What the Field had in its favor was that it was level, generally smooth, and free of obstructions. It was the Edwards Air Force Base of its era. The Wrights had made their pioneer flight from Kill Devil Hills near Kitty Hawk, North Carolina, because of its favorable wind conditions. But now, having established that their aircraft could fly, the Wrights did most of their flight testing and pilot training closer to their Dayton home.

When the two lieutenants arrived in Ohio, they met many of the civilian pilots whose names, while no longer household words, were important to the early years of American aviation. Hanging around at the Wright factory or out at the Field was nineteen-year-old Walter Brookins, the first pupil Orville had trained to fly, as well as Frank Coffyn, Phil Parmalee, Cliff Turpin, and Al Welsh, all of them working as Wright test pilots and instructors. Also on hand were Leonard Bonney and Howard Gill, both anxious to become exhibition flyers. Arnold met Lieutenant John Rodgers of the U.S. Navy and his cousin, Calbraith "Uncle Cal" Rodgers, who would later make the first transcontinental flight from New York to California.

The two young officers got to know Wilbur and Orville quite well and were often invited to Sunday dinner, where they met Wilbur and Orville's brother Lorin, sister Katherine, and stern father, Milton Wright, known to all as "the Bishop" because of the office he held in the United Brethren of Christ. Arnold agreed with Wright biographers who have theorized that the Bishop had inspired his sons with a flying toy that he had given them when they were children. In 1910, during his only flight in an airplane, the Bishop is said to have ordered Orville to "Go higher, higher!" Arnold thought the brothers unassuming, a little shy, and good-natured. "They never took themselves half so seriously as we took them," Arnold wrote in his memoirs. "Still, to Milling and me, sitting at their Sunday dinner table and listening to their quiet stories, what they had done was a miracle,—and it is a miracle to me today. Without any formal, scientific training whatever, two 'ordinary' young Americans from an ordinary town in the state of Ohio had not only grasped and advanced the whole known science of aerodynamics—they had become its admitted masters, even more appreciated in Europe than at home."

Arnold's first flight came on May 3, 1911, at the Field. He flew as a passenger of the Wright B2, with Al Welsh as the instructor pilot. It lasted only seven minutes, but it was followed by a five-minute second flight.

On a twelve-minute flight the next day, Welsh let Arnold get a feel for the controls, and by his tenth flight, the young student was handling the controls unaided. With another ten flights under his belt over the next few days, Arnold made the first of several unaided landings, duly recorded in his logbook with Welsh's notations.

After three hours and forty-eight minutes of flight time, Arnold's first solo flight came on May 13, five days after Tommy Milling had soloed.

"You can learn to ride a horse by reading about it, or by standing by and watching a horse jump around in a pasture, but you will never learn as well either of those ways as you will if you get on the horse and ride it," Wilbur Wright told Bill Bruce, Arnold's protagonist in his novel of pioneer aviators. He probably said the same to young Lieutenant Arnold.

Arnold and Milling learned more than how to fly a plane; they learned how a plane was built. This was essential because the Army not only lacked full-time pilots, it did not have any mechanics or ground crew. For Arnold and Milling, military aviation was equal parts flying and understanding the *mechanics* of flight, and they were responsible for two early innovations: Milling developed a standard seat belt design, and Arnold was the first Army pilot to wear goggles.

"The first goggles worn by Army airmen came as the result of a bug's hitting me in the eye as I was landing my plane," Arnold reminisced.

> On this particular flight, soon after I left Simms Station, I was coming back into the field when a bug hit me in the eye and left one of its transparent wings sticking to my eyeball. The pain was terrific; blinded by tears I could scarcely see to make my landing. As a matter of fact, it was some days before the doctors were able to find that transparent wing and remove it. The possibility of being rammed dead by a bug had not occurred to us before. After that we wore goggles.

Aviation was still a work in progress.

On July 6, 1911, Arnold and Milling received Fédération Aéronautique Internationale (FAI) pilot certificates, then the international standard for accreditation of pilots. One might say they had "earned their wings," although the U.S. Army's precursor to actual metal "wings," the military aviator's badge, was not introduced until 1912. As Hap Arnold's grandson Robert pointed out to me, none of

the signatories on Hap Arnold's military aviator's license, which
Robert still has framed on his wall, was a pilot. Arnold and Milling
were ordered to College Park, Maryland, where the Army was establishing its first official airfield and where, Arnold and Milling soon
discovered, they were the only two men on flight duty in the entire
service. Their predecessors either were dead or had been transferred
to other jobs, and it was not clear what Arnold and Milling were
expected to do. As Arnold noted, "The Army admitted now that the
airplane could fly, even if it didn't know yet quite what to do with
it."

They started by unpacking Signal Corps No.1, shipped from
Dayton by rail, and using it to teach their boss, the head of the Signal Corps Aeronautical Division, Captain Charles de Forest Chandler, and the division's adjutant, Lieutenant Roy Kirtland, how to
fly. Chandler had been an Army balloon pilot but had never soloed
in a heavier-than-air craft.

Flight times at the new Signal Corps Aviation School were usually in the early morning and late afternoon, when there was less air
turbulence. Between flights, the military aviators manned desks in
the Signal Corps wing at the War Department headquarters in
nearby Washington, D.C., where, initially at least, the pilots were
considered celebrities. They were recognized in restaurants and
beset by groupies at the airfield, where, if the *Los Angeles Times* of
December 17, 1911, is to be believed, Arnold was known, however
briefly, as "Silk Hat Harry" (the nickname did not stick).

Arnold provided flight training to new military aviators while
also establishing a series of firsts. In September 1911, for instance,
he became the first American pilot to carry mail. He also set a series
of world altitude records. The day after receiving his FAI certificate,
Arnold set an altitude record of 3,260 feet. Within the next eleven

months, he broke it twice, flying to 4,167 feet on August 18, 1911, and to 6,540 feet on June 1, 1912.

The Army authorized its young fliers to perform in motion pictures to promote military aviation. Arnold became a movie star of sorts, being featured as a pilot in the early silent films *The Military Air Scout* (1911) and *The Elopement* (1912). According to U.S. Air Force historian General John Huston, it was while working with the movie people that the good-natured Arnold earned the nickname "Happy," soon shortened to "Hap."

Flying was still a dangerous business. In July 1912, Arnold and Lieutenant Roy Kirtland, trying to fly a Burgess-Wright seaplane nonstop from Salem, Massachusetts, to Bridgeport, Connecticut, which would have set a distance record, were grounded near Plymouth by weather. Taking off the next day, the seaplane was forced into a crash landing on the water. The pilots were injured; the seaplane suffered a damaged wing. As Arnold recalled, "As we floated away toward the Atlantic, a sailboat came out manned by two [elderly] veterans from the Soldiers' Home at Plymouth. They approached the plane so closely I could almost touch them from my position on the tip of the wing, where I was trying to keep the half-floating aircraft from losing balance and going to the bottom of the bay. They sailed around us without a word, and then calmly sailed back to their dock." Eventually, the coast guard arrived and towed the damaged aircraft to Plymouth Rock.

But even with the occasional mishap, Arnold was making his mark as a pilot. He was the first recipient of the Clarence Hungerford Mackay trophy for the meritorious flight of the year. In this case, it was a "long distance" flight from College Park, Maryland, to Fort Myer, Virginia, in October 1912 that included spotting camouflaged troops on the ground. The Mackay Trophy is still awarded annually and is one of the most prestigious awards in American military aviation.

Among Arnold's duties at the War Department was monitoring dispatches from war zones, including the First and Second Balkan Wars of 1912 and 1913 and Italy's campaign in Libya, the first instance of aerial bombing in warfare. But while American airmen tested weapons and talked about arming planes, Arnold recalled that "older officers said, 'No, no, there is no such idea.' The plane would remain a reconnaissance vehicle." This shortsightedness turned up again in 1911 when a former Army officer named Riley Scott invented a crude bombsight, using a small telescope and a table to calculate speed and altitude. Arnold observed that it offered better precision than just tossing bombs out of a plane, but the Army did not buy it. The following year, Scott sold it in Europe, and during World War I, bombsights based on Scott's design were used by the Germans.

In November 1912, the aviators of the Aeronautical Division participated in the most intensive coordinated air-ground exercises yet conducted by the U.S. Army. During these exercises at Fort Riley, Kansas, Lieutenant Arnold was one of the first pilots to communicate with ground forces via radio to direct artillery fire. Before this, a pilot would scribble his observations on a colored paper card, attach it to a weight, and drop it to a soldier on horseback, who would take it to the command post; even after this test, the use of radio was still limited.

Arnold almost did not survive the exercises at Fort Riley. On November 5, he was flying with an observer, A. L. P. "Sandy" Sands, when, as Arnold wrote,

> the plane spun completely around in a small 360-degree circle. As we started to plunge down he looked back quickly, thinking one of the propeller chains had broken. It hadn't. Now in a whistling vertical nose dive, I took in everything, as you do at such a time. Everything was all

right, nothing broken, my hands doing all the right things on the controls. Nevertheless, we were diving straight down without a chance. My observer didn't realize this and was taking photos. Somehow, after every frantic yank and twist I could make, just a few feet over the ground I managed to pull the plane out of the dive.

Arnold was lucky. There was a mounting list of military aviators who had died in crashes, many of them Arnold's friends. Al Welsh, the man who had taught him to fly, died in a crash. His West Point classmate, Lewis Rockwell, had been killed a few weeks before Arnold had gone to Fort Riley.

"If I had not been as high as I was, I would have never gotten out alive," he admitted in a letter to Captain Chandler of the Aeronautical Division dated two days later. "I cannot even look at a machine in the air without feeling that some accident is going to happen to it. For the past year and a half I have been flying in almost any kind of weather at almost any time. That being the case, it would take some awful strain to put me out of commission the way this has."

He asked that the chief of the Aeronautical Division relieve him of flying duties.

CHAPTER 3

A YOUNG OFFICER ON THE CAREER LADDER

O n November 15, 1912, ten days after skillfully pulling his
aircraft out of a deadly nosedive over the Kansas prairie,
Second Lieutenant Henry Harley Arnold was "flying a desk"
in Washington, D.C., as assistant to Major Edgar Russel,
soon to be named head of the Signal Corps Aeronautical
Division. Unlike Captain Chandler, who took command of the 1st
Aero Squadron (established by the War Department in March 1913),
Russel was not a pilot, but by the end of 1912, neither was Hap
Arnold.

Arnold assumed his flying days were behind him. "In those
days," he later recalled, "you didn't plan to continue flying after you
were married—unless you were an optimist," and by the spring of
1913, marriage was on his mind.

Blond, blue-eyed Eleanor Alexander Pool had first met Harley in 1907, during his last year at West Point. But when Arnold left for the Philippines, "Bee," as she was known, went to study in Germany.

"For her time she was more highly educated than most women," Robert Arnold told me. "She read German and spoke German fluently" and was "certified to teach in German schools. She danced with the Kaiser before World War I. Prussians fought duels over her."

Hap and Bee reconnected around Christmas in 1912, and in April 1913, shortly after Hap received his long-awaited silver first lieutenant's bars, Bee visited him in Washington. In place of the unpolished and clumsy cadet of 1907, she now saw a dashing, even if deskbound, aviator with several world records and a Mackay Trophy.

He proposed, and she accepted, just as she was about to board the train back to Philadelphia. He gave her his West Point class ring in lieu of an engagement ring, and a week later, he formally asked Sidney Pool for his daughter's hand. The cheerful banker told Arnold that his daughter could marry anyone she wished, so long as it wasn't a "goddamn foreigner." She had previously dated an Italian her father did not like.

The wedding took place on September 10, 1913, at the First Unitarian Church in Philadelphia, with Tommy Milling as best man, and the bride's younger sister, Lois, as maid of honor. The teetotaling Arnolds, who had reluctantly accepted his daughter-in-law's refusal to become a Baptist, insisted that the reception at the Pools' home remain "dry." The Pools, who were light to moderate drinkers, surreptitiously served booze in Mr. Pool's study upstairs. When one of the guests got out of hand and Dr. Arnold found out, it soured relations between the doctor and his patient (and newly acquired in-law) for many years to come.

After spending their honeymoon aboard an Army transport ship bound for Panama, Hap and Bee returned to Hap's new post with the 9th Infantry Regiment at Fort Thomas in Kentucky. After this brief assignment, they traveled to the Philippines, where Hap reported for duty with the 13th Infantry at Fort William McKinley on January 5, 1914. It was here, a year later, that their daughter, Lois Elizabeth Arnold, was born on January 17, 1915.

The hot, muggy weather was hard on Bee, and shortly after giving birth, she suffered a severe intestinal disorder, which the doctors could not accurately diagnose. Arnold sent his wife to Baguio, in the cooler, higher elevations of northern Luzon. The illness was further complicated by a botched operation that almost killed her. She was left with intermittent pain for the rest of her life, and permanent, albeit subtle, damage that would contribute to her death six decades later.

As during Arnold's last tour of duty in the Philippines, American officers talked often about a possible Japanese invasion, and even war-gamed it. In fact, during maneuvers south of Manila designed to simulate a Japanese attack, Arnold made the most important professional connection of his career. Halting his infantry company for a rest, he chatted with a young lieutenant from another company. The officer was studying a map and sketching an attack plan with the skill, Arnold thought, of a lieutenant colonel. Arnold was so impressed that he told his wife that Lieutenant George Catlett Marshall would be chief of staff of the Army one day—a prediction that became true in 1939.

The friendship formed that day at Batangas would blossom into one of the most successful internal alliances in the history of the U.S. Army's high command. During World War II, the two men, by then both wearing four-star—and ultimately five-star—general's rank, would be close collaborators at the Pentagon and two of the half dozen most influential architects of the strategic direction of the American victory.

In January 1916, Hap Arnold and his family were steaming across the Pacific from the Philippines, headed for an infantry assignment at Madison Barracks in upstate New York when he received a radiogram from the adjutant general asking whether Arnold would volunteer for duty with the Aviation Section—the successor of the Aeronautical Division (in July 1914)—of the Signal Corps. A second radiogram elaborated: "If you apply for detail in the Aviation Section, Signal Corps, you will come in with the rank of Captain. If not, you will be detailed and come in with the rank of First Lieutenant."

Arnold immediately detected the hand of an old friend, Major William Lendrum "Billy" Mitchell. Arnold had met Billy Mitchell years before in Washington:

> One day a sharp-faced, eager young captain of the General Staff came in to see me. He was not a flyer himself, but was working on a paper concerning the military future of aviation which he intended to present to the Army War College. He had recently returned from Alaska, where he had apparently put in a highly interesting and most observant tour of duty. Afterward he had been in Japan where he had a look at the Japanese Army. He said the Japanese Air Force was bigger than ours—it had ten planes. His questions about the air were intelligent and to the point; in fact, it was he who did most of the talking, asking questions only to get concrete facts and accurate data. It seemed that as far back as April 1906, he had written in the *Cavalry Journal* that "Conflicts, no doubt, will be carried out in the future in the air, on the surface of the earth and water, and under the earth and water."

Arnold was fascinated with Mitchell as an advocate of military aviation, but the admiration ran both ways. Mitchell had been impressed with Arnold both as an airman and as an officer. If anything, he had more faith in Arnold's future as both than did Arnold himself, steering him back into Army aviation in 1916.

On May 20, after serving two months with the 3rd Infantry, Captain Arnold reported for duty as the Aviation Section supply officer at Rockwell Field (named after Arnold's deceased West Point classmate) on North Island in San Diego, California. Arnold had to face down his fear of flying. He flew again, albeit not alone, on October 18, determined to get into the air daily for fifteen or twenty minutes, gradually reacquainting himself with the controls. Finally, on November 26, he flew solo for the first time in just over forty-eight months.

A lot had happened with U.S. Army aviation in those four years. For one thing, the rickety, first-generation Wright Flyers had been superseded by more modern types, including the first of the ubiquitous Curtiss JN series aircraft, the famous "Jennys," which would be standard equipment for the U.S. Army for the better part of a decade, and that would see action in the punitive expedition against Pancho Villa in 1916. Then there was the size of the service. The Aeronautical Division had an average of twenty-five men assigned to it between 1908 and 1912. When the organization became the Aviation Section in 1914, it was 122-men strong. By 1916, it had 311 men, including about twenty-five qualified pilots. While the division was growing, more than a dozen countries had larger air arms than the United States—and aerial combat, once merely theoretical, was now a common occurrence in the "Great War" raging in Europe since 1914. By force of necessity, the European powers had better-designed aircraft and engines.

American pilots were not yet in mortal combat—except for the American volunteer pilots fighting for the French in the Lafayette Escadrille—but flying could still be hazardous enough. On January 10, 1917, an aircraft piloted by Lieutenant W. A. Robertson took off from Rockwell Field bound for El Centro, California, about one hundred miles inland, in what should have been relatively routine flight, even though, as Arnold noted, aircraft navigation was not easy, with compasses that were "still not too good" and maps that were "only fair." On board as a passenger was an artillery officer, Colonel Harry Bishop.

When the plane did not arrive on time, Robertson's fellow pilots, Arnold included, thought they should fly out in search of the missing plane. Their commander, Colonel Edgar Gorrell, thought otherwise and forbade such a mission. Arnold deliberately disobeyed orders, went to look for the missing men, and was reprimanded. In his report, Gorrell called Arnold a "trouble maker," and "not suited for an independent command." Robertson's plane had in fact crashed in the desert, but both he and Colonel Bishop survived the crash and an arduous nine-day hike to Arizona.

Within a matter of weeks, thanks perhaps to the hand of Billy Mitchell, Arnold was once again reassigned. On January 30, 1917, the day after the birth of his first son, Henry Harley Arnold Jr., Captain Arnold was en route to the Panama Canal Zone, tasked with locating a suitable airfield for the new 7th Aero Squadron.

The Aviation Section had four squadrons located within the United States, plus the 2nd Aero Squadron in the Philippines and the 6th Aero Squadron in Hawaii. The 7th Aero Squadron would be activated in Panama as soon as Hap Arnold could find it a base, which meant navigating the strong and divergent opinions of the Signal Corps, the Coast Artillery, and the U.S. Navy. Major General Clarence Edwards, the senior officer in the Canal Zone, told Arnold the decision should be made not in Panama but in Washington by General Leonard Wood, the commanding general of the U.S. Army Atlantic Department.

On April 6, Arnold was aboard a steamer en route to Washington, D.C., when the ship's radio operator received the news that President Woodrow Wilson had signed a declaration of war against Germany, which had waged unrestricted submarine warfare against American ships and even secretly proposed an alliance with Mexico to attack the United States (this was in the intercepted "Zimmermann telegram" between German foreign minister Arthur Zimmermann and the German ambassador in Mexico). On April 2, Wilson had declared to Congress that neutrality was no longer an option: "The world must be made safe for democracy."

The first task for Arnold, however, was simply to make it back safely to the United States. "We had read about darkened ships, lifeboats, and all that," Arnold wrote later. "But our skipper hadn't had any first-hand experience with wartime sailing. He turned out all lights, swung our lifeboats, and the ship crept on to New York. It was an eerie feeling, but at the same time, a relief. Now we really knew where we stood as far as Germany was concerned."

To Arnold's relief, finding the site for an airbase in Panama was no longer a priority. Instead, he was made executive officer of the Signal Corps Aviation Section, under Lieutenant Colonel John Bennett at the War Department, which had the staggering challenge of raising, training, and equipping an American Expeditionary Force that could fight effectively in Europe. To put that task into perspective, the U.S. Army of April 1917 was essentially a 127,000-man constabulary force, which had most recently seen action chasing Mexican bandits along the border and keeping the peace in the Philippines. The war in Europe was something different altogether. To take one compelling statistic as an example, the number of French army casualties in April 1917 equaled the entire manpower of the regular U.S. Army. But it was not just the scale of the war in Europe, it was the technology. The United States had little experience with the ghastly sophistication of modern industrial warfare.

The most optimistic American estimates concluded that an American Expeditionary Force of five hundred thousand would not be available for nearly a year, while the British General Staff estimated that only half that number could be in the field by the middle of 1918. In fact, in the space of nineteen months, the number of personnel in the U.S. Army would rise to 4,057,000. Two million American troops, soldiers and Marines, were sent to France as the American Expeditionary Force (AEF). In the closing months of the war, the AEF led offensive operations against the best-defended sectors of the Western Front, and by November 1918, the last month of the war, occupied more of the Western Front than all the forces of the British Empire combined.

By Arnold's estimate, in May 1917 the Army had fifty-five airplanes, none of them configured for combat and most of them outdated by European standards, and twenty-six qualified pilots. The Army was charged to have 4,500 aircraft, five thousand pilots, and fifty thousand mechanics in France within a year, and it was Arnold's job to make this happen. The expansion plan he and his staff drafted carried an unprecedented price tag of $639,241,452. As Arnold noted, this compared to an annual average U.S. Army aviation budget of $100,000. Although the General Staff looked aghast at the request by the upstart airmen, Congress did not. It was passed on July 21 and signed by President Wilson three days later.

Against the backdrop of the mobilization, promotions came rapidly, especially in the Aviation Section, where pilots were at a premium. Effective on June 30, 1917, Arnold, still technically an infantry captain, became a major in the Aviation Section. Two months later, he was briefly promoted to the brevet rank of colonel—the youngest in the Army. He recalled that the eagles on his shoulders seemed unreal. "There had been 30-year-old colonels in the Civil War," he quipped. "But that was before my time."

Robert Arnold pointed out to me that his grandfather ran U.S. Army aviation in both world wars. "A lot of people miss the fact," he noted, "that he did this *twice*. In World War I, he had generals in charge, but they didn't know anything about airpower."

Working with Arnold at the War Department was Donald Wills Douglas, who became a lifelong friend and eventually his son's father-in-law. In 1914, Douglas had been the first student to earn a degree in aeronautical engineering from MIT. He helped the Navy design its first dirigible before joining the Glenn Martin Company as its chief engineer. In November 1916, the twenty-four-year-old "boy engineer" became chief civilian aeronautical engineer for the Aviation Section. Before the war ended, he returned to the Glenn Martin Company, where he designed Martin's MB-1 bomber.

Robert Arnold, the grandson of both men, explains that Hap and Douglas "became good friends, seeing one another as men who didn't have a lot of fluff. Douglas saw Arnold as a visionary who was open to learning. Arnold saw Douglas as a straight shooter who would tell him the truth. They hit it off magically."

Among Arnold's challenges was that not only had America fallen behind the Europeans in aircraft design but also that aircraft companies were not geared for mass production. Arnold quickly realized that America's contribution to the air war would not be made through aircraft production—indeed, no American-built combat aircraft reached the front during the war—because it would take too long to turn aircraft factories from jobs shops into mass assembly lines. American aviators learned to fly in American-built Jennys but fought their battles in planes made in Britain and France. America's contribution would be pilots.

Arnold established an archipelago of new training fields, twenty-five stateside, and sixteen in France, including a major base complex, the 3rd Aviation Instruction Center, outside of Issoudun in central France. When the Aviation Section became the U.S. Army Air Service, independent of the Signal Corps, on May 24, 1918, its personnel strength had grown from just over 1,200 in June 1917 to more than 195,000.

While Hap Arnold grappled with aircraft production and stateside pilot training—Arnold estimated that by war's end, there were 2,768 American combat pilots and observers on the Western Front—Colonel Billy Mitchell had the job of putting airpower to work on the battlefield. During the Battle of Saint-Mihiel in September 1918, Mitchell launched a coordinated 1,500-plane air attack that devastated German forces at the front as well as enemy supply lines. It was the first such coordinated air-ground offensive on this scale.

Pershing, like most ground Army officers, saw airpower strictly as an implement for tactical ground support. Mitchell, on the other hand, saw the potential for a broader application. He envisioned his airmen striking the enemy at his source of supply rather than being simply another weapon for ground commanders to use as they would use battlefield artillery.

Mitchell became the first major American exponent of strategic airpower, although his ideas were never implemented during World War I. Nevertheless, Mitchell's theories impressed Arnold, as well as many of his Air Service contemporaries, and Arnold put Mitchell's ideas to work in World War II.

Though the work Arnold did in Washington was indispensable, he yearned for command of a combat squadron. Indeed, his old friends Tommy Milling and Frank Lahm had gone to France as air commanders. It was one of Arnold's greatest career disappointments that he did not get the chance to join them.

"My ambition to take an air outfit to France was never realized," Hap Arnold wrote in his memoirs. "In a sense, it remains a disappointment to this day [1949]. During World War II, in Washington, I deliberately deprived myself of the aid of a whole series of fine Chiefs of Staff and valuable topflight advisers so that these men would not miss out on wartime experience that I never had."

When Arnold *did* finally get overseas, it was in a non-combat but highly interesting and little known "secret weapon" role, helping to develop what one might think of as America's first combat drone and its first cruise missile. Invented by Charles Kettering, the "Bug," as it was known, was a piston-engined, pilotless biplane, directed by a gyroscope that carried an explosive payload. Arnold described stateside tests of the Kettering Bug as "highly successful." In his memoirs, he compared the Bug to the German V-1, the most widely used cruise missile of World War II. General John J. "Black Jack" Pershing, commander of the American Expeditionary Force, invited Arnold to bring the Bug overseas for an operational demonstration.

Arnold's long awaited deployment to the Western Front in October 1918 almost cost him his life, but not in combat. At the time, the world was gripped by an influenza pandemic that, by some estimates, infected more than a quarter of the earth's population and killed more than a hundred million people. Arnold was so badly stricken by the flu that when he arrived at Southampton aboard the SS *Olympic*, he had to be taken ashore on a stretcher.

After eight days in a hospital in England, Arnold finally recovered sufficiently to travel on to France. By the time he reached the headquarters of the First Army on the Western Front, there was already talk of an impending armistice.

He managed to reach the front in the 103rd Infantry sector, later noting the irony of seeing the war from an infantryman's eye view. He planned a flight over the battlefront for November 11, but morning fog canceled it. It was the last day of the war. There being no more use for the Kettering Bug, nor indeed for the bulk of the Air Service that he had helped to build, Hap Arnold bade farewell to Tommy Milling, commander of the air assets of the U.S. First Army, and headed for home. In his diary entry for Armistice Day, he lamented, "It looks like I will go down in history as a desk soldier."

≡ CHAPTER 4 ≡

THE STRUGGLE FOR AIRPOWER

Scant consolation it might have been, but Arnold did manage to spend three weeks flying over the now-quiet Western Front before he returned to Washington and the unhappy chore of dismantling the Air Service he had worked so hard to build. The number of Air Service personnel peaked at around two hundred thousand during the war. That number dropped to 25,603 by June 1919. A year later it was down to 9,050. In the process of demobilizing the wartime air force, Arnold had, in his own words, "worked myself out of a job."

In January 1919, less than two months after the Armistice, Arnold was back at Rockwell Field in San Diego, discharging officers and mustering out airmen. His own wartime promotion was rescinded. Brevet Colonel Arnold became a captain on June 30, 1920, although he was promoted to major the next day. Still, amid the shrinking Army Air Service, some men stood out— including two young pilots on Arnold's staff, Captain Carl "Tooey" Spaatz and Lieutenant Ira Eaker, both of whom later played a major role in shaping the Air Force that fought World War II—and there was still good, and even dramatic, work to be done, including the flight of five Curtiss JN-4s from Rockwell across the country to Florida and back. "It was quite a feat," Arnold reminisced, "for the Jenny was far from a cross-country airplane."

Arnold's tenure at Rockwell was short. In June, he was reassigned as air commander of the IX Corps area, headquartered at the Presidio in San Francisco, and covering, essentially, the western half of the United States. Arnold and his family spent three years in San Francisco. He was also now the father of three, after William Bruce Arnold was born on July 17, 1918. Bruce's son, Robert, tells the story of how his father came to be known by his middle name. He was called "William" because nearly every family in the Army Air Service had a son named after Billy Mitchell. This reached a point of confusion when mothers were calling for their children, so they got together and decided which of their boys would be called William, Will, Bill, Billy, and so on. As Robert explains, "Pop says, 'Mom drew badly, so I'm Bruce.'"

Hap and Bee's third son, John Arnold, born in 1921, died at age two of acute appendicitis, just after Bruce almost lost his life to rheumatic fever. Robert remembered that half a century later, his father still got teary-eyed at the mention of his "wonderful brother." By all accounts, this was the point when Hap and Bee, both still relatively young people, watched their hair begin to turn gray.

The Air Service was still keen on publicity. Arnold was authorized to make demonstration flights for the motion pictures, and military airmen were encouraged to take part in well-publicized cross-country flights. As Arnold later noted, "regardless of where they were, all air officers did what they could to keep the air arm before the public." In 1921, Arnold got involved in a flight stunt after the press in San Francisco debated whether a carrier pigeon was faster over a long distance than an airplane.

"I accepted the challenge for the airplane and the Signal Corps accepted the challenge for the pigeon," Arnold recalled. "Soon I was carrying a coop of pigeons with me to Portland, Oregon, from whence the race was to start to San Francisco. These pigeons were all known by name, rank, and serial number, and some of them had distinguished combat records.... The excitement was terrific. Betting was taking place just as at a race track. There were even 'bookies' there offering odds on which would win." Oregon's governor, Ben Olcott, decided to get involved, flying as Arnold's passenger.

Things began badly for the airman and the politician when the engine would not start. By the time they finally got it purring, the pigeons had a 45-minute lead.

"As pigeon after pigeon neared its home coop, Governor Olcott and I munched sandwiches and refueled at Medford, practically ready to concede the race," Arnold recalled in his memoirs. "But apparently pigeons, as well as pilots, make private plans in flying their cross-country missions, for none of the feathered war heroes reached their home base until 48 hours later. The Governor and I had completed our flight in about seven and a half hours. Our Air Force was small in those days, but the pilots were good. I think it might well be said that any one of our boys, picked at random, could have made nonstop flights across oceans or continents had the planes been available."

This was demonstrated perhaps most dramatically when a pair of Air Service aircraft conducted a flight around the world. These two (of four that started) Douglas World Cruisers (modified observation planes) completed the historic feat in just over five months in 1924. There were other feats too. In 1927 came the momentous solo flight of Charles Lindbergh, an officer in the Air Service Reserve, across the Atlantic. Among regular Army air officers making their mark in the 1920s was James Harold "Jimmy" Doolittle, the first to fly across country using navigational instruments (in 1922).

"Billy [Mitchell] and I used to talk over the developments in flying and the men who were responsible for them," Arnold recalled. "We both agreed there was one outstanding young man who would make a name for himself and be present in a big way when airpower really came into being. His name was Doolittle." Though Doolittle was, indeed, making a name for himself in the early 1920s, Arnold was right: his presence "in a big way" was yet to come.

Among the other airmen who set records in this period, and whose presence "in a big way" was yet to come, were Arnold's Rockwell Field subordinates, Tooey Spaatz and Ira Eaker. In January 1929, they participated in a dramatic early demonstration of aerial refueling in which they succeeded in remaining aloft for seven days aboard an Atlantic-Fokker C-2A nicknamed *Question Mark*, during which they were refueled thirty-seven times. Two other men aboard the aircraft, Elwood "Pete" Quesada and Harry Halverson, would also play important roles in the future of U.S. Army aviation in World War II.

Another outstanding Army pilot who garnered headlines in this era, and who would become a household name during World War II, was Claire Lee Chennault. He had joined the Air Service in 1917 but did not complete flight training until after World War I. At the same time that many of his contemporaries, such as Arnold and Spaatz, were concentrating on the bomber capabilities of the Air Corps, Chennault was an advocate of fighter aviation and was chief of the Pursuit Section at the Air Corps Tactical School.

Like Doolittle, Chennault was no stranger to air races and aviation shows. He flew a Boeing PW-9 pursuit plane with the Army aerobatic team, the Three Musketeers, in the 1920s, and organized a second team, the Men on the Flying Trapeze, who flew demonstration flights with Boeing P-12s between 1932 and 1936. Both teams can be seen as predecessors of the current U.S. Air Force demonstration team, the Thunderbirds, which was formed in 1953.

In the 1920s and early 1930s, however, there were matters other than daring airmanship and record-setting flights that were demanding the attention of Hap Arnold and the Air Service men of his generation.

As far as they, and the public, were concerned, the central figure within the Air Service was Brigadier General Billy Mitchell. Although the colorful Mitchell would never be given the top job at the Air Service, he was its second in command from 1920 to 1925.

At the end of 1918, immediately after the war, Secretary of War Newton Baker had gone with a safe, traditional nomination, picking Major General Charles Thomas Menoher to command the Air Service. A member of the West Point class of 1886, he was not an airman, but an artillery officer who had risen through the ranks to command the 42nd "Rainbow" Division during World War I. The Air Service was the comfortable desk job that he had earned. In this position, he was greatly overshadowed by the colorful and outspoken Mitchell, who was not just an airman but also, among his fellow pilots, an *airman's* airman, and whose eloquence on the importance of aviation inspired junior Air Service officers.

"The world stands on the threshold of the 'aeronautical era,'" Mitchell wrote in his 1925 book, *Winged Victory*.

> During this epoch the destinies of all people will be controlled through the air. Airpower has come to stay. But

what, it may be asked, is airpower? Airpower is the ability to do something in or through the air, and, as the air covers the whole world, aircraft are able to go anywhere on the planet. They are not dependent on the water as a means of sustentation, nor on the land, to keep them up. Mountains, deserts, oceans, rivers, and forests, offer no obstacles. In a trice, aircraft have set aside all ideas of frontiers. The whole country now becomes the frontier and, in case of war, one place is just as exposed to attack as another place.

But just as Mitchell could be eloquent, his blunt advocacy of airpower made him enemies in the U.S. Army high command. Menoher felt that Mitchell's outspokenness bordered on insubordination. It also irritated the Navy, especially when, in 1921, Mitchell told Congress that his bombers could sink any ship afloat. The Air Service, he asserted, could defend America more economically than could the Navy with its battleships.

"Mitchell's fight with the Navy over the battleships was not just a simple fight between the Army, the Navy, and the little Air Service," Hap Arnold observed. "It was really a battle of ideas, involving air-minded people and non-air-minded people in both services. But Mitchell's constant use of the press to put his ideas across oversimplified the question.... Our Chief, General Menoher, was not only unable and wholly unwilling to cope with Mitchell's ideas, but he could not handle Billy Mitchell."

Secretary of the Navy Josephus Daniels took Mitchell's claims as a slap in the face, like a challenge to a duel. Rather than pistols at ten paces, the Navy agreed to battleships versus aerial bombs. The Navy had captured German warships they were going to scuttle anyway, so why not let Mitchell's bombers try their luck on them? The Navy's Atlantic Fleet commander wrote the rules of engagement.

The Navy would regulate the weight of the bombs and the number of planes, and it reserved the right to call off the engagement at any time.

The demonstrations, which took place over the space of several weeks in June and July on Chesapeake Bay, vindicated Mitchell's assertions. The Air Service attacked and sunk a German destroyer, the light cruiser *Frankfurt*, and the heavily armored battleship *Ostfriesland*.

"Everybody throughout the [Air Service] celebrated," Hap Arnold recalled. "At Langley Field they put planes in the air to meet the returning bombers; and every man, woman, and child was down at the line to meet the men as they got out of their planes."

Despite this success for his own service, General Pershing, who had just taken over the post of U.S. Army chief of staff, downplayed the results in the interest of not ruffling the feathers of the Army's embarrassed sister service.

Menoher congratulated Mitchell publicly, but privately he reacted angrily—jealous of Mitchell's popularity and annoyed at his continuing impolitic remarks.

"General Menoher, who had not been getting along too well with Mitchell, made a request to Mr. [John W.] Weeks, the Secretary of War, that Mitchell be relieved from his job," Hap Arnold wrote. "Mr. Weeks probably would not have minded such a change very much. He was getting fed up with Mitchell's activities and complained at a Washington press conference that Mitchell 'had greatly annoyed the Navy on numerous occasions.' But nobody in Washington, least of all Mr. Harding's Secretary of War, wanted to tangle with the popular Billy Mitchell."

The simmering row between Menoher and Mitchell reached its crescendo in September 1921. It turned out that Mitchell's Chesapeake Bay successes had not merely been downplayed by his own service, but that his own report on the operation had been suppressed.

As so often happens to controversial documents in Washington, it was leaked to the press. As Hap Arnold tells it, "Suddenly, somehow—no one quite knew how—a report of Billy Mitchell's, believed to be safely pigeonholed in General Menoher's confidential files, was published throughout the entire country. It mentioned no names, but it tore the battleships, the Admirals, and the Pershing report to shreds. General Menoher resigned as Chief of the Air Service [effective October 5]."

In turn, Pershing replaced him with a West Point classmate, General Mason Patrick. A member of Pershing's staff during World War I, Pershing trusted Patrick to keep Mitchell under control. Patrick was not an airman, but soon after taking the job, he learned to fly—at age 59—and became an advocate for his newly adopted service. He was a critic, for instance, of subordinating air combat units to corps commanders on the ground, instead favoring centralized Air Service command of these units.

In October 1922, Hap Arnold was transferred to Rockwell Field, where the training facility had become a large regional air depot. After two years in San Diego, Arnold returned to Washington for a six-month session at the Army Industrial College, which trained would-be senior officers in how to understand, and cooperate with, civilian industrial production to secure wartime materiel. The school, which had General Dwight Eisenhower on the faculty for four years in the 1930s, grew in stature and eventually evolved into today's Industrial College of the Armed Forces. Arnold had plenty of practical experience on the subject, but he found this academic training extremely useful in better understanding that experience, which would greatly benefit him, and the country, in the war to come.

While it appears General Mason Patrick had a hand in Arnold's return to Washington—grooming Arnold as a talented and forward-thinking, but more tactful, version of Mitchell—it was on this tour of duty that Arnold got to know Mitchell especially well. Their families socialized, and while Arnold liked Mitchell, he frequently had to talk him down from tirades about how the Air Service was being mistreated or misused or ignored.

"Billy, take it easy," he recalled saying to Mitchell repeatedly. "We need you. Don't throw everything away just to beat out some guy who doesn't understand! Airpower is coming! Calm down, Billy. Get a balance wheel in your office! Let him look over some of the things you write before you put them out! Stop saying all these things about the independent air arm that are driving these old Army and Navy people crazy!"

"When senior officers won't see facts, something unorthodox, perhaps an explosion, is necessary," Arnold recalled Mitchell saying in reply. "I'm doing it for the good of the Air Force, for the future Air Force, for the good of you fellows. I can afford to do it. You can't."

But Arnold did express what was on the airmen's minds, though with more tact and in writing. U.S. Air Force historian General John Huston notes that Arnold's final essay at the Army Industrial College was entitled "What's the Matter with the Air Service," raising questions about professional standards and about a general staff of non-aviators making decisions regarding aviation.

When Arnold graduated from the school in March 1925, Mason Patrick brought him into the Air Service headquarters, where he would serve for a year as chief of the information section. It was during that same month that Billy Mitchell was denied reappointment as Mason Patrick's number-two man. President Calvin Coolidge, who had just been inaugurated, was in favor of deep budget cuts in the Army and strongly disliked Mitchell and his advocacy for an expanded air arm. Mitchell was promptly reassigned to Kelly Field near San Antonio, Texas, where his voice would be less audible to the national media.

In September 1925, after the loss of life from the crash of the Navy dirigible *Shenandoah*, Mitchell called the management of national defense by the War and Navy Departments "incompetent" and "treasonable." He even used the term "criminal negligence." That was the last straw. Mitchell was summoned to the nation's capital to face a court-martial on charges of "conduct prejudicial to good order and military discipline."

The witnesses called for the defense included Captain Eddie Rickenbacker, who had been America's ace of aces during World War I, as well as Tooey Spaatz, Arnold, and many other airmen who would become senior general officers in World War II.

When the media denounced the court-martial as an unfair attack on a popular hero, President Coolidge appointed a commission to investigate Mitchell's charges against the U.S. Army's treatment of the Air Service and to study American aviation in general. To head the commission, he picked an old Amherst College classmate, now a successful financier, Dwight Morrow. Coincidentally, Morrow was the future father-in-law of the soon-to-be-famous aviator Charles Lindbergh.

During the court-martial, Morrow's panel of military and civilian aviation experts confirmed much of what Mitchell had asserted, and recommended that the Air Service be given a position comparable to the Quartermaster Corps and Signal Corps. Hap Arnold testified before the commission, and so did Mitchell, although Arnold was later critical of his mentor for reading ad nauseam from his recent book, *Winged Victory*, rather than actually testifying. This alienated friends and foes alike. At one point Senator Hiram Bingham, himself an aviator, assured Mitchell that the commissioners had read his book, but Mitchell became argumentative.

"Billy himself was in strong form at the trial, often putting the prosecution and even the Court on the defense," Arnold wrote in his memoirs. "He could be as affable with a foe or a judge as with a friend, but he was a hard man to make peace with. He was a fighter, the public was on his side, he was righter than hell and he knew it, and whoever wasn't with him a hundred per cent was against him."

Mitchell's tongue won him no new friends among those it lashed, though some of what he said proved prophetic—warning, as Hap Arnold later recalled, that Japan would attack Pearl Harbor from the air on "some fine Sunday morning." Despite having the Morrow Commission and popular opinion in his favor, Mitchell was convicted, suspended from duty, and put in a position where essentially his only choice was resignation. The thirteen-man panel convicting him voted by secret ballot, but General Douglas MacArthur openly insisted that he had voted to acquit. As he wrote in his memoirs, "A senior officer should not be silenced for being at variance with his superiors in rank and with accepted doctrine."

Putting Mitchell's conviction aside, the Army *did* adopt many of the Morrow Commission recommendations, and on July 2, 1926, the Air Service was upgraded in status to become the U.S. Army Air Corps. Mason Patrick continued as its chief until December 1927, when General James Fechet, who had been an Army pilot since 1920, succeeded him.

CHAPTER 5

YEARS OF EXILE

After the Billy Mitchell trial, Arnold was assigned as air commander at Fort Riley, Kansas. His children loved it there—his fourth son, David Lee Arnold, was born at Fort Riley in 1927—but Arnold believed he had been "exiled" for critical comments he had made about the Coolidge Administration during the trial. Nevertheless, the commander at Fort Riley, General Ewing Booth, whom Arnold described as "a stern old cavalryman," greeted Arnold warmly. "Arnold, I'm glad to see you. I'm proud to have you in this command. I know why you're here, my boy. And as long as you're here you can write and say any damned thing you want. All I ask is that you let me see it first!"

Arnold technically had responsibility for the air operations of VII Corps—covering Arkansas, Kansas, Minnesota, Nebraska, Wisconsin, and the Dakotas—but in fact he had fewer than twenty aircraft to manage. With nearly twenty years of service and the prospect of a dull posting at Fort Riley, Arnold thought about retiring.

Instead, of course, he became Mitchell's diplomatic apostle, following Mitchell's vision, but in his own way. As his grandson Robert Arnold remembered, unlike the abrasive Mitchell, Arnold had "an easy working relationship with all types of people, which none of his contemporaries did." Among his friends he could number not only officers who would reach high rank, but politicians, scientists, and aircraft manufacturers, many of whom were fellow Freemasons (Freemasonry being very popular at the time). Moreover, Arnold realized his "exile" was "a wonderful opportunity to indoctrinate ground officers all through the Army with the possibilities and capabilities of the airplane...." To that end he took officers from other branches of the service into the air as observers.

He also, taking a longer view, wrote a series of adventure novels for young people promoting aviation. The six-book series—all of the books were published in 1928—was inspired in part by his own son Bruce's reading difficulties in the third grade. The titles were *Bill Bruce and the Pioneer Aviators*; *Bill Bruce, The Flying Cadet*; *Bill Bruce Becomes an Ace*; *Bill Bruce on Border Patrol*; *Bill Bruce in the Transcontinental Race*; and *Bill Bruce on Forest Patrol*. The series ended when Arnold asked to be paid more than $200 per book and the publisher refused. Arnold remained proud of his writing and kept his hand in by writing a column on aviation for *Modern Mechanix* magazine and coauthoring three books with fellow air officer Ira Eaker.

Arnold also became, amazingly, an airline executive. Arnold knew that the Colombian-German Air Transport Society (or SCADTA, Sociedad Colombo Alemana de Transporte Aéreo) wanted the contract to carry airmail between Bogotá and the United States via Panama. SCADTA was managed and operated by German airmen.

Arnold, for national security reasons, wanted to give the United States postmaster general, Harry New, an alternative, so Arnold and fellow Air Service Majors Tooey Spaatz and Jack Jouett created a competing airline, at least on paper—Pan American Airways, Incorporated (Pan Am)—on March 14, 1927. On June 23, 1928, Pan American was merged into the Aviation Corporation of the Americas. The merged airline retained the Pan American name and beat out SCADTA for the airmail contract.

In 1928, General James Fechet, the Air Corps chief, submitted Arnold's name for the Command and General Staff School at Fort Leavenworth, Kansas. The commandant, General E. L. King, however, wrote back that Arnold's reputation for being critical of the Army establishment had preceded him. According to Arnold, the commandant told Fechet that the school "didn't want me, but if I did come I would naturally be accepted...." Arnold did go and enjoyed the ten-month course, though he did think that the school's teaching about airpower was out of date.

Arnold's next assignment was as chief of the Field Service Section of the Air Corps Materiel Division at the Fairfield Air Depot, part of the sprawling complex of installations that had grown up around the Wright brothers' operations northeast of Dayton, Ohio, and that were now collectively called "Wright Field." Wilbur Wright had died of typhoid fever in 1912, but Arnold renewed his friendship with Orville, who occasionally came for dinner at the Arnolds' home.

Arnold's work at Wright Field was focused on providing logistical support for the growing Air Corps and its large-scale field exercises, which included 250 planes in Sacramento in 1930 and seven hundred planes near Wright Field in 1931. By 1932, the Air Corps had 1,700 aircraft and about fifteen thousand men. "I soon found out it was the transportation, supply, and maintenance of such an air armada that decided, in the first place, how much of the listed 'air strength' would ever get into the air at all," Arnold observed.

"The maneuvers were principally to get experience in supply, oper-ations, and command. Supply, as we were to learn, meant more than merely furnishing gasoline and oil. It meant preparation of the airdromes; providing airdrome space for parking; providing shops and temporary buildings for maintenance and overhaul at all the minor airdromes; sleeping accommodations and messing arrange-ments for the men [1,400 officers and men were involved in Ohio]; it also necessitated securing communications of some kind or another, mainly telephone, between each Group and the next higher headquarters. But above all, supplies had always to be available when they were needed."

In 1931, General Douglas MacArthur and Chief of Naval Opera-tions Admiral William Pratt agreed that the Air Corps—as opposed to *naval* aviation—would have the responsibility for defending the coastlines against enemy ships, which in turn meant the Army needed longer range aircraft. March Field, near Riverside, Califor-nia, was designated as the hub for long-range aviation operations on the West Coast. Hap wanted to be a part of it, and on November 26, 1931, the recently promoted Lieutenant Colonel Arnold became the commander at March Field. Major Tooey Spaatz became his executive officer. The immediate task was to turn an erstwhile flight training base into an operational base for the 7th Pursuit Group and the 17th Bombardment Group.

One of his first tasks was finding a suitable bombing range. With burgeoning Los Angeles lying between March Field and the Pacific Ocean, he had to look in a different direction. Sparsely populated Kern County, one hundred miles north of Los Angeles, seemed prom-ising. Arnold took a road trip to look around. "At six a.m. we reached the little town of Muroc, adjacent to a big dry lake, fourteen miles long, seven miles wide, with a hard surface as smooth as glass. The texture of the soil was the finest kind of clay.... It made about the best and smoothest landing field imaginable. It was a 'natural' for a bombing range.... Returning to March Field with a boiling radiator in our car, we started a title search at the County Courthouse, covering a piece of the Muroc desert land about nineteen miles long by nine miles wide." This was how the U.S. Air Force came to own the 301,000 acres of what is now Edwards Air Force Base.

The proximity of March Field to Los Angeles and to Hollywood, then in its "Golden Age," meant that movie studios shot flying scenes at the base and movie stars were frequent guests. Arnold showed off his airplanes to a galaxy of stars from Errol Flynn and Hedy Lamarr to silent film star Mary Pickford (to whom he had already presented honorary wings at a Los Angeles air show back in 1919) and Clark Gable (who would serve under him during World War II). Arnold also arranged for aerial demonstrations at the 1932 Los Angeles Olympic Games.

"He figured out that if he had a Hollywood star stand next to an Army airplane, media people would take pictures of it and report about it," Robert Arnold recalls. "If you needed an airplane in your movie, he could help out with that. The whole idea was how to get airpower in front of a people. He was a guy trying to tell the story, to get access to the American people to support the Air Corps, because they could influence Congress."

During the winter following the Olympics, Arnold's March Field aircrews were able to demonstrate the ability of aircraft to deliver humanitarian relief. When heavy snowfall isolated communities across Arizona and New Mexico, especially on the Navajo and Hopi Reservations, Arnold was asked to help. His crews developed a method for airdropping supplies by parachute. In the end, they were able to parachute cartons of eggs without them breaking. In

March 1933, the March Field crews responded quickly in the wake of the Long Beach earthquake.

The most important contacts Hap Arnold made in Southern California were at the California Institute of Technology (Caltech). He had met Robert Millikan, chairman of Caltech's executive council, in Washington during World War I, when the physicist had been vice chairman of the National Research Council. Since then, Millikan had become a Nobel laureate in 1923 for his work with charged electrons and the photoelectric effect. When he and Arnold reconnected, he was at Caltech doing research into cosmic rays and high-energy photons. Arnold's aircrews even aided in some of Millikan's cosmic ray research.

Through Millikan, Arnold met Theodore von Kármán, a Hungarian-born mathematician and physicist who had immigrated to the United States by way of Germany in 1930. He became director of the Guggenheim Aeronautical Laboratory at Caltech. Today, he is regarded as the outstanding aerodynamic theoretician of the twentieth century, and at the time that he and Arnold met, he was already doing some of the most advanced aerodynamic work in the world. Arnold was also interested in the work being done by Dr. Irving P. Krick, who had just founded the Department of Meteorology at Caltech. Krick had become famous for making long-range weather predictions based off historical weather patterns. Arnold was impressed by Krick's track record as a weather predictor—and predicting weather, of course, would be hugely important for subsequent air campaigns. Actually, it was important right away in the biggest fiasco to involve the Air Corps.

Originally, airmail had been carried by Army pilots in Army aircraft. Later, the Post Office Department took over the job with its own pilots and fleet of airplanes. Beginning in 1925, the post office had contracted with commercial airlines to carry the mail.

However, the suggestion of overcharging and political shenanigans led an exasperated President Franklin Roosevelt to abruptly cancel the existing airmail contracts on February 9, 1934. Secretary of War George Dern confidently told Roosevelt and Postmaster General Jim Farley—without any consultation with Army Chief of Staff Douglas MacArthur or Chief of the Air Corps Benny Foulois—that the Air Corps would have no problem flying the mail. The Air Corps was given ten days to get ready for delivering millions of pounds of correspondence on air routes covering twenty-five thousand miles, mainly at night. The commercial airliners had better instrumentation for nighttime and foul-weather flying, had been designed for delivering the mail, and had maintenance crews along the various routes. The Air Corps lacked these advantages but did the best it could. Brigadier General Oscar Westover, given command of the effort, divided the country into airmail zones. The eastern section was commanded by Major B. Q. Jones, the central zone went to Lieutenant Colonel Horace Hickam, while the western third was assigned to Lieutenant Colonel Hap Arnold.

"Foulois, who has always taken the responsibility for this decision, has been harshly criticized for it," Arnold recalled.

> In view of…the Air Corps' willingness to accept any and all challenges, with or without previous experience, I think it is doubtful if any other air leader in his place would have answered differently…. Within two weeks we were forced to realize that although the "will to do" might get the job done, the price of our doing it was to equal the sacrifice of a wartime combat operation. Courage alone could not substitute for years of cross-country experience; for properly equipped planes; and for suitable blind flying instruments, such as the regular airline mail pilots were

using.... There was not—especially in the case of the open-cockpit fighter types that had to be flown—even enough space for the mail bags.

The results were worse than imagined. Extremely bad weather compounded the other factors. Ten Air Corps pilots lost their lives in crashes during the first three weeks as the failures of the Army Air Corps Mail Operation (AACMO) program became headline news nationwide.

"At first the editorials and radio commentators, especially those who wished to see the President win his fight against the commercial air lines, blamed us," Arnold wrote. "'What was the matter with our Air Corps, anyway? If it couldn't carry out a job like this, how could it ever fight a war? Wouldn't the Air Corps be expected to meet any and all flying conditions in wartime?'"

These arguments, oft-repeated, did a great deal to harm the image of the Air Corps. The Roosevelt administration went into damage control as the experiment they had initiated began to fail. Routes were changed or suspended as efforts were made to save face. Finally, the government relented, temporary airmail contracts were issued, and the airlines began to resume service after May 8. Nevertheless, under the Air Mail Act passed in June, new airmail contracts were issued only to airlines that had not had them before. In most cases, this was accomplished by reincorporating airlines under a new name. Also forbidden now was the ownership of airlines by plane-makers. This resulted, for example, in Boeing being compelled to divest itself of United Air Lines.

Two commissions were set up to study the Air Corps mail fiasco, one headed by Major General Hugh Drum, and a civilian board chaired by former Secretary of War Newton Baker. The recommendations of the Baker Board led to the creation, effective on March 1, 1935, of a new organization, the General Headquarters (GHQ)

Air Force. This entity did not supersede the Air Corps, but existed in parallel with it, and reported directly to the Army chief of staff, rather than the Air Corps. Major General Foulois of the Air Corps and Major General Frank Andrews of the GHQ Air Force both wore Air Corps uniforms but now reported separately to MacArthur.

The plan was for the Air Corps to retain responsibility for such activities as training and procurement, while operational units, the "air striking force," would be under the control of GHQ Air Force. As a field commander, Arnold came under the umbrella of the latter. Further complicating the chain of command was the continuing control of the physical air bases by the Army's regional corps commanders.

While many have agreed that GHQ Air Force was, in Hap Arnold's words, "the first real step ever taken toward an independent United States Air Force," the duplication of effort, the bureaucracy, and the parallel chains of command would serve to complicate operations over the next several years. Arnold, however, regarded the arrangement as an opportunity to improve the tactical readiness of the operational units.

Structuring the new entity called for organizing the air striking force into regional wings. Under this structure, Hap Arnold became commander of the 1st Wing, with control not only of units at March Field, but at Rockwell Field in San Diego, Hamilton Field near San Francisco, McChord Field near Seattle, and other bases throughout the West. Commensurate with his new responsibilities, Lieutenant Colonel Arnold was given the brevet rank of brigadier general.

In his role as the senior Air Corps man in the West, Arnold evaluated the vulnerability of Southern California to enemy attack. In an article published in the *Los Angeles Times* on January 12, 1936, he was quoted as explaining, "Forty high-speed heavy bombers, launched from a carrier off this coast, could in a few minutes completely demoralize the Los Angeles area by the simple expedient of bombing the exposed siphons or the Los Angeles Aqueduct in Owens Valley.... In so doing these enemy planes need not even approach the air defenses of Los Angeles, yet the havoc created by such a well-directed attack would be far more effective than if they dropped their bombs on the very heart or the city. Some 2,000,000 people are absolutely dependent on Los Angeles' water supply." Arnold warned that "a one-minute rain of bombs" could make the area as arid "as it was when Cabrillo first sighted this coast" in 1542. It was a scenario that not many took seriously—at least not yet.

CHAPTER 6

WASHINGTON AND WAR CLOUDS

By all accounts, including his own, Brigadier General Arnold greatly enjoyed his nine months at March Field as commander of the 1st Wing. It was an exciting time in terms of the new equipment that was coming on line, such as the modern, 200-mph Martin B-10 and B-12 bombers, all-metal, low-wing monoplanes far removed from the ungainly open-cockpit Keystone biplanes they replaced.

Arnold had good reason for his fondness for the Martin bombers. He earned his second Mackay Trophy in 1934 for leading a flight of ten B-10s from Bolling Field, near Washington, D.C., to Fairbanks, Alaska, in July, and back in August. The mission was the first on this scale, and it was welcome publicity for U.S. Army airpower. The flight also netted Arnold an audience with President Roosevelt and the beginnings of an acquaintance that would be important for Arnold in later years. After the air mail debacle, Roosevelt was happy to have some good publicity by way of his Army airmen.

Arnold relished the performance that newer aircraft brought to maneuvers and to various tactical experiments he was able to run. He liked being able to work on the development of such new innovations, and he derived great satisfaction from the constant improvements in bombing accuracy from high altitude, which would prove vital during World War II. There was much to enjoy, but that which he seems to have found most pleasing was being thousands of miles, out of sight and out of mind, from Washington, D.C. He mentions that the 1st Wing came to feel like an "independent air force."

In December 1935, however, it all came to an end.

Arnold received a telegram from General Malin Craig, who had, in October, succeeded MacArthur as U.S. Army chief of staff. The message was that General Oscar Westover, replacing the retiring General Benny Foulois as chief of the Army Air Corps, had requested Arnold as his assistant.

Westover had graduated from West Point a year ahead of Arnold, had joined the Air Service after World War I, had headed the air mail operation in 1934, and was an outspoken advocate for airpower. Arnold regarded Westover as a friend, and the offer was an enormous boost to his career, but he also had such a deep aversion to Washington that he replied, "I would rather stay on the Coast with my silver leaves back; really, would rather be a lieutenant colonel running my present command than a staff general in Washington!"

It was too late for protests. Craig had already signed the orders for Arnold to go to Washington. Arnold left March Field, he conceded in his memoirs, "a gloomy man." When he thought of Washington, he thought of "the honking traffic jams, the waiting in anterooms, clerks colliding with their stacks of papers in the endless corridors, the sharp tongues at cocktail parties confiding what they seldom really knew.... Friends or no friends, I thought, it was no place for me. Also, it was goodbye to Command! If I had realized then that I would stay in Washington for ten consecutive years, right up to my retirement, I would almost have dared to turn my over-loaded car around and drive straight back to California."

His daughter Lois did, in fact, return to California, where she met naval aviator Ensign Ernest Maynard Snowden, the twenty-six-year-old naval officer from Wildwood, North Carolina, whom she would marry at the end of 1937. A 1932 graduate of the Naval Academy at Annapolis, he had begun his career aboard surface ships but had moved to naval aviation.

In 1936, Hap Arnold entered the vast Munitions Building on Constitution Avenue, which the War Department shared with the Navy Department. Arnold and a few of his colleagues were increasingly cognizant of the threat of war in Europe. Arnold traced his own wake-up call to a blustery summer day back in 1934, even as Hitler was consolidating his power in Germany. It was while he was in Alaska, working on an aerial photography assignment, when he met a German, a pilot in World War I, who had since drifted around the world in aviation-related jobs and was now setting up a bush pilot service out of Fairbanks and hoping to become an American citizen. He had seen the B-10s parked at the airport and wanted to meet the man in charge of them.

"You think you have a good bomber out there, don't you?" the man asked.

"The best bomber in the world," Arnold replied.

"What would you say if I told you the Germans have a far better bomber today than you have in that B-10 out there?"

"I couldn't say anything, except you're a damned liar!"

"Well, they have," the man insisted.

Arnold told him pointedly that Germany had been forbidden by the terms of the Treaty of Versailles to build warplanes, adding that Allied inspection officers were monitoring German industry to prevent this.

"Just have your military attaché go to the Junkers plant, the Heinkel plant, or the Dornier plant, and take a good look at the ships they are calling 'high altitude transport planes,'" the man said with a smile. "They are making pursuit planes, as well. The component factories are well dispersed from the parent assembly plants, but if your attaché is smart, he'll find them. These are things that you should know."

On August 2, one week after Arnold first touched down in Fairbanks, Adolf Hitler, already chancellor of Germany, also became its all-powerful Führer.

On his return from Alaska, Arnold reported what he had heard to War Department intelligence. They had no information on the subject of the Germans building such aircraft. But a few months later, in March 1935, Hitler announced that he was reconstituting the German armed forces. His designated commander for his air arm, Hermann Göring, announced that the new Luftwaffe would be bigger and better than ever. At the Junkers, Heinkel, and Dornier factories, work was already progressing on the bombers that would be cornerstones of Luftwaffe operations during World War II, including the He 111 and Do 17, which were both developed under cover of being commercial, not military, aircraft.

As the Luftwaffe expanded, Britain's Royal Air Force struggled to keep pace. Dennis Richards wrote in *The Fight at Odds*, the first volume of his history of the RAF, that in March 1935, when British secretary of state for foreign affairs Sir John Simon and foreign secretary Anthony Eden flew to Berlin to try to negotiate an air pact with Hitler, the Luftwaffe, "which had enjoyed an official existence of only a fortnight, was already as strong as the Royal Air Force."

The Air Corps, meanwhile, was not a separate force, as were the RAF and the Luftwaffe, and was tiny by comparison. The Air Corps Act of July 1926, which had created the Air Corps, authorized its strength "not to exceed" 1,800 aircraft, and even as late as 1938, it had not. By 1938, personnel strength was 21,089, up from just 9,674 in 1926, but the Air Corps was still not even in the top five among the world's air forces.

The B-10 bomber, which Hap Arnold had called the "best in the world" when he was in Alaska in 1934, was no longer that; and when the Curtiss P-36 Hawk entered service as a fighter in 1938, it, too, was already obsolete by world standards.

"Looking at things as they were in 1936–1938, how did our little Army Air Corps stand in relation to the airpower of other countries as the war clouds took definite shape over Europe, Africa, and Asia?" Arnold asks rhetorically in his memoirs. "Well, to be realistic, we were practically nonexistent."

The U.S. Army's senior leadership still cast airpower in a defensive role—protecting the coastline—or with a limited supporting role on the battlefield. The Germans, on the other hand, were developing their Luftwaffe to have a key offensive role in a fast, integrated air-ground type of warfare they called "blitzkrieg," or "lightning war."

The irony of the situation was that there were men within the Air Corps who were actually looking *beyond* what the Germans were doing, developing a doctrine described as "*strategic* airpower" aimed at destroying the ability of an enemy to wage war, targeting factories, power plants, and cities. Billy Mitchell had seen the potential for strategic airpower as early as World War I. He and his acolytes pushed it constantly in their bureaucratic battles in the Air Service, achieving at least some peripheral victories in aircraft production.

Arnold, as assistant chief of the Air Corps, believed the future belonged to the long-range, "four-engine bomber," in particular the

Boeing Model 299, which had made its first flight in Seattle on July 28, 1935. At the rollout, *Seattle Times* reporter Richard Williams described the huge, four-engine bomber as a "flying fortress," which became its official name. Designated as B-17, the Flying Fortress operated at very high altitudes, up to thirty-six thousand feet, and had a ferry range of 3,600 miles and a top speed of 292 miles per hour. (The B-10B, in comparison, had a ceiling of 24,200 feet, a ferry range of 1,830 miles, and a top speed of 213 miles per hour.) The Army still thought of bombers not in strategic terms but in terms of coastal defense. For that purpose they had a much cheaper, two-engine alternative, the B-18. The B-17 had to be defended on the grounds that it was even better at coastal defense.

"The 'strategic' function of this new plane, as laid down by the over-all plans for national defense at that time, was still only a 'tactical' employment," Arnold wrote. "The B-17, too, was intended to sink enemy ships approaching our shores. It was some time later that General Frank M. Andrews still had to argue in the struggle for its procurement that the B-17 was 'especially useful for coastal patrol.' But even at that, the interception would be hundreds of miles farther at sea [than was possible for a B-18] and formations of Flying Fortresses could cover in an hour more distance than a fast enemy ship could be expected to cover in a night."

The first baker's dozen of Flying Fortresses, which in World War II would vindicate the doctrine of strategic airpower, were ordered in January 1936, just thirty-three days before Billy Mitchell died, a sick and broken man, in a New York hospital, on February 19.

As Hap Arnold wrote, "Unbelieving men in high places, battleship admirals, generals, and others who seized on Billy Mitchell's sins to eliminate him, didn't eliminate airpower at all, nor retard it half so much as has been said. Actually, they didn't even eliminate Billy. They broke his heart, but from the day of his trial, public opinion was mostly on his side."

If there was any place where opinion was almost unanimously on his side, and on that of the airpower doctrine which he had preached, it was among the men who were young officers at the time of his trial and who were now in a position to start building the kind of air force that Mitchell had envisioned.

The shortsighted penny-pinching being practiced by the War Department and the U.S. Army General Staff disregarded the gathering war clouds in both Europe and Asia. Japan had invaded China in 1937, and in March 1938, Adolf Hitler annexed Austria—while insisting that Czechoslovakia's German-speaking Sudetenland region should also be folded into his Third Reich.

Britain and France, meanwhile, took notice, but did nothing. They might have called Hitler's bluff, but instead, they let it be known by their actions that they would do anything to avoid war. As was discussed at the time, a big part of their apprehension about Germany was a fear of having to face the Luftwaffe, which, by Hap Arnold's own reckoning, now outnumbered their combined combat aircraft strength by more than two to one. In September 1938, with Europe in crisis, Britain's prime minister Neville Chamberlain and France's president Édouard Daladier flew to Munich to meet with Adolf Hitler. To avoid war, Chamberlain and Daladier ignored Czech concerns and gave the Sudetenland to Hitler. When Chamberlain flew home, he happily announced that he had helped to negotiate "peace for our time."

Across the globe, Hap Arnold would read the news from the vantage point of a new and unanticipated job.

On Wednesday, September 21, Arnold had arrived home from work when the phone rang. It was Major Kenneth B. "K. B." Wolfe. Wolfe was the Air Corps representative at the Lockheed plant in Burbank, California. He had bad news. General Westover, chief of the Air Corps, had just crashed his A-17 on the runway on Burbank.

"He said that as he was talking to me the plane was still burning on the runway," Arnold recalled. "I joined my wife and we went down to wait in the lobby of the Kennedy Warren [apartment building on Connecticut Avenue] hoping to reach Mrs. Westover before she heard about it over the radio.... Westover worked harder than anybody. Too hard. He flew all over the country, always flying his own plane.... It was too much for any man his age [he was 55; Hap was 52] whose flying reflexes were being sapped day after day."

On September 29, the same day that Chamberlain, Daladier, and Hitler were wrapping up their negotiations in Munich, Henry Harley Arnold took on a new job. He was sworn in as the chief of staff of the U.S. Army Air Corps, with the brevet rank of major general.

CHAPTER 7

THE MAGNA CARTA
OF AMERICAN AIRPOWER

he new chief of staff hit the ground running. Indeed, as
assistant chief, he had frequently filled in while Westover was
out of Washington visiting field locations.

In retrospect, his promotion was an obvious choice, but
during the week following Westover's death, there was some
discussion that Frank Andrews might come over from GHQ Air
Force. There was even an unsubstantiated rumor going around
suggesting that Arnold drank too much. No wonder he despised the
Washington gossip mill. In his memoirs, he recalled that he never
ascertained the source of the rumor, and he insisted that he didn't
care. Ultimately, it did not matter. The announcement of Arnold's
promotion was issued by the White House. The fact that he had
Franklin D. Roosevelt's endorsement quieted the naysayers.

It is naturally important for a man operating within Washington's bureaucratic jungle to have the support of the president, but Arnold also benefited greatly from a working relationship—and eventually a close friendship—that he had developed with Harry Hopkins, Roosevelt's closest advisor, special envoy, and all-around troubleshooter. He had deliberately cultivated Hopkins as an ally and had found him a ready convert to airpower doctrine. In turn, Hopkins would become an advocate of that doctrine with the president.

On September 28, Arnold was summoned to the White House along with General Malin Craig, Army chief of staff; his assistant George Marshall; Admiral Harold Stark, chief of naval operations; Secretary of the Navy Claude Swanson; Secretary of War Harry Woodring; Assistant Secretary of War Louis Johnson; and Secretary of the Treasury Henry Morgenthau, among others. The president wanted to talk about the conference in Munich, where it appeared that Britain, France, and Italy were about to sign an agreement giving Hitler's Germany the Sudetenland region of Czechoslovakia.

"The heavy part played by [fear of] the Luftwaffe in the appeasement at Munich was not lost on the President," Arnold recalled of the meeting.

> To the surprise, I think, of practically everyone in the room except Harry [Hopkins] and myself, and to my own delight, the President came straight out for airpower. Airplanes—now—and lots of them! At that time, the War Department was handling the entire expansion for the ground and air forces, but FDR was not satisfied with their submitted report. A new regiment of field artillery, or new barracks at an Army post in Wyoming, or new machine tools in an ordnance arsenal, he said sharply, would not scare Hitler one blankety-blank-blank bit!

What he wanted was airplanes! Airplanes were the war implements that would have an influence on Hitler's activities!

Only three days later, French prime minister Édouard Daladier told the American ambassador to France, William Bullitt, that "if France would have had 3,000 or 4,000 planes, there would have been no [capitulation to Hitler at] Munich."

Munich had made the president not simply commander in chief, but "airpower-advocate-in-chief." "Some of those present were obviously unprepared for the forceful way in which he had made up his mind," Arnold recalled. "It was plainly a bolt from the blue, but the President, with equal plainness, made it clear that he had assembled this meeting to discuss aircraft production and airpower in general. He himself had some potent proposals which were obviously not made up on the spur of the moment."

In 1936, Congress had authorized 2,230 aircraft as a "minimum safe peacetime strength" for the Air Corps, though as of September 1938, the service had just 1,792. This was fewer than the number that had been authorized before 1936. Roosevelt thought that, in light of events, 2,230 was on the low side. He said that perhaps the number should be increased to ten thousand, with production capacity for twice that.

"I left that meeting of the 28th of September 1938, with the feeling that the Air Corps had finally 'achieved its Magna Carta,'" Arnold said. "It was the first time in history we had ever had a program—the first time we could shoot toward a definite goal of planes from the factories and men from the training fields. A battle was won in the White House that day which took its place with—or at least led to—the victories in combat later."

Though the president himself was using numbers in the low five figures, the practical implementation of the Magna Carta would travel a bumpy road. At a press conference on October 14, Roosevelt spoke in general terms about his desire to expand the Air Corps, mentioning fifteen thousand aircraft. Five days later, Arnold handed Woodring a detailed plan for a very modest—by Roosevelt's numbers—expansion to 6,360 aircraft by 1944. In 1938, this was considered excessive in some quarters.

General Craig, Arnold's senior uniformed boss, took exception, not only to Arnold's figures, but those of his own boss, the president. On October 24, Craig complained to Lewis Douglas, director of the Bureau of the Budget, that the "defense of the country... rests with ground troops. What are we going to do with 15,000 airplanes?" Craig went on to tell Douglas that the money was better spent on weapons, because airplanes had a rapid rate of obsolescence.

As has often been observed, when Roosevelt took a personal interest in a particular policy initiative, he personally ruled its momentum.

Another White House summit was held on November 14, just after the midterm elections. Most of the same faces from the September meeting were again present. Roosevelt said pointedly that the Air Corps needed twenty thousand aircraft, but that Congress would probably authorize only half that number. With that in mind, Secretary of War Louis Johnson directed Army chief Malin Craig to budget for ten thousand aircraft over two years.

Craig would not go quietly, however, insisting once again in a December 17 memo to the White House that "the ultimate defense of our own territory rests with the ground forces." Roosevelt responded by putting Treasury Secretary Morgenthau in charge of all weapons and aircraft procurement. This move naturally irritated Craig, but it had the added advantage of opening the door for Britain and France to buy American planes.

Britain and France were now expanding their own air forces as rapidly as possible. Under the "cash and carry" provision of the 1937

Neutrality Act, foreign powers could buy American arms for cash and carry them away on their own ships.

Nobody within the War Department was pleased to have the Treasury in charge of allocating and selling warplanes. Part of it was simple turf warfare, but Secretary Woodring, who considered himself a non-interventionist, strongly opposed the sales on the grounds that the United States should not become involved in Europe's wars. For his part, Hap Arnold was irritated with the idea of foreign airmen getting a look at proprietary American hardware and of foreign air forces getting aircraft that he desired for his Air Corps.

"Does the Secretary of the Treasury run the Air Corps?" Arnold struggled to respond to the irate questioning of a Senate Military Affairs Committee meeting on January 24, 1939. "Does he give orders about Air Corps procurement?"

In his memoirs, Arnold wrote that

> the responsibility for building up an Army Air Force was not that of the Secretary of the Treasury. He might give away, sell, or what-have-you, every plane produced, the latest planes which our engineers could develop, the most modern gadgets and devices out of our factories, and would lose nothing by it. It was someone else's responsibility. It was mine. To build up our Air Force was an obligation that I had to Congress, to the President, to the people of the United States. It was a job that was still ahead of me, for at that time we had no Air Force. The job could not be done without careful planning. There could be no planning with a hit-and-miss policy that permitted the Secretary of the Treasury to give away to the French and English whatever he desired.

Arnold's unconvincing response put him into abrupt disfavor with the president. He had, to paraphrase his own words, gone from the White House to the "dog house."

"I felt that I was about to lose my job," Arnold later confided in his memoirs. "In the presence of the key Military and Naval personnel from the two Secretaries down, the President, in unmistakable language, covered the necessity for cooperation and coordination concerning foreign sales for aircraft and latest equipment. Bringing out the desirability for everyone to be on his guard in answering questions before congressional committees, he expressed dissatisfaction with the manner in which questions had been answered in the past, particularly by War Department witnesses. And then, looking directly at me, he said there were places to which officers who did not 'play ball' might be sent—such as Guam." Little did anyone realize at the time that Guam would play a key role in the projection of American airpower in 1945.

Roosevelt did not fire Arnold, but his being ostracized from White House conferences for the foreseeable future was deeply troubling. As he wrote, "I had a genuine worry because I had lost the President's confidence at probably the most critical period of my professional career."

Morgenthau responded to Arnold's criticism by pointing out that foreign customers shopping at American factories translated into more work for American workers, and it was hard for most, especially Roosevelt, to find fault with that.

Britain and France placed orders for more than 1,200 aircraft during the first quarter of 1939. Smaller countries, including Australia, Belgium, Finland, and Sweden, also ordered aircraft.

American plane-makers certainly benefited from these orders, and so, too, did the Air Corps, as the influx of cash would help pay for plant expansion that would later benefit the American armed forces. American workers were also gaining experience, and American engineers would soon benefit from what they learned from American aircraft flying in combat with other air forces.

In 1939, according to the Civil Aeronautics Administration *Statistical Handbook*, the American aircraft industry built only 921 aircraft for the U.S. Army and U.S. Navy, while building 4,935 for export. The five-figure aircraft acquisitions promised—or *suggested*—for the Air Corps were yet to materialize. In April 1939, Congress authorized an increase to six thousand aircraft for the service, although they appropriated funds for fewer than 5,500. Meanwhile, the Luftwaffe took delivery from German manufacturers of 8,295 aircraft in 1939 and hoped to acquire more than ten thousand planes the following year.

Aside from the realization that it had developed into the world's premier air force, the Air Corps had little specific information about the Luftwaffe. Details about German airpower were few and hard to come by. The intelligence capabilities of the Air Corps were nearly as limited when Arnold assumed command in 1938 as they had been when he met the German mystery man in Fairbanks four years earlier. In his memoirs, Arnold notes that "there were American journalists and ordinary travelers in Germany who knew more about the Luftwaffe's preparations than I."

Arnold did have the perspective of one American traveler who was far from ordinary. The legendary aviator Charles Lindbergh, who had moved to Europe in 1936 to escape media attention resulting from the kidnapping and murder of his son, had made a visit to Germany. He had spent three weeks in 1938 visiting German aircraft factories and research facilities. He reported to Arnold in November 1938 that "Germany is undoubtedly the most powerful nation in the world in military aviation and her margin of leadership is increasing with each month that passes."

In May 1939, shortly after Lindbergh and his family moved back to the United States, and two months after Nazi Germany annexed

Czechoslovakia, Lindbergh met with Arnold at the Thayer Hotel at West Point. Among other things, Lindbergh told Arnold that the Germans were ignoring the development of long-range strategic bombers; moreover, they were training for a future European war that would be intense, but short.

In May, Hitler and Italy's fascist dictator Benito Mussolini formed a military alliance, the Pact of Steel (joined by Japan in 1940 to form the Tripartite Pact). On August 24, Hitler signed a nonaggression pact with the Soviet Union, trading *eastern* Poland to Josef Stalin in exchange for a free hand in *western* Poland. On September 1, the German Wehrmacht launched a blitzkrieg into Poland; Britain and France protested with ultimatums, invoking their mutual assistance treaties with Poland. On September 3, Britain and France declared that they were at war with Nazi Germany. "The news from Poland hit us full force," Arnold recalled. "It was plain, not only to American airmen but to everyone, that our worry about the German Luftwaffe had been well founded. Only some 40 per cent of Göring's front-line air strength,—between 1,500 and 2,000 combat airplanes ... were employed. But it was the Luftwaffe ... that made the advance of the Wehrmacht's ground forces a walk-in. Poland died on its airfields, from which the Luftwaffe never allowed the Polish planes to take off."

Also on September 1, by coincidence, George Catlett Marshall was sworn in as chief of staff. The cantankerous Malin Craig had retired one day before the war. Though Marshall still opposed divorcing the Air Corps from the Army, he was otherwise a firm Arnold ally in rapidly expanding American airpower.

After Poland's defeat and occupation by German and Soviet forces, an anticipated westward strike by Hitler's war machine failed to materialize. The Germans glared at the French armies and at the British Expeditionary Force that came to the continent—and the Western Allies glared back. For the remainder of 1939, and through the winter, a nervous standoff ensued. The blitzkrieg was replaced by what commentators called a "sitzkrieg."

The British and French continued buying weapons in the United States—the 1939 Neutrality Act, passed in November, made it legal to sell to nations now at war—and Hap Arnold bit his tongue.

In April, the sitzkrieg abruptly reverted to blitzkrieg, as the Wehrmacht swept through Denmark and Norway, and in May occupied Luxembourg, Belgium, and the Netherlands. On June 14, Hitler's armies marched into Paris, having accomplished in five weeks what Germany had been unable to do in four years of protracted fighting in World War I. If there was any doubt that Germany's war machine was the most formidable in the world, it ended when France formally surrendered on June 22. After the surrender, France dissolved its Third Republic and formed a new pro-German government based in the city of Vichy.

On June 11, Arnold's son, Henry Harley "Hank" Arnold Jr. graduated from the U.S. Military Academy at West Point, commissioned as an artilleryman. Hank's brother Bruce began his West Point career in 1940, having already put in a year at the U.S. Naval Academy in Annapolis. As Bruce explained many years later, his father had in his mind "the idea that he would like me to go to the Naval Academy. He used to drive us down to Annapolis and we'd drive around.... As I child I wasn't interested in that at all. I wanted to be a flier in the United States Army Air Corps.... I told Dad that I wanted to go to West Point."

Bruce changed his mind after talking with some naval officers to whom his father introduced him, and he entered Annapolis in 1938. His enthusiasm lasted until Christmas of that year, when he came home from school to tell his father that he had learned that an airplane cannot sink a battleship. Even if the bridge was blown off, it was "still a fighting unit of the United States Navy."

Hap's reaction was, "Don't you ever believe any of that crap they teach you down there." Having admitted that he had "lost most of the motivation I had in graduating," Bruce dropped out of Annapolis. According to his son Robert, he considered joining the Foreign Legion. Bruce spoke to the captain of a sailing ship about running away to sea "because I knew that once you got kicked out of an Academy you didn't go home."

"Dad was very clever," Bruce continues. "He sent an officer down to pick me up one day before I was supposed to ship out. And this officer was an Air Force officer who'd gone to the Naval Academy and also had been kicked out."

At this point, Bruce enlisted in the U.S. Army as a cavalry private. He was sent to Fort Myer, just across the river from Washington, where his commander was Colonel George S. Patton. Bruce spent a year in the cavalry and loved it, but in June 1940 he was discharged to attend a military prep school that would prepare him for West Point.

By that time, the debate over airpower was over. The Battle of Britain in 1940, featuring the Luftwaffe versus the RAF, had demonstrated the essential effectiveness of aviation in modern warfare. President Roosevelt had already asked Congress to fund a fleet of fifty thousand aircraft, a tenfold increase over what the services possessed. Then he replaced his isolationist Secretary of War Harry Woodring with Henry Lewis Stimson, an outspoken internationalist. Stimson, a Republican, had previously served as secretary of war under William Howard Taft and as secretary of state under Herbert Hoover.

Morgenthau approached Stimson shortly after he took office on July 10, 1940, insisting that he fire Arnold. Stimson declined, understanding that Arnold's criticism of arms sales to Britain grew not from isolationism, but from a paternalist's concern for the interests of his Air Corps. That understanding also made its way to the White

House. Arnold was invited back to the executive mansion, where Roosevelt greeted him cordially and personally mixed him an old-fashioned. Arnold later observed that he was finally "out of the dog house," although Roosevelt did keep the leash short. A May 16, 1941, memo from Marshall to Stimson, for example, notes that Arnold's promotion to permanent major general was being blocked by the president.

In May 1940, Roosevelt created his National Defense Advisory Commission, and in September, Congress passed the Selective Training and Service Act, paving the way for the first peacetime draft in American history. The role of the Commission would be to mobilize American industry, including its aircraft industry, as part of the general mobilization for war which many people now feared to be inevitable.

One of Arnold's tasks was to plan the great expansion of American airpower. Working with the U.S. Navy's Bureau of Aeronautics (BuAer), his staff came to an agreement on a 73–27 split of President Roosevelt's proposed fifty thousand planes. Unique among the Army's top brass, Hap Arnold understood aircraft production, especially the nuances of logistics chains, lead times, and financing issues, and he was a trusted friend of the industry's leaders, including Don Douglas, whose company was one of the nation's leading aircraft manufacturers. As the National Defense Advisory Commission established quotas for American industry, the quantities expected from plane-makers were immense in comparison to existing plant capacity. New factories had to be built, and Congress was asked to authorize funds both for expanding existing facilities and constructing new government-owned factories, operated by individual manufacturers at new locations.

In a December 29, 1940, radio broadcast, Roosevelt unambiguously called American industry "the Arsenal of Democracy." In so doing, he lifted from an earlier comment by playwright Robert

Emmet Sherwood, who was quoted in the May 18, 1940, *New York Times* as having said "this country is already, in effect, an arsenal for the democratic Allies." Roosevelt's paraphrase became an iconic phrase which still resonates in any recollection of the role of American industry in World War II.

Early in 1941, public opinion was shifting away from isolationism, but not to the extent that the American people were ready to go to war. Indeed, in November 1940, Roosevelt had just won an unprecedented third term in office partly by promising to keep the United States *out* of the war. The United States was not in a position to undertake military action against Germany. Roosevelt's goal was to keep the British fighting by supplying them with American arms. The British, however, were running out of money, so Roosevelt came up with an arrangement to supply arms to the British under a deferred payment scheme known as "lend-lease." With popular opinion narrowly in support of the concept, Congress passed the Lend-Lease Act on March 11, 1941.

In turn, Roosevelt sent Harry Hopkins, as well as his special envoy at large, financier Averell Harriman, to Britain to meet with Prime Minister Winston Churchill, and authorized American military officers to plan for future Anglo-American cooperation in the event of American involvement in the war. As these talks progressed, Hopkins and Stimson recommended that Hap Arnold be sent to Britain to join them.

Departing from New York on April 9 aboard a Pan American flying boat, Arnold reached London three days later via Bermuda and Lisbon. Here, he had his first meeting with his opposite number, Air Chief Marshal Charles "Peter" Portal, the chief of the air staff and commander of the Royal Air Force. Arnold envied the fact that Portal commanded an independent air force, while Portal envied the fact that Arnold sat astride the Arsenal of Democracy.

As the two got down to business, Arnold explained that he was there "to find a practical way in which the Army Air Corps can be of maximum aid to Britain."

On his previous trip to Britain in 1918, Arnold had been unimpressed with the British, complaining of their arrogance toward American troops. Now Arnold found them bending over backward to be accommodating. Though he grumbled about the food, he had nothing but compliments for the people, admiring how well they were holding up to serious shortages and Luftwaffe bombardment.

Over the course of two weeks in Britain, Arnold toured factories and RAF facilities, often accompanied by Averell Harriman. They experienced Luftwaffe bombing raids and dined with Portal and Churchill, as well as with the leaders of Britain's army and navy, Field Marshal Sir John Dill, chief of Imperial General Staff, and Fleet Admiral Dudley Pound. There was in all their meetings, Arnold wrote, "an undercurrent among all those present that suggested a fear of losing the war; at the same time, there seemed to be a calm determination to fight on to the last defense."

In his diary for April 19, Arnold wrote that "Portal is a brilliant man who does things, is capable and knows his job. Prime Minister a huge personality and has a most wonderful mind." At dinner that night, both men "started working on me, saying that we, the United States, must come into the fight, and soon."

In his memoirs, Arnold observed that he

found that Churchill had a wonderfully detailed knowledge of all phases of military operations, past and present. He had a remarkably retentive mind. [A tour of a military post with Churchill] reminded me of one of Roosevelt's in that everywhere he was received with great enthusiasm and spontaneous ovations. I noticed Churchill was able to change his manner, his approach, depending entirely upon the particular situation confronting him, or the plight or circumstances of the people with whom he was talking. He could register pathos; he could be gracious and winning in his ways; he could register sorrow or great joy, or be enthusiastic, or sympathetic.

When Arnold met with King George VI, coincidentally a fellow Freemason, it made headlines in the American papers. Observed Arnold in his diary, he seemed to be "a fine gentleman ... the kind of man I always imagined a British King would be."

Arnold's tour guide for much of his visit was Lord Beaverbrook, William Maxwell Aitken, Britain's minister of aircraft production, whom Arnold referred to in his diaries as "the Beaver." During dinner with Averell Harriman at Beaverbrook's country house on April 21, Arnold's possessiveness of the American aircraft industry at the expense of British interests became a topic of conversation. The Beaver suddenly turned to Arnold and asked, "What would you do if Churchill were hanged and the rest of us in hiding in Scotland or being run over by the Germans, what would the people in America do? We are against the mightiest Army the world has ever seen."

"Naturally, such a question coming out of a blue sky threw me back on my haunches," Arnold admitted, "particularly when I was making my first appearance among the British leaders."

The following day, they returned to London to find that Beaverbrook's house in the city had been destroyed in a Luftwaffe raid overnight.

★ ★ ★ ★ ★

On May 6, 1941, shortly after he returned to Washington, Arnold was called to the White House to brief the president, as well as

Stimson, Marshall, Morgenthau, and Secretary of State Cordell Hull. The Air Corps chief went over the British concerns in detail—from their overarching fear of German U-boats, which were strangling the shipping lanes and causing food shortages, to their eagerness for American aircraft and their longing for American participation in a war which they viewed as being against a common enemy.

"One thing was apparent," wrote Arnold, "either the British were actually in an awfully tight spot, and knew it, or they were deliberately trying to paint the picture as black as they could possibly make it so that I would take that picture back to the President of the United States. Now, with a perspective on the period, I am inclined to the former opinion. The British were desperate—so desperate that for once their cloak of conservatism was cast aside; their inbred policy of understatement thrown into the discard. They needed help, needed it badly, and were frank to admit it."

Stimson later recalled that Roosevelt reacted to Arnold's briefing by saying that it was the best account that he had yet heard of the situation in Britain.

An article in the May 13 *New York Times* quoted a speech Arnold gave to the Woman's National Democratic Club. He spoke of Britain's "hard task" and said America's aircraft industry would surmount all problems in order to supply the British with what they needed. Roosevelt must have been pleased that Arnold had softened his reluctance to help supply the British.

In a later memo to the secretary of war, Arnold stated explicitly that "England must have aid in the form of American airplanes if she is to survive and provide bases for decisive American offensives."

On May 23, the White House included Arnold's name on a list of recommended promotions that was sent to the Senate to be rubber-stamped. Arnold's permanent rank of colonel was jumped two grades to that of permanent major general. Hap Arnold was officially out of the White House "dog house."

Within days of his promotion, Arnold fulfilled a promise to the British by creating the Air Corps Ferrying Command to help deliver American-made aircraft across the North Atlantic to Britain. He assigned Colonel Robert Olds, a bomber pilot with extensive long-range flying experience, to command the new organization.

Arnold also drafted a detailed summary of his perspective on the situation in Britain for the secretary of war. According to his memoirs, Arnold told Stimson that

> a powerful air offensive must be carried on by the United States if Germany is to be invaded. England probably cannot conduct such an air offensive, even if adequate material is furnished by the United States. She is having great difficulty at this moment in operating the small Air Force she now has [but] the United States is capable of creating an adequate Air Force, and conducting a decisive air offensive in about two years if England survives to provide air bases. [However] the United States is not capable of creating the Air Force necessary to take decisive action if large quantities of long-range aircraft are exported and expended in a nondecisive effort.

According to Arnold, Stimson agreed and passed it along to Roosevelt, telling him that "I believe the moment has now come when we should give our primary attention to a prompt development of a well-armed, well-rounded and well-trained American Air Force, and I have, after a most careful study, reached the conclusion that it would be unwise to divert further production from our Air Force until such time as the main requirements for the Air Force are fully completed."

Curiously, just as Arnold was coming around to accept Roosevelt's arguments in favor of arming the British, Stimson was coming around to Arnold's original point of view of putting American airpower needs first.

CHAPTER 8

A NEW AIR FORCE GOES TO WAR

The Air Corps was growing not just in planes and personnel but in technological sophistication. Between 1938 and 1941, Arnold helped assemble an arsenal of exceptional aircraft that became household names during the war, including the Curtiss P-40 Warhawk, the Lockheed P-38 Lightning, the Bell P-39 Airacobra, the Republic P-47 Thunderbolt, the Boeing B-17 Flying Fortress, the Consolidated B-24 Liberator, the North American Aviation B-25 [Billy] Mitchell, and the Martin B-26 Marauder. From fewer than 1,800 aircraft on hand when Arnold took over as chief in 1938, the Air Corps had nearly five thousand two years later, and this number doubled by the fall of 1941.

Meanwhile, on his visit to Britain, Arnold had been shown Frank Whittle's jet engine and had seen the jet-propelled Gloster E.28/39 during taxi tests. Under a cloak of secrecy, Lord Beaverbrook had even given him the blueprints for this remarkable innovation. He did not share his thoughts on the jet engine with his own diary, but when he got home, according to his memoirs, "I called Mr. Larry Bell, of the Bell Aircraft Company, and Mr. D.R. Schoultz, of the General Electric Company, to a conference in my office. I explained just what the jet-propelled airplane was—its advantages and its disadvantages, and told them I should like very much to have General Electric go ahead with the engine, and Bell build the plane. Their engineers should be tied in close enough to work together as a team. I hoped this collaboration would weld the jet engine and the jet plane into one single project."

The formal contract was issued in October 1941, and the Bell XP-59 Airacomet, powered by a General Electric J31 engine, first flew a year later. Although no Airacomet, nor any American jet, would see service in the war, the anecdote illustrates Arnold's commitment to leading-edge technology that dated back to his interaction with Caltech a decade earlier.

On June 20, 1941, Army Regulation 95-5 formally merged the parallel staffs and functions of the GHQ Air Force and U.S. Army Air Corps into a single entity that would be called the United States Army Air Forces. Arnold became the chief of the new USAAF, as well as deputy chief of staff for air, answering directly to George Marshall.

Full autonomy for the USAAF, and a third star for Arnold, would come with Roosevelt's Executive Order 9082 of February 28, 1942. Effective on March 9, the U.S. Army was reorganized into three components: the USAAF, the Army Ground Forces, and the Services of Supply (Army Service Forces after March 1943). The USAAF effectively fulfilled the operational goal of an independent air force—if not in name—though Arnold and Marshall agreed to put the formal separation on hold until after the war. The reasons were practical, as explained in a conversation Arnold had with his son, and which Bruce Arnold related to Murray Green many years later.

"You know, we're screaming for our separate air force and suddenly it's offered to us on a plate and we had to turn it down," Hap Arnold had said. "They'll probably be kicking me around for the rest of my life on this, but I had to write to all the guys who had been fighting so hard ... and I [asked] them: what if they gave us this separate air force now? And of course this would mean our own logistics, our own administration, our own everything, just as much as the Army is separated from the Navy. Could you do it? You know they all answered the same way. They said, 'We can't do it at this time.'"

As the plural in U.S. Army Air *Forces* implies, the USAAF would be composed of multiple regional air forces. The original four were created in the four quadrants of the continental United States. The Fifth was the former Far East Air Force (FEAF) in the Philippines, the Sixth originated as the Panama Canal Air Force, and the Seventh came out of the Hawaiian Air Force. All of these had been components of the Air Corps. An additional eight air forces would be added after the United States entered World War II.

On June 22, just two days after the creation of the USAAF, Germany launched Operation Barbarossa, the largest military offensive in history, against the Soviet Union. It came as no surprise to anyone in Arnold's office that a major component of Barbarossa was the Luftwaffe assault upon Soviet airpower. Indeed, much of the Red Air Force was caught on the ground and destroyed within the first few days.

Arnold formed an Air Staff, analogous to the U.S. Army General Staff, and brought his old friend, General Carl "Tooey" Spaatz to be its chief. Arnold ordered Spaatz, who had spent time in London earlier in the year, working with the Royal Air Force Air Staff, to build an independent Air War Plans Division (AWPD).

In turn, the AWPD would be headed by Lieutenant Colonel Harold L. "Hal" George, who had been a fighter pilot in World War I. George brought together a group of young staff officers who would play key roles in USAAF operations. Among them were Lieutenant Colonel Orvil Anderson, Major Hoyt Vandenberg, Major Laurence Kuter, and Major Haywood Hansell.

Beginning work in July 1941, the AWPD men established aircraft production goals within a global strategy for defeating Hitler and Mussolini with American airpower. Indeed, their report, delivered on August 12, was entitled *Munitions Requirements of the Army Air Forces to Defeat Our Potential Enemies*, though it was referred to as AWPD-1. The subsequent AWPD-2 of September 1941 considered aircraft production in the context of the strategic outlines of AWPD-1.

As AWPD-1 was taking shape, Hap Arnold was out of town on a secret mission. On August 3, while touring flight training facilities near San Antonio, he received a cryptic message from George Marshall, telling him to pack a warm uniform, fly to New York City, and be prepared for a ten-day trip to an undisclosed location.

"He did not tell me anything about where we were going, or what we were to do," Arnold recalled. "I must admit my imagination did not measure up to the occasion; I could not even guess our destination."

The first face-to-face summit meeting between Franklin Roosevelt and Winston Churchill took place in Placentia Bay, off Argentia, Newfoundland, on August 9, 1941. Churchill and Roosevelt brought their top military leadership; on Roosevelt's side that included Hap Arnold. Churchill arrived aboard the HMS *Prince of Wales*—which had been part of the task force that ran down and sank the *Bismarck* a few weeks before—and anchored near the

American battleship USS *Arizona*. Nobody present in Newfoundland that week could have predicted that in four months, over the space of just three days, these two formidable battleships would *both* be sunk—by *airplanes*.

The result of the meeting was the Atlantic Charter, a broadly worded joint declaration that verbalized an Anglo-American vision for the postwar world. It called for freedom of the seas, disarmament, national self-determination, and global economic cooperation.

As a practical matter, however, much of what was discussed centered on the cooperation necessary to bring about Germany's defeat. In the months following the conference, it seemed that Hitler's vision of the future would trump the Anglo-American dream. German U-boats wrought havoc on the Atlantic sea lanes, while Hitler's armies raced toward Moscow and the Suez Canal. They had already occupied a swath of the Soviet Union twice the size of prewar Germany.

At home, Hap Arnold's biggest concern, as it had been for the past year, was not the strategy outlined by the Atlantic Charter, nor even the strategy of his AWPD team, but aircraft production. Of the four-engine bombers that were the highest and most complex aircraft on his wish list for the USAAF, most of the Consolidated B-24 Liberators and about half of the Boeing B-17 Flying Fortresses were going overseas to the RAF. At the end of November, the USAAF possessed only eleven Liberators and 145 Flying Fortresses, and, as Arnold noted, they were scattered among various installations and were being used "for training purposes." At the same time, according to Arnold's own reckoning, the total number of aircraft in the service that were "actually fit for war service" stood at 1,100.

Most of the aircraft in the USAAF were trainers. Since he had become chief of the Air Corps in 1938, personnel strength had risen from 20,196 to 152,125 at the end of 1941. The number of pilots had increased proportionally.

★ ★ ★ ★ ★

Throughout the fall of 1941, Arnold visited air bases across the United States. Saturday, December 6, found him at Hamilton Field, north of San Francisco. The chief spoke to the crews of thirteen Flying Fortresses that would be departing for Hickam Field in Hawaii, and from there flying to the Philippines.

On December 7, he flew to Southern California to meet Donald Douglas for a round of quail hunting. When the two men returned to Douglas's cabin after their shoot, Douglas's father was standing next to the car listening to the radio.

"The Japanese have stuck Pearl Harbor," he said as the hunters approached.

Nearly two decades before, when he had spoken of airpower in terms of geopolitical strategy, Billy Mitchell had occasionally made the ludicrous suggestion that one day the Japanese would attack Pearl Harbor from the air on "some fine Sunday morning."

Arnold admitted that few people, besides Billy Mitchell, could have guessed that the Japanese would actually attack Hawaii. "The general assumption seemed to have been that they would hit the Philippines first," he wrote in his memoirs. "Perhaps some of the [intelligence] officers who had been following the radio intercepts might have been able to come to a better conclusion. Certainly I could not."

As it was, the Japanese attacked the Philippines *simultaneously*.

Arnold got in touch with George Marshall, who asked him to fly to San Francisco before returning to Washington. He wanted Arnold to check in with General John DeWitt, the commander of the Western Defense Command. Ordering the units at his "old stamping grounds" at March Field on alert "for a possible sneak attack in the Los Angeles area," Arnold flew on to San Francisco, where he found the high-strung DeWitt "much worried over the possibility of what the Japanese might do to the West Coast. Frankly, I could not share all his apprehensions."

On December 8, Franklin Roosevelt addressed a joint session of Congress, describing the previous "fine Sunday morning" as "a date which will live in infamy," and asked for a declaration of war. At eight o'clock on the morning of December 11, the German declaration of war against the United States was delivered to the State Department, and by the end of the day, Congress had reciprocated and sent the American counter-declaration to Roosevelt's desk.

On December 21, President Roosevelt called his first wartime meeting of his military leadership. Secretary of War Stimson and Secretary of the Navy Frank Knox were there. The U.S. Navy was represented by Admiral Harold Stark, the chief of naval operations, and by Admiral Ernest King, commander in chief of the United States Fleet, who would hold both posts after Stark's retirement in March 1942. The U.S. Army was represented by its chief of staff, General Marshall; the USAAF by Hap Arnold. When the Joint Chiefs of Staff (JCS) was formally established as an entity in February, it would be comprised of Marshall, King, and Arnold, and would be chaired by Admiral William Leahy, Roosevelt's military advisor.

In the previous two weeks, the Japanese had used airpower to decimate the United States Pacific Fleet and sink two of Britain's biggest warships. They had landed in the Philippines and were headed for Manila, rolling over American and Filipino defenders with ease—*and* with air superiority. USAAF forces in the Philippines had essentially been erased.

On Monday, December 22, the British arrived. Winston Churchill came to the White House with Lord Beaverbrook and the Chiefs of Staff Committee, the British organization upon which the American JCS would be based. Many of the same faces from the August summit were there, including Royal Air Force chief Peter Portal.

As the conferees at the so-called Arcadia Conference discussed strategy, the Japanese overwhelmed the American defenders of Wake Island, closed in on Manila, and captured the British Crown Colony of Hong Kong on Christmas Day. Manila fell a week later. The Germans, meanwhile, controlled most of the European continent, were inching closer to Suez, and were banging on Moscow's door.

The outlook was beyond bleak; the task ahead was beyond daunting.

"It is one thing to sit on the sidelines and say what should or should not have been done in order to prevent this or that from happening," Arnold observed in his memoirs. "It is another when you have the responsibility for the task staring you right in the face."

CHAPTER 9

BUILDING
THE AIR FORCES

The Arcadia Conference lasted until January 14, 1942. The British staff and the American JCS formed a new Combined Chiefs of Staff (CCS), which would remain in place throughout the war and would include among its number Lieutenant General Arnold and Air Chief Marshal Portal and the other respective service chiefs, General George Marshall and Admiral Ernest King on the American side, and their opposite numbers, Field Marshal Alan Brooke, who had succeeded Sir John Dill as chief of Imperial General Staff, and Fleet Admiral Dudley Pound. The senior members were Admiral William Leahy, who chaired the American Joint Chiefs of Staff, and Dill, whom Churchill had now appointed as chief of the British mission in Washington. Over the coming months and years, Hap Arnold and Sir John would not only see eye-to-eye strategically, but would become close personal friends.

Arcadia's biggest strategic decision from a historical perspective can be summarized in the phrase "Germany first, contain Japan." Roosevelt and Churchill decided on putting the lion's share of their resources into defeating Germany. Indeed, the combined resources of the Anglo-American Allies were barely up to *this* task.

There was a great deal of talk about how to utilize these resources. The Allies discussed Operation Sledgehammer, an Anglo-American invasion of continental Europe in 1942, but given the weakness of the Allies relative to the strength and defensive advantage then held by the Germans, it was decided that such an operation should be postponed until 1943 (ultimately it was postponed until 1944).

In looking at the map, it was decided that the earliest effective major land action that the U.S. Army could undertake would be a landing in Northwest Africa. Ideally, this operation, code-named Gymnast, would take pressure off the British, who were fighting the German Afrika Korps on the opposite side of North Africa, not to mention provide some measure of relief for the Soviets, who could benefit from any diversion of German resources.

For Hap Arnold, the Arcadia discussions underscored the need to expand the aerial ferry routes across the Atlantic to Britain and to establish an air bridge to Australia, where the last ditch defense against the still-unstoppable Japanese would be made. Flowing through these corridors would be not only American aircraft on lend-lease, but USAAF aircraft destined to fight the Axis powers.

As Gymnast became the primary focus of American offensive ground strategy, talk turned to an offensive air strategy. It was almost as though the ghost of Billy Mitchell was present in the room and whispering in their ears, as the Arcadia conferees began discussing a *strategic* air offensive against Germany's industrial capacity. Even as American aircraft production had been a topic of Anglo-American discussions for at least a year, both parties realized that Germany's state-of-the-art factories were as much a part of their war machine as were the German armed forces. The only way to touch this industrial machine was from the air, and through the use of long-range, four-engine bombers.

Though they would differ in operational nuances, when it came to the *theory* of strategic air operations, Air Chief Marshal Portal and the commander of RAF Bomber Command, Air Marshal Arthur Travers "Bomber" Harris, were on the same page as the long-time Mitchell disciples running the USAAF, Hap Arnold and Tooey Spaatz.

On January 19, Arnold and his staff formed the VIII Bomber Command, which on February 22 was incorporated into the new Eighth Air Force, the umbrella organization for operational USAAF units in Britain. While the VIII Bomber Command was the centerpiece of the Eighth Air Force, the Air Force also contained a VIII Fighter Command to supply fighters to escort the bombers and a VIII Service Command to maintain the aircraft. In the beginning, the Eighth also contained the VIII Ground Air Support Command (later Air Support Command), which was formed for tactical operations, but its assets were later transferred to the Ninth Air Force.

Also on February 22, a Combined Chiefs of Staff memorandum, entitled *Policy for Disposition of US and British Air Forces*, promised that the Eighth Air Force would be joining the RAF in the strategic air offensive against Germany "at the earliest dates practicable." Harris was already conducting long-range bombing operations against Germany, and the British were anxious to have the Yanks on board. Hap Arnold had hoped that this would be as early as April, but with the small number of four-engine bombers then available and the need to share these with the RAF, Arnold and Spaatz had to admit that "the earliest dates practicable" was not going to be soon.

Roosevelt decided that the target for the American aircraft industry should be sixty thousand new aircraft for 1942. It was left to Arnold and Portal to work out how these numbers were to be allocated. Though there is no record of how the chiefs arrived at their figures, the Arnold-Portal agreement of January 14 called for 34,830 to be delivered to the USAAF; 10,382 to the RAF; and 10,220 to the U.S. Navy. In retrospect, the Arnold-Portal agreement was more a framework for an interim goal than a precise prescription of numbers.

In March 1942, George Marshall had insisted that for security reasons, Hap and Bee should move from their rented home in Maryland to quarters at Fort Myer, Virginia, which was located much nearer to the office complex in Washington that was used by the U.S. Army, and very close to the Pentagon building, then under construction and already about half-occupied.

As Robert Arnold recalls, Bee was especially upset about this. For the past several years, they had "finally been living in a normal house, and not the usual military quarters that they were used to. They were happy there. Bee didn't want to ever live in military quarters again." Marshall intervened with her personally, and she agreed to the move.

Hap's new house backed directly to the rear of Marshall's. The two generals could sit outside on their screened-in back porches on cool evenings and talk across the way to one another.

"After dinner, Marshall would wander over and Hap would run USAAF strike films," remembered Robert Arnold. "He would also run one-reel Westerns which his Hollywood friends had sent him. Marshall liked Westerns. This was an opportunity to entertain, and talk at length with Marshall. Whenever they were in public or in staff meetings, there was no gap because they had this relationship [and had already agreed on the points which were to be discussed]."

★　★　★　★　★

On February 15, 1942, the great British bastion at Singapore, considered impregnable, fell to the Japanese, along with its eighty-thousand-man garrison. Winston Churchill called Singapore's surrender the "worst disaster" in British history. At the same time, the United States was suffering its greatest defeat since the Civil War in the Philippines, where one hundred thousand American troops were surrounded. The tide of bad news, week after week, infected home-front morale like a debilitating sickness.

As Arnold wrote in his memoirs, Roosevelt had taken him aside immediately following Pearl Harbor, and asked—insisted, in fact—that *something* be done to "find ways and means of carrying home to Japan proper, in the form of a bombing raid, the real meaning of war."

Arnold had no immediate way to do this, but put the problem to his air staff. The solution came from the U.S. Navy.

"Early in 1942, Admiral King came to see me and asked if I thought it was feasible to use [USAAF] B-25 [twin-engine, medium bombers, with a longer range than Navy bombers] launched from the deck of a carrier," Arnold recalled. (A four-engine bomber was physically too large.) "I assured him I thought it was, provided the carrier deck was large enough to accommodate the number of B-25s that should be sent out on such a mission."

Next came choosing a leader for the mission: Jimmy Doolittle.

"The selection of Doolittle to lead this nearly suicidal mission was a natural one," Arnold recalled in his memoirs. "He was fearless, technically brilliant, a leader who not only could be counted upon to do a task himself if it were humanly possible, but could impart his spirit to others."

In the years since Arnold had first spent time with him in the early 1920s, Doolittle had gone on to make a name for himself on the air racing circuit, having won the "big three" air race trophies:

the Schneider Cup, the Bendix Trophy, and the Thompson Trophy. In the meantime, he had also earned the Mackay Trophy in 1926 and set a world speed record in the 1932 Shell Speed Dash. The "technically brilliant" aviator had earned a doctorate from MIT, had helped develop the artificial horizon and directional gyroscope, and had pioneered methods for teaching instrument flying. He had returned to active duty in 1940, and, like Arnold, had made a fact-finding trip to Britain.

"From that time on, the Doolittle Tokyo Raid was an approved, and Top Secret, project, very few officers in the Air Force, or in the Navy, knew it was to take place," Arnold continues. "President Roosevelt was kept constantly advised on the details. Closest cooperation was maintained with the Navy to insure proper carrier [take-off] technique."

Doolittle, his crews, and his B-25s sailed under the Golden Gate Bridge aboard the USS *Hornet* on April 2, 1942. On April 18, all sixteen managed to get off the flight deck and reach the skies above five Japanese cities, including Tokyo. Because it would not be possible to land on the carrier, the crews were briefed to continue westward and land in China. None of the aircraft were able to reach an airfield, but sixty-nine of eighty crewmen—including Doolittle—bailed out, survived, and were repatriated. Hap Arnold was pleased with his airmen. As Jimmy Doolittle later told Robert Arnold personally, "Hap Arnold was a man you did not want to disappoint." Doolittle hadn't.

The material damage done was slight, but the impact to morale was immense, because the raid demonstrated that the United States, specifically the USAAF, was capable of bombing Japan, albeit with the help of the U.S. Navy.

Meanwhile, Colonel Harry "Hurry-Up" Halverson was leading a contingent of B-24 Liberators around the world in the opposite direction, with the intention of attacking Japan from bases in China.

Crossing the South Atlantic by way of Brazil, the Halverson Project (HALPRO) had reached Khartoum in Sudan, en route to India, by early June. By then, the situation in China had deteriorated to the point that it was no longer feasible to base American long-range bombers there, so HALPRO was diverted to attack the oil refineries at Ploesti, Romania. This was the largest refinery complex in continental Europe, and given that Romania had joined the Axis, Ploesti was a key source of the petrochemicals that oiled and fueled the German war machine.

Launched from a British base at Benghazi in Libya, the HALPRO mission took place on June 12 and came as a complete surprise to the enemy. Wrote Hap Arnold, "The improbability of this two thousand-mile round trip was its best protection, and enemy opposition was not heavy."

As with the Doolittle mission in April, the actual physical damage was minimal, but it served notice that the USAAF was capable of attacking distant enemy targets. Of course, no one knew better than Hap Arnold that such missions were at the extreme limits of USAAF capability, and that much hard work would need to be done before the USAAF was capable of a sustained strategic air offensive against either Germany or Japan.

The means by which this strategic offensive would be undertaken was the USAAF Eighth Air Force, which was being formed in Britain even as the HALPRO raiders were preparing for Ploesti. The Eighth was one of the topics on Hap Arnold's agenda as he departed on May 23 for his second wartime trip to Britain.

The primary reason for the trip, however, was that Roosevelt wanted Arnold to renegotiate the earlier agreement that had been made with Portal regarding allocation to the RAF of a proportion of American aircraft production. In his memoirs, Arnold mentions a May 19 memo from Roosevelt to Churchill in which the president "expressed the thought that a reallocation of airplanes should be made—more airplanes should go to the United States Air Force, and the number of airplanes scheduled to go to the British Air Force should be cut down."

Accompanied by Admiral John Henry Towers, head of naval aviation, Arnold traveled the northern route through Labrador and Newfoundland that was now being flown by his Air Corps Ferrying Command aboard a USAAF C-54. This was the military variant of the four-engine DC-4 airliner that Don Douglas had on his assembly line in December 1941. They were to have been the "next big thing" in commercial aviation for Arnold's old friend, but their service for the airlines had been postponed "for the duration."

Traveling across the North Atlantic with Arnold and Towers was General Dwight Eisenhower, who in June would assume command of the European Theater of Operations, U.S. Army (ETOUSA), making him the highest-ranking American officer in Europe.

Despite the purpose of his mission, Arnold found RAF chief Peter Portal quite conciliatory when they sat down on the morning of May 26 for a talk ahead of a full conference later in the morning at 10 Downing Street with Churchill and their respective staffs. Arnold later described their meeting as "promising."

Arnold wrote of Churchill's opening remarks that the prime minister called for "the maximum number [of bombers] in action at all times and the greatest possible number of bombs must be dropped. It was a question of maintaining strength for the next few months—not a year from now."

Arnold replied by insisting that the American heavy bombers carrying the war to the Germans should be flown by American crews. As he summarized in his notes from the meeting, Arnold explained that the American people—and Congress—wanted to see the USAAF "in action in Europe, [but the] present allocation would not permit us to meet our Australian, Indian, Hawaiian [and] coast defense commitments. We wanted above all things to retain strength in defense areas and build up in other areas [and] had no intention of allowing any theater to have smaller number."

When the meeting adjourned, the prime minister took Arnold out to the Downing Street garden for a one-on-one discussion, after which Arnold recorded in his diary that "I may be mistaken but believe that we can sell our point."

In his own account of the negotiations, Arnold describes Churchill and Portal as being extremely willing to see things from his perspective. In so doing, he modestly downplays his own skills as a negotiator, which are evident in the results. The ongoing discussions over the next several days resulted in a revised Arnold-Portal agreement that called for a much larger proportion of American aircraft remaining with the Americans.

In a memo Portal prepared for Churchill on June 16, he outlined specifics. From an original allocation of 5,413 American aircraft for the first half of 1942, the RAF would now receive 2,339. Of these, the number of four-engine bombers was trimmed from 447 to just fifty-four. Totals for fighters were reduced from 2,105 to 704, but light bombers remained roughly unchanged.

With the horse-trading done, Arnold was anxious to see the effects of the strategic bombing that the RAF was already undertaking against Germany. On May 27, he traveled out to RAF Bomber Command headquarters at High Wycombe to meet with Air Marshal Arthur "Bomber" Harris. Here, he got his first extensive look at aerial reconnaissance photos of destroyed factories from Rostock to Augsburg, which showed the effects of the strategic air offensive. Arnold's comment, knowing that the RAF was anxious to have the Americans also involved, was that "their operations gave us something to shoot at."

At that moment, the USAAF Eighth Air Force was in England with high hopes, but not yet with the critical mass of men and equipment necessary to start shooting at much of anything. Thanks to Arnold's negotiating, there would be more in the allocation, but it was just an empty number until the trickle from the factories became a steady flow. In May 1942, the Eighth was just a shell, an air force in name only, but that was soon to change. When he returned to Washington, Arnold sent two of his most trusted officers—and long-time associates—to Britain to take command. Major General Tooey Spaatz, who had headed the AWPD, would now command the Eighth Air Force itself, while Brigadier General Ira Eaker would command its constituent VIII Bomber Command. Arnold successfully lobbied Eisenhower to give Spaatz the additional post as the air officer for Eisenhower's ETOUSA command, which would give the USAAF a role in theater planning.

Spaatz arrived on June 18 to find that the advance echelon of the 97th Bombardment Group, the first USAAF combat unit destined for his command, had been in England for three days. They were not, however, combat-ready, nor would they have their full complement of Flying Fortresses for several weeks.

Despite the reality on the ground in Britain, Hap Arnold was brimming with confidence on June 10 when he casually drafted a memo to Churchill in which he said, "We will be fighting with you" by the fourth of July. It was an improbable promise that sounded good at the time, but was an embarrassing mistake in retrospect. Henry Stimson wrote in his diary that the statement was "half-baked." Others have not been so kind to Arnold for this overly optimistic misjudgment.

Nevertheless, the symbolism of the date demanded that there could be no postponement. The show had to go on. Because there were only two Eighth Air Force Flying Fortresses in Britain at the time, Spaatz and Eaker had to borrow a half dozen lend-lease Bostons from the RAF. At least they were aircraft made in America, and the crews were American. Seven of the crewmen died in the mission, which targeted Luftwaffe fields in the Netherlands. It was an inauspicious beginning to the Eighth's coming offensive, but, as with the Doolittle mission and HALPRO, the news played well at home.

Six weeks later, on August 17, the Eighth Air Force offensive finally did get underway. A dozen Flying Fortresses of the 97th Bombardment Group, led by Eaker personally, struck railroad marshalling yards near Rouen in occupied northern France.

Two days afterward, nearly two dozen Flying Fortresses attacked airfields near Abbeville that were the home of Jagdgeschwader 26, one of the Luftwaffe's most highly regarded fighter wings. The latter mission was coordinated so as to sidetrack German aircraft as the Allies made their ill-fated commando raid on the French coastal city of Dieppe. The six-thousand-man Allied force lost more than half its troops as casualties or prisoners, and the remainder was compelled to withdraw under fire after just a few hours ashore.

When Eaker's bombers were able to follow up with additional missions on August 20 and 21, Arnold was elated. It mattered little that only nine Flying Fortresses took part in the latter mission. "Our heavy bomber missions were started, even if their communiqués, self conscious about the RAF's tons, announced the number of 'pounds' they had dropped," he wrote in his memoirs. "What a pattern it became! In Washington our hearts soared."

Meanwhile, the USAAF was expanding organizationally. Through August, Arnold oversaw the addition of four new numbered air forces. The Ninth Air Force was created as a tactical air support organization in the eastern Mediterranean Theater; the Tenth Air Force was formed as an umbrella organization for USAAF operations in the China-Burma-India Theater; the Eleventh Air Force came into being as a redesignation of the Alaskan Air Force; and the Twelfth Air Force was created in the western Mediterranean Theater primarily to support Operation Torch, the American landings in Northwest Africa that had been decided upon during the Arcadia Conference.

Commanding these new air forces were General Lewis Brereton with the Ninth, General Clayton Bissell at the Tenth, General William Butler with the Eleventh, and—back in the field after receiving his Medal of Honor from President Roosevelt—General Jimmy Doolittle with the Twelfth.

Meanwhile, Arnold re-designated the USAAF Air Ferrying Command as the Air Transport Command because units and operations of the command were "extended to all parts of the world" and not just doing ferry work.

To command this new organization, Arnold picked General Hal George, late of the AWPD, and as George's deputy, he "drafted" C. R. Smith, the president of American Airlines and commissioned him as a USAAF colonel. Indeed, the pilots and aircraft of all the nation's airlines would be a vital element in the development of the Air Transport Command and its global route structure.

"They made a wonderful pair," Arnold wrote in his memoirs. "No matter what mission I gave them, I could count on its being carried out 100 percent. The two officers complemented each other in ability, experience, and judgment—they made a perfect team. The growth of the Air Transport Command paralleled closely the expansion of the whole Air Force. It started out with two officers and one clerk in a small room and within two years totaled over 85,000 officers and men, and had lines extending to practically every corner of the world."

Having won his battle over production allotments and now finally seeing his Flying Fortresses in action, Hap Arnold should have been able to breathe more easily about the European Theater. However, two further internal battles now loomed, both of which threatened to limit the effectiveness, at least in the near term, of his plans for a strategic offensive against the Third Reich.

The first of these again put him at odds with Portal, with Bomber Harris, and with the rest of the RAF establishment. The crux of the matter was the beginning of a long-running doctrinal dispute over tactics. The USAAF located targets visually and bombed them with as much precision as possible. For this purpose, the USAAF had developed and deployed the Norden bombsight aboard its Flying Fortresses and Liberators. Developed in the United States by a Netherlands-born engineer named Carl Lukas Norden, the bombsight was the most sophisticated aiming device in history not to use electronics. Having worked for the Sperry Gyroscope Company before World War I, Norden was a recognized pioneer in the field of gyroscopically stabilized naval gun platforms when he went out on his own to build his bombsight.

The Eighth Air Force bombers were equipped with the Norden M-Series, which was capable of targeting within a fifty-foot radius from an altitude of more than twenty thousand feet, a level of precision eight times that afforded by the British Mk.XIV bombsight. The USAAF was confident that the Norden validated the doctrine of daylight precision attacks.

The British, however, were skeptical of both the bombsight and the doctrine, insisting that the Eighth Air Force abandon precision strikes in favor of area attacks, such as the RAF was doing. Unlike precision attacks, which were only possible in the daytime, area or "carpet" bombing could be done at night, when it was harder for enemy antiaircraft gunners or interceptor pilots to track and shoot down the bombers. The British advocacy of this doctrine verged on insistence. The Americans countered that carpet bombing was wasteful and imprecise and it led to widespread civilian casualties.

Having seen what the Luftwaffe Blitz of 1940 had done to London, Bomber Command's Harris was outspoken in his disregard for the drawbacks of area bombing. As he famously told Portal, "The Nazis entered this war under the rather childish delusion that they were going to bomb everyone else, and nobody was going to bomb them. At Rotterdam, London, Warsaw, and half a hundred other places, they put their rather naive theory into operation. They sowed the wind, and now they are going to reap the whirlwind."

As James Lea Cate wrote in the official history of the USAAF, the Americans stuck to their doctrine, believing that "paralysis of selected key spots would be as effective as, and far cheaper than, total obliteration." Although the USAAF and RAF agreed to disagree, and fly by day and night, respectively, the RAF continued to urge the USAAF to join them in nighttime area bombing.

The second challenge confronting Arnold and Spaatz involved Operation Torch, now set for November. The Combined Chiefs of Staff decided to focus the majority of Allied resources to the support of Torch and to divert bombers to the Mediterranean Theater and away from the build-up in Britain.

Tooey Spaatz went to General Eisenhower, who was given the supreme command of Allied forces for Operation Torch, and argued that the Eighth Air Force should continue to amass forces for strategic operations against Germany. Eisenhower agreed to Spaatz's demands, but only with the caveat that any resources deemed necessary for Torch would have to be diverted. As a result, the Eighth lost entire bombardment groups. It also lost Tooey Spaatz. When Eisenhower moved to the Mediterranean to assume the supreme command of Allied forces for Operation Torch, Spaatz, as the chief airman on his staff, went with him. Ira Eaker now moved up from VIII Bomber Command to head the entire Eighth Air Force. To command the VIII Bomber Command, Arnold picked Major General Frederick Lewis Anderson Jr., who had been the deputy director of bombardment at USAAF Headquarters before coming to England in 1941 as Arnold's personal representative "on bombardment matters" in the European Theater.

Eisenhower's gain would be Arnold's loss, but only for the moment. A year and a half later, both men would be back in Britain. As 1944 began, Eisenhower would be the supreme Allied commander in Europe, and Spaatz would be right where Arnold needed him for the climactic campaigns of World War II in Europe.

CHAPTER 10

THE PACIFIC THEATER

The "Germany first" policy had made the Pacific a secondary theater in the conference rooms of Anglo-American military planners, but to people on the street in the United States, it was just the opposite. It was Japan that had attacked Pearl Harbor, and it seemed to many that the war against Japan should come first.

As the planners anxiously awaited the start of the land war in Northwest Africa, the United States was *already* fighting a land war in the Pacific. American soldiers had fought, died, and lost at Bataan. American Marines had fought, died, and lost at Wake Island. Even as most Americans were blissfully unaware of Operation Torch, the headlines they were reading every day told of the hard, close combat in Guadalcanal, where the Marines had landed in August, and in New Guinea, where American and Australian troops were fighting desperately to halt the vigorous Japanese advance toward Australia. In June, the Japanese had even occupied American territory—the islands of Attu and Kiska in the Aleutian chain, which were part of Alaska.

In June 1942, U.S. Navy airpower sank four Japanese aircraft carriers and a cruiser at the Battle of Midway. For Hap Arnold and his staff, this remarkable victory only made it harder to justify their crusade to concentrate strategic airpower in Britain.

So far as public opinion was concerned, the buildup in Europe didn't seem to be accomplishing very much. When Americans looked across the Atlantic, they saw small results from small USAAF air raids against an enemy against which American ground troops were not yet engaged.

"The Navy's carrier-based air victory at Midway did not settle, but vindicated in the press the immediate need for more planes in the Pacific," Arnold complained in his memoirs. "To come from where? From us! From the Army Air Forces! The cries naturally included a plea for heavy bombers. The press and the American people didn't know about Torch. Early in the summer, the various commanders in the South West Pacific began yelling their heads off for airplanes. Nine heavy groups were supposed to go to the Middle East; eleven to the projected North African operations, and nine more were to go to the South West Pacific Area. Out of a total of fifty-four groups originally slated for the air offensive based in England, this left only twenty-five."

If Arnold and the strategic thinkers saw the big-picture implications of the "Germany first" policy, people who read the headlines perceived that the war was being fought, and fought desperately, by the soldiers and Marines in the South West Pacific Area. The SWPA was the swath of the Pacific Theater centering on New Guinea that stretched from Australia to the Philippines, and from Java to the

Solomon Islands—including Guadalcanal, the date line of the most attention-grabbing news stories. Nevertheless, in keeping with the prevailing strategic paradigm, Arnold had gone so far as to recommend *against* sending the nine groups earmarked for the SWPA. In a July 29 memo to Chief of Staff General George Marshall, he asserted that in the SWPA, "the initiative still rests with the enemy, and suitable objectives may not be available for effective full scale operations. It should also be noted this theater cannot, at this time, safely and properly sustain operations of an Air Force augmented over nine additional Groups because of the dangerous concentration which would result from limited base areas and base facilities."

In the same memo, Arnold confirmed his own "Germany first" bias as he reiterated to Marshall that "air action is the only direct offensive operation against the Germans which is not completely contingent upon the status of the Russian Front. Successful air operations depend upon the continual application of massed air-power against critical objectives. Germany remains our primary objective, and I feel strongly that the Air Force operating directly against her, which is permitted only from bases in the United Kingdom, must be maintained in sufficient strength to permit strict adherence to this principle."

A turn of events whose irony would not have been lost on Billy Mitchell, had he been in the room, came at a Joint Chiefs of Staff meeting two months later on September 16, 1942. The chief of naval operations practically begged the commanding general of the USAAF for *more airplanes*!

"There was quite a flare-up at the Joint Chiefs of Staff meeting, when Admiral [Ernest] King asked for more planes for the South Pacific," Arnold wrote. "I said planes were not what they needed; landing fields were the determining factor; not planes. All they could do with the planes, in excess of 80 or 100, was to let them sit on the few landing fields they then had. With no training, the pilots would get stale, while in England they could be used against the Germans every day."

"We must keep the South West Pacific saturated," King insisted.

"What is the saturation point?" Arnold asked. "Certainly, not several hundred planes sitting on airdromes so far in the rear [in Australia] that they cannot be used. They will not do us any good, and may do us some harm."

The tension, even in Arnold's measured recollections, is palpable.

"I was not surprised when General Marshall said he thought it was a good time for me to go to the South West Pacific and have a look around," Arnold recalled of the aftermath of the "flare-up" meeting. Marshall diplomatically told Arnold that "the most imme-diate way I could help Torch and the Eighth Air Force was to turn my back on both and go to the Pacific."

Before leaving for the South West Pacific two days later on Sep-tember 18, Arnold asked Marshall for "some hints about what I should or should not do."

"Listen to the other fellow's story," Marshall advised. "Don't get mad, and let the other fellow tell his story first."

Topping the checklist of "other fellows" who would be visited by Arnold was General Douglas MacArthur, the supreme Allied com-mander for the SWPA.

Next below MacArthur on the checklist was his USAAF com-mander, General George Kenney, who commanded the Fifth Air Force and whose responsibilities coincided with the boundaries of the SWPA. The relationship of MacArthur to Kenney was analogous to that between Eisenhower and Spaatz on the other side of the world.

The SWPA was bounded on the east by the Pacific Ocean Area (POA), under the overall command of Admiral Chester Nimitz, the commander in chief, Pacific Ocean Areas (CINCPOA). In turn, the POA were composed of the Northern Pacific Area (NORPAC), the Central Pacific Area (CENPAC), and the South Pacific Area (SOPAC). Virtually all of the land area involving actions by American forces in the Pacific prior to 1944 was under MacArthur's command. The major exception was Guadalcanal, which was in the SOPAC and under Nimitz's command.

Vice Admiral Robert Ghormley commanded the SOPAC at the time of Arnold's trip, while the naval air commander for the SOPAC was Admiral John S. "Slew" McCain, grandfather of the naval aviator and future presidential candidate, John S. McCain III.

The U.S. Army commander for the SOPAC was General Millard "Miff" Harmon, who was actually a USAAF officer. The idea of having an airman in command of both ground and air forces was a turnabout from the old days of having ground officers commanding the airmen in the Signal Corps. Harmon had known Arnold from the time they served together as young airmen on Governor's Island until Arnold made him his chief of staff in Washington just before the war.

The USAAF air commander under Harmon was General Nathan "Nate" Twining, while Harmon's ground force commander was General Alexander "Sandy" Patch, who would achieve his place in history two years later as commander of the U.S. Seventh Army in the European Theater.

Flying aboard a Consolidated C-87—the transport variant of the B-24 Liberator—Arnold and his staff reached Hawaii on September 20. Here, they were joined for the next leg of their trip by General Delos Emmons, formerly of GHQ Air Force, who had been in Hawaii for the past year. As Arnold wrote, Emmons had just returned from the South Pacific, "where he had spent considerable time with General Harmon, Admiral Ghormley, and General MacArthur. I was somewhat depressed after hearing Emmons' report on MacArthur's estimate of the situation. MacArthur, at the time, he thought, seemed not to be in too good health; and blamed our Air Force commanders for failure of the Air in the Philippine Islands."

When he met Nimitz at Pearl Harbor, Arnold found him to be "far more optimistic" than Emmons. He wrote that "Emmons was convinced that Guadalcanal could not be held; Nimitz was just as sure it could be. Nimitz' idea was that the Japanese shipping losses were so great they could not keep up such operations indefinitely."

As Arnold recorded in his diary for September 21, Nimitz believed that the Japanese "are getting worried.... The Japanese losses [from Midway through Guadalcanal] had been terrific.... The Japanese planes and pilots are both of inferior quality, and the war could be won in the Pacific."

Arnold and Emmons headed southwest, through Tonga and Fiji, to Noumea, New Caledonia, to meet with Ghormley, McCain, Twining, and Patch. If Nimitz was upbeat, Arnold discovered that Ghormley was extremely pessimistic and "particularly concerned about the logistics of his operations." Arnold noted that Ghormley "feared another big movement by the Japanese to the southeast, and the Marines were holding on [at Guadalcanal] only by a shoestring.... Gasoline and supplies at Guadalcanal were very short. Ships were hard to get into Guadalcanal.... It was obvious the Navy could not hold Guadalcanal if they could not get supplies in, and they could not get supplies in if the Japanese bombers continued to come down and bomb the ships unloading supplies."

Arnold left Ghormley's headquarters with the impression that the Navy "did not have a logistic setup efficient enough to insure success. The Marines were very tired and would grab at anything as a possible aid—something to restore their confidence.... Talk among the Navy staff officers indicated that conditions in New Guinea were very, very bad.... The Japanese would take over all of New Guinea soon. It looked to me as if everybody on that South Pacific Front had a bad case of jitters." Arnold later described Ghormley as "suffering mentally, physically and nervously." A month after Arnold's visit, Nimitz replaced Ghormley with Vice Admiral William Halsey Jr.

Arnold took exception when Admiral McCain asked for USAAF Flying Fortresses for long-range reconnaissance missions, writing that this was "amazing to me, in view of the propaganda we had heard prior to the war, that the big PBYs, the Navy flying boats, were the airplanes the Navy was [originally] going to use for reconnaissance and on long-range patrols. Here they were asking for our long-range bombers to do their work for them."

The maximum range of the twin-engine PBY was actually greater than that of the Flying Fortress, but the patrol bombers had relatively minimal bomb-carrying capacity. In his diary entry for September 23, Arnold noted that McCain "finally admitted the possibility of using PBYs."

"Everyone just happened to be thinking of B-17s and P-38s," Arnold observed about the Navy's desire for the most up-to-date USAAF aircraft. "When I went into the question of using P-38s out of Noumea, I was confronted with the fact that they had no way to get them from the ships on which they arrived to flying fields. They were too big to get over the roads, and there were no docks near the airfields."

As with Admiral King's pleas at the Joint Chiefs of Staff meeting on September 16, Billy Mitchell would have laughed at the admirals lusting for USAAF aircraft.

Everyone with whom Arnold had met—Army, Navy, and USAAF—was disdainful of the "Germany first" paradigm, and argued eloquently for a realignment of priorities. They saw no reason why the grand strategy should put so much emphasis on Operation Torch to the detriment of the desperate campaign to stop the Japanese onslaught.

They were equally derisive of the USAAF plan to use long-range bombers in a strategic air offensive against Germany. Nimitz had told Arnold pointedly that "the bombardment of Germany was of no use."

Hap Arnold complained both about the "uninformed pressures" of "American popular opinion" back home and about the parochialism of the admirals in the South West Pacific. In his diary entry of September 16, the day of the "flare-up" at the Joint Chiefs meeting, he paraphrased Frederick the Great, writing that "small minds want to defend everything. Intelligent men concentrate on the main issue, parry the heavy blows and tolerate small evils to avoid a greater one. He who wants to defend everything saves nothing."

Of course, it can also be said that those, like Arnold, who had become adherents to the "Germany first" policy were no less parochial than the Pacific commanders. Indeed, in September 1942, based on the best available information, Australia was in greater danger of a Japanese invasion than Britain was from Nazi Germany, and Operation Torch might have seemed far more parochial than the fighting in the SOPAC.

In his diary, Arnold posed the questions: "Where is this war to be won? What is our plan for winning the war? Is this [the SOPAC] not a local affair and should it not be treated as such? In any event, everyone from the Chief of Naval Operations on down should be indoctrinated with one plan for winning the war."

Before sunrise on September 25, Arnold took off for the 850-mile flight from Noumea to Brisbane, Australia, where MacArthur and Kenney had their headquarters.

By early afternoon, Arnold sat down with MacArthur, an outspoken, charismatic figure who was lionized on the home front and respected—if not universally loved—in the field. Like the admirals with whom Arnold had been meeting, he was not shy about sharing his perspective on the war in the Pacific and on global strategy. If anything, he was more forceful in expressing his views because it was the nature of his personality to be sure that his convictions were fact, not merely opinion.

Unlike many who met MacArthur for the first time, Arnold was not overawed by the colorful general's larger-than-life presence. Indeed, Arnold had known him for nearly two decades. They were not close friends, but they knew each other reasonably well.

MacArthur told Arnold flat out that the aim of the Japanese was to "control the Pacific Ocean ... move into the Aleutians and be ready for a general move into Alaska."

As had the others with whom Arnold had met, he dismissed the "Germany first" doctrine out of hand, stating that Britain was merely a "besieged citadel," and that "it would be very difficult to establish a Second Front from England, [the] movements into North Africa would be a waste of effort, [and] a sufficient number of air bases could never be established in England to provide air cover for a Second Front."

MacArthur recommended that the Allies should "build up Australia as a reservoir of supplies, troops, and planes, and use them in any direction against the Japanese."

Far from being swayed by MacArthur, Arnold felt a sympathy that bordered on pity.

"Thinking it over, MacArthur's two hour talk gives me the impression of a brilliant mind, obsessed by a plan he can't carry out; frustrated, dramatic to the extreme, much more nervous than when I formerly knew him, hands twitch and tremble, shell-shocked," Arnold wrote in his diary that night.

It was early to bed for the USAAF chief. He was up at 2:00 a.m. for his first flight into a combat zone since World War I. As he boarded an armed Flying Fortress at the field in Townsville, Australia, the copilot introduced himself. He was Captain Bill Stoddard, who had been a member of the West Point class of 1940, along with Arnold's son Hank.

In his diary, Arnold describes the scene aboard the crowded aircraft as he and his drowsy staff officers sought a place for a nap. "Everybody hunting a bunk, sleeping on catwalks, around ball turrets and everywhere they can find a place," he wrote. "Awake at 6:00, New Guinea coast at 6:30, supposed to be met by fighters, all guns manned and tested, a fine wide-awake crew. Just heard that Japs raided Darwin [Australia] last night."

The plane touched down at the Allied stronghold of Port Moresby on New Guinea's southeast coast at a quarter past seven o'clock, where Arnold was greeted by Australian Generals Thomas Blarney and S. F. Roswell, and USAAF Brigadier General Ken Walker. The commander of the Fifth Air Force's V Bomber Command, Walker was not a "desk-flying" commander, but rather one who managed to fly frequent combat missions despite orders from both Kenney and MacArthur himself to stay out of harm's way.

Arnold sat down to breakfast with Walker and General Ennis Whitehead, Kenney's deputy. The discussions focused on the aircrews of the 19th Bombardment Group, a unit that had been under Arnold's direct command at March Field a decade earlier, and which was now bearing the brunt of heavy bomber operations in the SWPA. Among other missions, they were carrying out raids against the big Japanese bastion at Rabaul, the center of enemy power in the region.

In his diary, Arnold described the 19th Bombardment Group men as including "war-weary pilots, experienced but indifferent [who had] been in war since the Philippines ... too many stars; know all the answers."

This description, along with Walker's maverick reputation, was illustrative of the status of the USAAF in a theater at the ends of the earth, making do with limited equipment and informal organization, thousands of miles from a USAAF headquarters ruled by the "Germany first" doctrine.

In his diary, Arnold jotted down some observations about the strategic situation in the SWPA: "If we don't take the offensive soon, the Japanese will drive us out [of New Guinea]. We have enough troops to do it.... Taking the offensive, we can secure bases at Buna, Lae, Salamaua, and operate strongly against Rabaul. If we don't take the offensive, we will lose Port Moresby, the south side of New Guinea, and open up the north shore of Australia to attack and possible occupation by the Japs."

Having seen his men at war, on the front lines, for the first time, Arnold was greatly heartened by what he had found: "The youngsters who were actually doing the fighting, actually meeting the Japanese in combat, were not the people who were jittery. They had no doubts about their ability to lick the Japanese and they were positive of the action that could and must be taken."

In his memoirs, Arnold extolled the virtues of his Fifth Air Force commander and his men, writing that "Kenney had certainly developed into a real leader and he had one of the finest groups of pilots and combat crews I have ever seen. Many of those who were nervous and worn out, and who had wanted to go home when he first got there, had withdrawn their requests and now wanted to stay."

Arnold may have remained wedded to the idea that Germany was the Allies' first priority, but he was gaining useful insight into, and appreciation for, the work being done by Allied soldiers and airmen facing Japan. As for the naval war, it was another matter.

At Noumea, Arnold met once again with Ghormley, and with Nimitz, who had come down from Pearl Harbor. At this meeting, he was struck by the way that Nimitz and his POA Theater command operated with such a profound lack of cooperation and coordination with MacArthur and his SWPA Theater command.

Arnold noted that

> the US Navy for years had been thinking toward a state
> of readiness to lick the Japanese. They knew they could
> do it with little, if any, trouble!—"with one hand tied
> behind them." Pearl Harbor came as a distinct shock to
> all of us, but to our Navy more than anyone. It upset years
> of their planning. It was only natural for them to figure
> on regaining their position in the sun. They must do
> everything possible to make the Pacific campaign not only
> the first-priority war theater, but also to make it a Navy
> war theater, run by the Navy.

"I was more convinced than ever that there must be unity of command in our Pacific operations if we were to get economy and maximum effectiveness," Arnold wrote.

On the afternoon of October 2, 1942, Arnold touched down at Bolling Field in the District of Columbia. Much to his surprise, he was met by a band, the press corps, Chief of Staff Marshall, and Robert Lovett, the assistant secretary of war for air. Lovett greeted Arnold by pinning a Distinguished Service Medal on him in recognition of the mission he had just completed. This journey had taken him through fifteen time zones in as many days. By his own reckoning, he had covered 9,830 miles and had logged 127 hours and thirty-five minutes of flying time, an average of more than eight hours a day.

Arnold's questions about where the war was to be won and with what plan were about to have an unexpected answer.

CHAPTER 11

THE PLAN

Within a week of Hap Arnold's return to Washington, the Japanese succeeded in reinforcing their forces on Guadalcanal with a contingent of three thousand troops. Aware of both the impending Operation Torch and the midterm elections, a startled Franklin Roosevelt reacted by ordering a renewed emphasis on the Pacific. The "Germany first" doctrine may have remained as the key strategic policy among military leaders, but in the president's perception, it was first among equals.

In an October 24 memo to the Joint Chiefs of Staff, the president wrote that "my anxiety about the Southwest Pacific is to make sure that every possible weapon gets into the area to hold Guadalcanal, and that, having held in this crisis, munitions, planes, and crews are on the way to take advantage of our success. We will soon find ourselves engaged on two active fronts [Southwest Pacific and Northwest Africa], and we must have adequate air support in both places, even though it means delay in our commitments, particularly, to England."

Arnold responded to the phrases about "two active fronts" and "delay in our commitments," writing in his memoirs that "those two quotations in themselves might have changed completely our strategic planning for operations against Germany, for if aid to the Pacific meant delay in our commitments to England, it could not help but delay our operations against the Germans."

Indeed, operations against the Germans, outside those surrounding the requirements of Operation Torch, *would* be delayed. The Eighth Air Force strategic air offensive from bases in Britain was evolving at a far slower pace than Arnold and his commanders on the scene, such as Ira Eaker, would have liked.

Operation Torch took place on November 8, five days after the midterm elections. The Democrats lost forty-six seats in the House and eight in the Senate, although they retained control of both houses. While the president mourned that modest political defeat, he celebrated the fact that Operation Torch was a success, with five landings across Morocco and Algeria. A week later, the Vichy French resistance crumbled, the USAAF quickly took advantage of newly captured airfields, and American airpower was established in the Mediterranean. Moreover, the tides of the war had shifted, thanks to the stubborn American defense of Guadalcanal, the British victory at the battle of El Alamein in November, and the looming defeat of the German army at Stalingrad.

As Hap Arnold wrote in his memoirs, "It had become obvious to the members of the Joint [American] and the Combined [Anglo-American] Chiefs of Staff that there must be a meeting with the

President and the Prime Minister to determine 'where do we go from here.' Not until [Operation Torch] was actually accomplished had we been ready, positively, to plan for what, where, and when our next action should be."

It was agreed that there would be an Allied conference, with Roosevelt, Churchill, and their chiefs of staff, at Casablanca, Morocco—recently captured by American forces—during the third week of 1943.

Hap Arnold, Chief of Staff George Marshall, Sir John Dill, and a collection of staff officers departed Washington on January 9, 1943, flying aboard a C-54, with stops at Belém, Brazil, and Dakar in French West Africa. On the nighttime flight across the Atlantic, Arnold took the controls for three hours. An accompanying C-54 carried Admiral King and his staff, as well as General Brehon "Bill" Somervell, commander of U.S. Army Service Forces, and General Albert Wedemeyer, destined for a command role with the Allied Southeast Asia Command.

Arriving in Casablanca on January 13, a day ahead of Roosevelt, the officers were met by General Eisenhower, the Allied commander of the recent Torch success, and by other key figures in the operation such as General George Patton and General Mark Clark. Among the British officers was RAF boss Peter Portal. Also present, and significant because of Morocco's status as a French colony, were Charles DeGaulle and Henri Giraud. The two French generals had each escaped the clutches of the Germans and were now bitter rivals for recognition as leaders of the Free French, anti-Vichy forces who wished to liberate France from German domination. Their presence was long on political drama, but short on substance, as the Free French Forces that existed at the time were tiny by comparison to the armed forces of Britain and America.

Meanwhile, Arnold was also met at the Anfa Hotel by his son, Hank, now a young officer assigned to the sizable U.S. Army contingent guarding and providing logistical support for the conference. Hap brought Hank belated Christmas presents, and father and son made a short sightseeing trip through Casablanca. In his diary, Hap noted the "beautiful villas along coast, land very fertile, city has clean, wide streets, see very few natives in foreign section. Large, freshly painted buildings. At the docks, [French battleship] *Jean Bart* with holes in bow and stern large enough to take a small bungalow, made by 1,000-pound bombs as it fired at our fleet."

That night, January 14, Arnold was invited to a dinner with Roosevelt and Churchill. Arnold, Marshall, and King sat across from Portal, Field Marshal Alan Brooke, and Admiral of the Fleet Dudley Pound. Hank Arnold did not attend, but the president's son—Major Elliott "Bunny" Roosevelt, a USAAF officer and a P-38 pilot with the Twelfth Air Force—did, acting as his father's military attaché.

Both Roosevelt and Churchill, to the horror of everyone else, let it be known that they were anxious to make a field trip to the battlefront east of Algiers. "Everyone tried to keep President and Prime Minister from making plans to get too near front, both seemed determined, could see no real danger," Arnold confided in his diary. Ultimately, Roosevelt reviewed frontline troops, but at a considerable distance from the actual front.

Among the many staff meetings, the most important for Arnold was when he sat down with Portal to discuss the air campaign against Germany. Portal was joined by Bomber Harris and by Air Chief Marshal Arthur Tedder, who had been picked to head the joint Mediterranean Air Command (MAC). Arnold was accompanied by Spaatz and Ira Eaker, who had flown down from England for the conference.

The British opened by saying that they were disappointed with the American participation in the air campaign. After a year of hopes and promises, the Eighth Air Force had relatively little to show for itself. It had taken until August 1942 to get the Eighth's

Flying Fortresses into action, and they had yet to establish a routine pattern of missions flown. The RAF Bomber Command had mustered a few *thousand* plane raids, while it had taken the Eighth until October 9 to launch a *hundred* plane raids, and this had not been possible to replicate. The British pointed out that the Eighth had yet to fly a mission into Germany itself.

The Americans countered by referencing a steeper-than-expected learning curve and the diversion of USAAF resources to Operation Torch and a campaign against U-boat pens in France. They also noted that northern Europe was almost continuously blanketed by overcast in December and January, which made precision bombing impossible.

Portal and Harris then pointed to the apparent effectiveness of the RAF's nighttime area bombardment raids and pointedly told Arnold and his men that it was time to terminate the American "experiment" with precision bombing and adopt the British doctrine of area bombing. They explained that area raids were not dependent on an unobstructed view of the targets, and flying at night made the bombers safer from antiaircraft fire and interceptors.

At Casablanca, Arnold took the American case to Churchill directly, outlining "to him why we were so sure we could carry out daylight precision bombing and why we figured the Germans could not stop us. I told him of the various experiments we had made and how we figured our formations of B-17s and B-24s, subsequently with long-legged fighters, could protect themselves against German aircraft. I also told him I had at Casablanca, General Frank Andrews, General Spaatz, and General Eaker; that I would like to have him talk with each of them, in turn, so they could give him additional data and information."

On January 18, Churchill sat down face-to-face with Eaker. When the prime minister brought up the recurring disagreement over the issue of nocturnal area raids versus daytime precision attacks, Eaker was able to show the prime minister how the Norden bombsight permitted a degree of accuracy that was five times more precise than what the RAF was accomplishing. This, in turn, dovetailed into the argument that the same volume of ordnance could be used by fewer bombers to effectively destroy more targets.

Eaker also cited specific data to demonstrate that the loss rate was actually less for the Eighth than for the Bomber Command. He pointed out improvements in Luftwaffe night fighter tactics, which militated against nighttime safety, as well as improvements in Eighth Air Force defensive tactics, which favored continued daytime operations.

"On January 19th, I had lunch with the Prime Minister," Arnold recalled in his memoirs.

> The Prime Minister seemed willing to let the matter drop. It was quite evident to me he had been harassed by some of his own people about our daylight bombing program and had to put up a fight on the subject. Whether they were fearful we would use our airplanes ineffectively in the daylight missions; whether they were afraid we would waste airplanes; or whether they feared we would do something they could not and had not been able to do, I do not know … the Prime Minister told me he was willing for us to give it a trial; that he would say nothing more about it. That was a great relief to me and to my command. We had won a major victory, for we would bomb in accordance with American principles, using the methods for which our planes were designed.

Arnold later had a separate meeting with Roosevelt and Marshall on the same subject and, "as far as they were concerned, the matter was settled."

"Go ahead with your daylight precision bombing!" Roosevelt and Marshall told him. It was now understood that a prerequisite to the defeat of the Third Reich was to hammer it from the air. That said, Roosevelt and Marshall—and even Churchill—were willing to leave the details to their experts in the USAAF and RAF.

On January 21, the Combined Chiefs of Staff approved what came to be known as the Casablanca Directive on the subject of *round-the-clock* strategic bombing. It called for the RAF to continue flying at night and for the Eighth Air Force to continue flying their daylight missions. The directive called for what was later formalized as the Combined Bomber Offensive, which would be an organizational structure that would coordinate the efforts of the Eighth Air Force and RAF Bomber Command to achieve "the progressive destruction and dislocation of the German military, industrial, and economic system, and the undermining of the morale of the German people to a point where their capacity for armed resistance is fatally weakened."

The crucial issue was not day bombing versus night bombing but designing a strategic bombing campaign that would destroy Germany's ability to make war. When Spaatz had arrived in Britain in the spring of 1942, he brought with him the nucleus of a target planning staff. These civilian experts, now commissioned into uniform, analyzed the German war economy, looking for supply routes and key industries—such as petrochemicals, aluminum, and aircraft production—identifying where strategic bombing could do the most damage.

In London, this organization, the Enemy Objectives Unit (EOU) of the Economic Warfare Division (EWD) took up residence at a secret location—40 Berkeley Square—known only to a handful of outsiders. Among those on its staff were economists and other experts, including many who had originally been recruited by William J. "Wild Bill" Donovan of the Office of Strategic Services (OSS).

Among them were the Ivy League–educated economists, Walt Whitman Rostow, the future security advisor to presidents Kennedy and Johnson, and Charles Poor "Charlie" Kindleberger, late of the Board of Governors of the Federal Reserve System. Another member of the team, recruited by Spaatz and the Air War Plans Division staff, was Richard D'Oyly Hughes, who by all accounts was the driving force at the EOU.

While the EOU was, in Rostow's words, "waging economic warfare from London," Hap Arnold had created his own economic warfare board closer to home. On December 9, 1942, he ordered Colonel Byron Gates to empanel a "group of operational analysts under your jurisdiction [to] prepare and submit to me a report analyzing the rate of progressive deterioration that should be anticipated in the German war effort as a result of the increasing air operations we are prepared to employ against its sustaining sources. This study should result in as accurate an estimate as can be arrived at as to the date when this deterioration will have progressed to a point to permit a successful invasion of Western Europe."

This organization, known as the Committee of Operations Analysts (COA), differed from the operational EOU in that it was designed to give Arnold the data that he would need to support the strategic air campaign politically in Washington.

With the Combined Bomber Offensive now formalized, Arnold could afford to turn his attention to the other items that had brought the Allied leaders together. In his memoirs, he wrote that the next "most important problem of the Combined Chiefs of Staff now was to figure out the next movement to follow the Tunisian campaign. The British talked about a movement through southern France, but the American Chiefs of Staff still thought the main offensive should come across the English Channel into northern France. Naturally, had the men, materiel, equipment, and air superiority all been available at that time, we could have carried on with that campaign against the main German Army at once, but we were still short in many things."

The cross-channel invasion, discussed a year earlier under the code name Operation Sledgehammer, had been postponed from 1942 to 1943, revised under the designation Operation Roundup, and then postponed again. Now, it was 1943, and it was time to put Roundup back on the agenda. The Allies were in a better position to consider this than they had been in 1942, but as Arnold points out, they "were still short in many things."

Instead of continuing to pursue the ambitious Roundup concept, Churchill now spoke in favor of action against what he called the "soft underbelly of Europe," meaning operations in the Mediterranean. Realizing that the Anglo-American Allies were, indeed, "still short in many things," Roosevelt agreed that the next major move, to take place during 1943, would be a two-part operation against the *third* Axis power—Italy.

The first step, after defeating the German Afrika Korps, would be the Allied invasion of Sicily, code-named Operation Husky. Once Sicily was in Allied hands, it would be the springboard for amphibious landings on the Italian mainland. The cross-channel invasion of northern France, meanwhile, was postponed until 1944.

But the most important decision made at Casablanca came from an apparently offhand comment by Roosevelt on the last day that took Churchill and others off guard. As Drew Pearson reported for the *New York Times*, Roosevelt told the press corps that "world peace will come only as a result of the total elimination of German and Japanese war power." The president, Pearson wrote, "borrowed a phrase from General Grant's famous letter to the Confederate commander at Forts Donelson and Henry—'unconditional surrender'—to describe the only terms on which the United Nations would

accept the conclusion of the war." Roosevelt added that unconditional surrender would not involve the annihilation of the German
or Japanese people, but "the destruction of the philosophies in those
countries which are based on conquest and the subjugation of other
people."

Many have argued that Roosevelt's policy of unconditional surrender stiffened enemy resolve and prolonged the war. But one can
just as easily argue that it gave the Allies a definite war-ending objective. In a June 30, 1943, speech at the Guildhall in London, Churchill
said the United States and Britain "shall continue like brothers,
certainly until unconditional surrender and until our goals have
been achieved and I trust until after all due measure has been taken
so as to secure our safety in future years."

For men like Hap Arnold, forcing the "unconditional surrender"
of the enemy became the objective for the strategic bombing campaign, and the answer to his earlier question, "What is our plan for
winning the war?"

CHAPTER 12

MISSION TO CHINA

With the conclusion of the Roosevelt-Churchill press conference on January 24, 1943, the Casablanca Conference broke up, and the participants went their separate ways. For Hap Arnold, this meant trading his C-54 with the airline interior for the more spartan confines of a B-17 dubbed *Argonaut* and heading east toward Algiers and Cairo. From there, Roosevelt had asked him to continue eastward to the China-Burma-India Theater to brief the Allied leaders in Asia on the discussions and decisions of the Casablanca Conference.

Roosevelt told Arnold that he wanted him to personally brief Generalissimo Chiang Kai-shek, the Nationalist leader of war-torn

China, a nation of immense importance geographically and strategically. Chiang's forces (and the Chinese Communist guerillas he was fighting simultaneously) were tying down more than three million Japanese troops.

After a stop in Algiers to visit Jimmy Doolittle and the aircrews of his Twelfth Air Force, Arnold reached the Egyptian capital on January 26. In his diary, he noted how cold Cairo was in midwinter and how little the Egyptian capital had changed since his last visit as a young lieutenant in 1909. While in Cairo, he was taken to see "the Caves," a quarry "perhaps the source of the lime and sandstone with which the Pyramids themselves were built [and which] were now used by the RAF as 'shops' in which to repair and rebuild salvaged engines, propellers, instruments and radio sets."

On January 29, now accompanied by Sir John Dill, Arnold headed out to Basra in Iraq, a city that became well known in a later war in another century. When Arnold and Dill arrived, the port was serving as a transshipment point for American lend-lease aircraft bound for the Soviet Union; about 1,500 Douglas Aircraft Company employees were preparing the last of nearly seven hundred A-20 light attack bombers to be delivered to Soviet crews. In his diary, Arnold used the "pulling teeth" metaphor to describe his efforts to get the complaining Soviet commander to admit that the aircraft were, in fact, battle-ready when they were turned over.

After stops in the Iranian oil town of Abadan and in Karachi, Arnold, Dill, and their party landed in New Delhi late on the night of January 30. The following day, Arnold and Dill dined with General Archibald Percival Wavell, the British commander in chief for India, as well as General Claude Auchinleck, his predecessor. During the early years of the war, the two men had alternated between the India job and that of commander of the British Middle East Command.

Arnold briefed Wavell and Auchinleck on the talks at Casablanca, they briefed Arnold on the campaign against the Japanese in Burma, and Arnold and Dill talked about the strategic importance of China (which Wavell and Auchinleck considered outside their area of concern).

Arnold and Dill explained that with China's ports in Japanese hands, the only land route to supply Chiang's forces was the narrow, seven-hundred-mile Burma Road, which ran across mountainous terrain from Burma to Kunming. In May 1942, however, the Japanese had defeated the mainly British force holding Burma, and had closed the road.

The delivery of supplies to the Chinese forces battling the Japanese was now in the hands of the USAAF. The air route was across the Himalayas, studded with cloud- and blizzard-shrouded mountain peaks topping fifteen thousand feet. This route—known as "the Hump"—was the most difficult supply route flown by any routine airlift operation during the war.

In his memoirs, Arnold recalled finding Wavell to be "a very brilliant man, but apparently more of a student, a planner, than a leader in the field. He seemed to be tired and worn out with his combat experiences." Arnold goes on to say that "I could not get the impression out of my head that the British had been using India as a place to which to send officers who had more or less outlived their usefulness in other theaters."

"At first it was the British in India who were dragging their feet," Arnold recalled in notes written as he was headed home from the Far East. "We managed to step up their thoughts.... Looking [back], it did not take long to get Wavell headed right; it took longer for his staff."

After nightfall on February 2, the American commander in China arrived in New Delhi to meet Arnold. General Joseph Warren "Vinegar Joe" Stilwell is one of the great, overshadowed figures of World

War II. He was in his final year at West Point when Arnold was a plebe, and he had gone on to earn a Distinguished Service Medal at St.-Mihiel during World War I. He had served three tours of duty in China and was the United States military attaché from 1936 to 1939, being present during the Japanese invasion and the evacuation of the Chinese government from Peking to Chungking.

Regarded as one of the top field commanders in the U.S. Army, Stilwell had been considered to command American forces in Operation Torch, the job that went to Eisenhower. Instead, Roosevelt and Marshall thought Stilwell was the obvious choice to command American forces in China, even though it was a job Stilwell did not want. Stilwell was in Burma during the Japanese invasion. The fifty-nine-year-old general led more than one hundred members of his staff to India *on foot*, with Stilwell himself setting the brisk pace.

Arnold's meeting with Stilwell in India was brief, with the two men deciding to continue their discussions in Chungking in three days' time. Stilwell, with Sir John Dill aboard his aircraft, departed first. Arnold, accompanied by Tenth Air Force commander General Clayton Bissell, took off from Delhi at half past seven o'clock on the morning of February 4, and made a short stop in Agra. At this stop, Arnold made a note in his diary that he was unimpressed with the city "until we saw the Taj Mahal." He also noted in his diary that as they flew over the Hump, they saw Mount Everest "in all its glory standing in the blue sky with its snow peak well above the haze."

As the plane touched down in Dinjan, China, in the mid-afternoon, the plan had been to spend the night. However, when Arnold learned that Stilwell and Dill had continued on to Kunming, he decided that he and Bissell would resume their travels and continue the 525 miles to Kunming after dark.

"After two hours flying we saw little or nothing," Arnold wrote in his diary. "I saw a red glare off to the south and asked what time we would land. The answer came: 20 minutes. We flew for another hour and then some more and still had not reached our destination. Then I learned that there was considerable apprehension among our combat crew as to our locality."

As Arnold wrote in his memoirs,

> I had not known that the crew had not put on their oxygen masks, although we were traveling at 19,000 feet. I talked with the radioman and told him to put on a mask right away and then start using the radio to see if he could get a check with any of the various stations in North Burma, India, or China. In the meantime, I asked the navigator whether he was taking oxygen. He told me he wasn't. I told him to start using it right away, then get on the job and find out where we were. I called the pilot back to the seats where General Bissell and I were and started talking with him. While he was standing there, he crumpled to the floor. No oxygen. I gave him my mask and soon got him back in shape. Lack of oxygen had certainly fixed up my crew.

Arnold's diary, written a few hours after the incident, betrays the profound concerns that were going through his mind as *Argonaut* rumbled through the night:

> There is always the possibility of Jap planes being abroad. They probably have radar and plot the course of all visiting aircraft such as ours. If we turn back into the wind do we run out of gas in the mountains? Do we jump? If so, when? Will we be captured over by Mandalay? What should we take with us if we have to jump? What will the people back home think if they hear that the Commanding General, US Army Air Forces and the Commanding

General, Tenth Air Force and others with us have been
taken prisoners? What are the best shoes to wear in hiking
through the jungle? Can we take emergency rations with
us if we jump?

He ordered the pilot to reverse course as the radio operator tried
to locate a radio beacon with which they could navigate to Kunming.
The navigator was finally able to plot their location, discerning that
they had overshot their destination by three hundred miles. The red
glare which Arnold had seen had, in fact, been Kunming. For reasons that were never explained, the radio station at the airport had
been off the air, but Arnold's radio operator was overheard by a
friendly ham radio operator in Kunming. The Flying Fortress landed
nearly five hours late.

Arnold and Bissell met with Stilwell and General Claire Lee
Chennault, commander of the USAAF's China Air Task Force. Chennault was a colorful, difficult, maverick officer who, like Douglas
MacArthur, saw Asia as the crucial theater of the war, in part because
he had spent a number of years in the Far East before the war. Chennault had left the service in 1937 and gone to China, where he
became Chiang Kai-shek's air advisor, organized and trained the
Chinese air force, and then, in 1940, with the Chinese forces on the
verge of collapse, created the American Volunteer Group (AVG),
better known as the Flying Tigers. The AVG, made up of former
American military fighter pilots, was authorized by President Roosevelt under a secret executive order. Roosevelt arranged for the AVG
to receive lend-lease P-40 Warhawks, whose cowlings were painted
with fierce shark teeth, hence the nickname "Flying Tigers." After
Pearl Harbor, the AVG was integrated into the USAAF, and Chennault was now Hap Arnold's senior airman in China.

Accompanied by Chennault, Arnold proceeded on to Chungking,
where he met with Chiang Kai-shek and delivered a personal memo

from President Roosevelt. The president promised Chiang that Arnold would

> tell you about the plans to intensify our efforts to drive the Japanese out of the Southwest Pacific. As I wired you, I have been meeting with the Prime Minister and our respective Chiefs of Staff to plan our offensive strategy against Japan and Germany during 1943. I want Arnold to talk all this over with you in the greatest detail because I think it would be best that I not put it on the cables.... I have great hopes for the war in 1943, and like you, I want to press it home on the Japanese with great vigor. I want to convey not only my warm regards for you personally, but my everlasting appreciation of the service which your armies are giving to our common cause.

On February 6, with heavy snow falling throughout the day, Arnold and his aide, Colonel Louis Parker, together with Stilwell and Chennault, were taken to Chiang's residence by T. V. Soong, the Harvard-educated financier who was Chiang's brother-in-law, closest advisor, and trusted international envoy. With Soong translating, Chiang let it be known that he was, in Arnold's words, "not particularly interested in the Casablanca Conference nor in the Combined Chiefs of Staff, except where Burma and China were concerned."

Chiang said he was bitterly opposed to the Roosevelt-Churchill "Germany first" doctrine and was keen to receive substantial aid and support from the Americans. In his notes, Arnold wrote that they spent five minutes on the Casablanca Conference and more than an hour discussing China's air force and an ideal independent command with Chennault running both Chinese and American airpower in China. The generalissimo called him "the only one who can handle operations on account of the many complications…the one outstanding tactician and strategist in the Far East today."

While Chiang was greatly enamored of Chennault and earnestly advocated that he be in charge of all American air operations throughout the China-Burma-India Theater, Stilwell's relations with Chiang were another matter entirely. He made no secret of his opinion that the generalissimo was a corrupt buffoon.

"No one dares to tell the Peanut (meaning the Generalissimo) the truth, if it is unpleasant," Stilwell told Arnold, who repeated the dialogue in his memoirs. "The big obstructions are the General Staff. They are due to jealousy, inertia, laziness, pride, and crass stupidity. They continue because the Peanut is too dumb to realize what is being done. Anything that is done in China will be done in spite of, and not because of, the Peanut and his military clique."

The following day, February 7, Arnold was summoned back to Chiang's cold and drafty house for further talks. At the generalissimo's insistence, he came alone. The two men were joined only by T. V. Soong, who translated.

"I am going to be very frank with you, more so than I usually am," Chiang said at the outset, as recorded in Arnold's diary. "The conference so far has been a failure and I want you to tell the President so for me. It has accomplished nothing. Our Army has been carrying on at war now for six years. We have gotten no supplies from anyone. Our movements have been made by our own legs; we have had no trucks, we have carried our artillery on our backs, our men have starved…. Tell your President that unless I can get [more supply tonnage and more airplanes] I cannot fight this war and he cannot count on me to have our Army participate in the campaigns."

Chiang continued to stress the importance of an independent air force for Chennault, with five hundred new aircraft, and insisted that Arnold's USAAF should deliver ten thousand tons of supplies each month over the Hump.

Arnold replied that he had "nothing but the highest praise for the splendid courage and heroism of the Chinese soldiers; their bravery and endurance of hardships are outstanding. I must tell you that I am sincerely disappointed in your message to the President for it is not in any way in accordance with my understanding of what has occurred."

Arnold then turned Chiang's admiration and reverence for Chennault back on him by telling him that "the officer in whom you have the greatest confidence" had told Arnold that heavy bombers could not operate in China until Chiang fulfilled his own long-standing promise to build and expand airfields in the country. Arnold promised that he would increase the supplies coming over the Hump to four thousand tons a month "as soon as it can be done," and to "build it up beyond that as soon as facilities are available," which put the ball back in Chiang's court.

The following day, February 8, in India, Arnold reflected on his meeting with Chiang Kai-shek. "The Generalissimo does not impress me as a big man; he casts aside logic and factual matters as so much trash," Arnold wrote. "Apparently he believes his power can force from his subjects the impossible. He never gave any indication of thoughts of the outside world, except insofar as it gave aid to China.... He does not have to think things through. It makes no difference as long as he has his way.... He did not impress me as being in the same class as the President [Roosevelt] or Prime Minister [Churchill]."

In his memoirs, Arnold wrote that "the personal clashes among the key leaders in China made it rather difficult for me to give the President a clean-cut report. Logistics, air and general military progress were one thing. Matters like Chiang's attitude toward Bissell, his unlimited confidence in Chennault, Chennault's own oversimplification, along Chinese lines, of various problems, and above all the personal position of Stilwell, who called Chiang Kai-shek

'Peanut Head' practically within the Generalissimo's hearing ... were complications a bit beyond the Book."

Nevertheless, against Arnold's recommendations, and under pressure from the White House, USAAF operations in China were carved from Bissell's Tenth Air Force. On March 5, the USAAF officially activated the new Fourteenth Air Force in China, placing it under Chennault's command. Two days earlier, Arnold sent a terse memo to Chennault in which he told him, "You have been accorded the status of independent commander of an air force. With this status comes, as you know, certain responsibilities that you must meet."

CHAPTER 13

PRESSURES OF OFFICE

A rnold arrived at Bolling Field on February 17, 1943, after stops in Calcutta, Karachi, Khartoum, Accra, Recife, and Puerto Rico. In Brazil, he met with Brigadier Eduardo Gomes, commander of the Força Aérea Brasileira's Northwest Air Zone. Brazil had declared war on the Axis the previous August and contributed to the war effort by functioning as an important link in the USAAF Air Transport Command's southern route across the Atlantic. Gomes wanted American supplies, as well as training for mechanics and pilots. Arnold promised that he would "see what can be done, if anything."

Arnold had traveled an exhausting 27,842 miles in forty days and was dreading the pile of paperwork that awaited him after reporting to the president and to Marshall. He was tired—some of his diary entries seemed despondent—and then on February 27, Brigadier General George Stratemeyer, Arnold's chief of staff, casually mentioned in a memo to Harry Hopkins that "as you know, General Arnold has been a bit under the weather and confined to his quarters the last two or three days. He expects to be back for duty, March 1st."

In fact, Arnold had just suffered the first of an eventual four wartime heart attacks, though he had not sought immediate medical attention. Under pressure from his family, he finally acquiesced to an electrocardiogram at the Army's Walter Reed Hospital, which confirmed the heart attack.

General David N. W. Grant, the chief flight surgeon for USAAF headquarters, insisted that Arnold interrupt his schedule for a couple of weeks of rest. On March 5, he was quietly flown to Florida, where he was put up in the Biltmore Hotel in Coral Gables, which the USAAF had taken over as a convalescent hospital.

In a March 15 letter to his daughter, Lois Snowden, which is preserved among his papers in the Library of Congress, he wrote that he was resting with "nothing to do and nobody can get at me to bother me so it is really a grand setup."

By this time, Lo's husband, Lieutenant Commander Ernie Snowden, had made quite a reputation for himself. As commander of the Douglas SBD Dauntlesses of Scout Bomber Squadron 72 (VS-72) aboard the carrier USS *Wasp*, he had earned a Navy Cross for extraordinary heroism against the Japanese on Guadalcanal in August 1942. Before the end of the 1943, he had earned the Legion of Merit for his actions in the Battle of Kwajalein in the Marshall Islands.

Meanwhile, like Hap, Bee was also pursuing a strenuous wartime schedule of her own. When the war started, she had been "drafted" as spokeswoman for the Army Air Forces Relief Society (now called the Air Force Aid Society), a charitable organization with which the wives of many USAAF officers volunteered. It had been formed in 1942 to provide financial and other assistance to families of airmen who were confronted with emergencies. In this job, she spent a great deal of time flying around the country, visiting the wounded and making public appearances.

As her grandson Robert recalls, "Bee was not by nature a public person, but she was a game and plucky soul and very charming. She was only about four foot eleven, but you never saw that until you were standing right next to her, because her personality was very large and she could really turn on the star power."

Arnold was not relieved of command, as was the customary protocol when a commander was incapacitated, but he was spared not only the pressures of his office but responsibility for its day-to-day control. The White House, for instance, nudged through the elevation of Claire Chennault's China Air Task Force to the status of Fourteenth Air Force while Arnold was convalescing.

On March 16, contrary to relieving him of duty, George Marshall recommended, and Henry Stimson concurred, that Arnold should be promoted from lieutenant general to full general. Three days later, it was announced to the media that Roosevelt had formally nominated Arnold for his fourth star. Arnold reacted modestly, but it had to have helped his recuperation to know that he still had the full confidence of his superiors.

Meanwhile, Arnold's USAAF continued to grow into an immense and potent war machine. At the end of 1942, he commanded 764,415 officers and men. By the time that he landed at the Biltmore, the number was approaching two million and heading for 2.2 million by the end of 1943. In the nine months since Arnold's last visit to Britain, the number of USAAF combat groups there had increased from two to a dozen, and the number in the Mediterranean Theater from only one to more than thirty. Since his visit to Douglas MacArthur and George Kenney in September 1942, the number of USAAF combat groups in the Pacific Ocean Areas and the South West Pacific Area had doubled from fourteen to twenty-eight.

From March 1942 to March 1943, the total number of USAAF aircraft had increased from 16,346 to 41,184, and the number of combat aircraft from 5,130 to 14,901. The inventory of Flying Fortresses had grown from 355 to 1,765, while the Liberator count had gone from 147 to 1,174. Among fighters, which Arnold readily conceded were of secondary importance to bombers in his global USAAF master plan, P-38s had increased from 309 to 1,068, and from only three P-47s, the number had risen to 678. A handful of P-51 Mustangs were making an appearance in the total count.

Though the number of training aircraft had doubled from 10,014 to 20,325, one of Arnold's biggest headaches involved training. He complained in one memo to the USAAF Training Command that "Replacement crews are going overseas who haven't fired a gun at altitudes over 16,000 feet. This is a hell of a way to send these boys overseas, and I will have to explain why they are sent. You might just as well start writing [condolences to families] telegrams now for me to sign when I get back [to Washington], and see that no more men are sent until they have had proper training at high altitudes."

In another memo, this one to General Spaatz overseas, he wrote about "the character of instruction being given at the Operational Training Units in the United States and [in North Africa], and the type of instructors. One of my difficulties is to get training at altitudes above 20,000 feet. On this side of the world I find it rather difficult to have my instructions carried out, and I presume you have the same difficulties over there."

To "all Air Force commanders and Air Force task commanders throughout the world," Arnold wrote, "The tactical doctrines learned at our schools were being followed too closely in bombing, and not enough initiative was being displayed to cope with combat conditions as they actually existed." Another memo complained of a "wishie-washie, indecisive program for cooperative training with ground troops."

The Air Transport Command was also on his mind. In military histories, a great deal of attention is devoted to combat commands, but the USAAF also built what was then the world's largest global air transport service. In a year, the number of transports had increased sevenfold from 423 to 2,984. Among Arnold's first memos after he returned from China was one to General Hal George, head of Air Transport Command, about increasing the delivery of supplies over the Hump. Already looking ahead, he also ordered George to put together policy recommendations "that we might have proper air bases for military operations in the future, after the war is over." In a similar vein, Arnold wrote to Harry Hopkins that "a United States airline be established across the Pacific which would not be dependent upon the French, the British, the Dutch, nor anyone else for maintenance."

He and Hopkins addressed the nuances of lend-lease deliveries of American aircraft to the Soviet Union via the Siberian Airplane Ferry Service, also known as the Alaska–Siberia Air Road (ALSIB), and a transfer point at Ladd Field in Fairbanks, Alaska. They discussed whether American crews should accompany the aircraft into Siberia despite the strong objections of the Soviets, who did not want American pilots flying over their territory.

But the biggest issue for Arnold was the strategic air campaign against Germany. Arnold wrote to Hopkins that there should be "a more aggressive attitude, [concentrating] on the plans for bombing Germany, so we could make the trans-Channel landings on the French coast possible."

These issues and others were on the agenda for the next conference between Roosevelt, Churchill, and the Combined Chiefs of

Staff, code-named Trident, which was scheduled for mid-May in Washington, D.C. But on the eve of the Trident Conference, Arnold was stricken with a second heart attack and was confined to Walter Reed. In his memoirs, Arnold does not mention his first heart attack and dismisses the second by saying he had "a bit of trouble with my 'ticker.'" He adds that Air Marshal Portal, as well as Averell Harriman, "were able to get to the hospital to see me and talk over the proceedings." By this time, Harriman had been serving as a frequent conferee in meetings with the Soviets and had represented Roosevelt at a meeting between Churchill and Stalin in Moscow nine months earlier.

The item heading the agenda at Trident was the impending Allied invasion of Sicily, which was to take place in eight weeks, and the landings in mainland Italy, which were to occur between September 3 and September 9.

Upon his release from Walter Reed, Arnold was ordered by Marshall, in a May 14 memo, to rest. Hap and Bee embarked on a fishing trip to Oregon, but much to Marshall's consternation, Arnold cut this short to accept an invitation from his alma mater to deliver the commencement address on June 1. How could Hap Arnold refuse when it meant handing a second lieutenant's commission to his son?

On that rainy day, William Bruce Arnold was one of the 514 men of the West Point class of June 1943 (another 409 had graduated as part of the class of January 1943 under the Academy's wartime expansion of the cadet corps and condensed curricula). His eyesight kept Bruce Arnold from a career in the cockpit. Instead, he was commissioned a field artillery officer, which, perhaps ironically, included antiaircraft artillery. (Among the 206 new lieutenants from the class who did go to flight training was Robin Olds, who has the distinction of being the only American fighter ace to achieve aerial victories in both World War II and the Vietnam War.)

General Arnold told the class that "we are now ready for a decisive year." The Axis, he said, could "see the handwriting on the wall [in the] destructive day and night hammering" of the Combined Bomber Offensive. "By such operations," Arnold predicted, "we will end the war [and] will cut down the casualties."

He spoke of "the tremendous speeds and distances of modern warfare [in which] supply lines are measured in thousands instead of hundreds of miles." He told the class that the great tide of aircraft then being produced by American industry would "enable Allied forces to drive the Axis from the skies and hold a protection umbrella over our ground forces as they triumphantly march to the roads that lead to Berlin and to Tokyo." Arnold said the question was no longer *whether* the war would be won, "but how it will be won." The answer, he said, was through airpower.

After Arnold's remarks at West Point, he returned to Washington to prepare for the summer's second top-level Allied summit meeting. Designated as the Quadrant Conference, this conclave was held in Quebec during the third week of August, and it included Canada's prime minister, William Lyon Mackenzie King, as well as Franklin Roosevelt and Winston Churchill. It took place against the backdrop of a successful operation in Sicily and had as its secret top priority the long-awaited cross-channel invasion of northern France. Known as Operation Overlord, this was now tentatively planned for May 1944.

"At those meetings in Quebec behind closed doors, there were some very rough, tough sessions," Arnold wrote in his memoirs. "Angry words were sometimes thrown back and forth. The Americans and the British did not always have the same ideas about what our future plans should be. The Americans were eager to get going and get the thing over with by making a landing in France as soon as the supplies, troops, and equipment could be gotten together. The British had a tendency to hold back until everything was carefully prepared. Many times the sessions were so hot that even the Planning Staff was not allowed to be present."

In Quebec, Arnold exhibited a much greater interest in the China-Burma-India Theater than he might have before he had visited it. He met with the British army's Brigadier Orde Wingate, the leader of the "Chindits," special operations forces (as we would call them today) who operated behind Japanese lines in Burma. "I liked his initiative and imagination, his resourcefulness and his courage," Arnold wrote, giving rare praise to a British officer. Roosevelt was also taken with the eccentric and daring Wingate, and he proposed that Arnold organize an equally unconventional air support unit to work with him. Arnold readily agreed and ordered the creation of the 5318th Air Unit (later the 1st Air Commando Group).

"I reviewed the qualifications and personal characteristics of the available Air Force officers to decide who could best work with him behind the Japanese lines in Burma," Arnold wrote of his search for men to command the 5318th. "I finally selected [veteran fighter pilots] Colonels Phil Cochran and John Allison, and directed them to report to Wingate. These two officers were naturals for the job. [Their] equipment included everything from helicopters to puddle-jumpers to light and medium bombers, to fighters, gliders, and transports and all the latest gadgets and means then known for snatching gliders off the ground. This Commando organization played a most important part in making Wingate's mission a success and in making interior Burma too hot for the Japanese." The same concept is seen in today's Air Force Special Operations Command (AFSOC).

But most important for Arnold was advancing the Combined Bomber Offensive because a prerequisite for the success of Operation Overlord was gaining air superiority in Europe. That was Arnold's primary task.

CHAPTER 14

STRATEGIC AIRPOWER AT THE CROSSROADS

O n the morning of February 18, 1943, Edmund T. "Eddie" Allen, one of the most highly regarded test pilots in the United States, was going through his preflight checklist before taking off from an airfield in Renton, Washington. Allen had been an Air Service pilot in World War I, the first test pilot for the National Advisory Committee on Aeronautics (NACA, the predecessor of NASA), and a test pilot for the nation's leading aircraft manufacturers. For Donald Douglas, he was the first man to pilot the DC-2. For Boeing, he had been the first man to fly the Model 307 Stratoliner, the Model 314 Clipper, and every Flying Fortress variant from B-17B through B-17F. Six months earlier, on September 21, 1942, he had been the first man to fly the prototype of the Boeing XB-29 Superfortress. Fifty percent bigger than the Boeing Flying Fortress, the four-engine Superfortress was designed to have nearly twice the range and triple the bomb load. With a pressurized cabin, the big bomber could operate at altitudes above thirty thousand feet. Whereas the Flying Fortress and Liberator were called "heavy" bombers, the Superfortress was officially designated as a *"very* heavy" bomber.

The Superfortress, developed under the tightest secrecy, was how Hap Arnold imagined the USAAF could bring the strategic air war to Japan. Indeed, no other bomber in the world had its range or payload.

Allen was about to fly the second prototype XB-29. The crew of ten included four flight test engineers. The Superfortress still had problems to be worked out. For one thing, its Wright R3350 engines sometimes caught fire. Allen lifted the big silver bird off shortly after noon and climbed to five thousand feet. Five minutes into the flight, a fire broke out in the number one engine nacelle. Allen feathered the prop, closed the throttle, declared an emergency, and started back to Renton.

As the XB-29 circled south over downtown Seattle, Allen was talking to the men in the control tower. In the background they heard someone tell Allen that he "better get this thing down in a hurry ... the wing spar's burning badly!" Within seconds, the faltering XB-29 struck the top of the five-story Frye meatpacking plant, killing Allen and destroying the plane. The loss of the XB-29 was a terrible blow. Eddie Allen was no ordinary test pilot, and the XB-29 was no ordinary prototype. It was the single most important airplane developed by the USAAF during World War II.

The Superfortress was so important to Hap Arnold's idea of strategic airpower that he had ordered 250 production Superfortresses in September 1941, upping that order to 750 at the start of 1942—*before* the first XB-29 test flight. Boeing even built an all-new Superfortress factory in Wichita, Kansas. With so much invested in

A medical tent of the Pennsylvania National Guard, circa 1900. The officer on the right is Dr. Herbert Alonzo Arnold, and the boy next to him is a young Henry Harley Arnold. (Source: Robert and Kathleen Arnold collection)

Lieutenant Henry Harley Arnold in civilian clothes in 1911 at the U.S. Army airfield at College Park in Maryland. He earned his lasting nickname "Hap" around this time, but at College Park, he was known as "Silk Hat Harry," for reasons now unknown.
(Source: Author's collection)

Colonel Henry Harley Arnold at his desk in Washington in 1918. The youngest colonel in the U.S. Army, he was the senior qualified pilot in the Signal Corps Aviation Section headquarters, where he was essentially running the whole show.
(Source: Robert and Kathleen Arnold collection)

Hap Arnold (right) with airpower pioneer General William Lendrum "Billy" Mitchell, some time after Mitchell's departure from the service in 1926.
(Source: U.S. Air Force)

The Arnold family at their home in Chevy Chase, Maryland, in 1937. From left to right, they are William Bruce Arnold; Hap Arnold; Eleanor Arnold, known as Bee; David Lee Arnold; Lois Elizabeth Arnold; and Henry Harley Arnold Jr.
(Source: Robert and Kathleen Arnold collection)

Lieutenant General Henry Harley Arnold with Brigadier General Jimmy Doolittle, shortly after the latter led his daring April 1942 raid on Tokyo.
(Source: Robert and Kathleen Arnold collection)

Hap Arnold visits the Douglas Aircraft Company in Santa Monica, California, circa 1942. On the left is company vice president Carl Cover, and on the right is company founder Donald Wills Douglas. Douglas and Arnold were close friends, and Arnold's son later married Douglas's daughter.
(Source: Author's collection)

A proud father, General Henry Harley Arnold hands a diploma to his son, newly minted Second Lieutenant William Bruce Arnold, at the June 1, 1943, commencement ceremonies at West Point. Hap had come off sick leave prematurely to deliver the commencement address to his son's class.
(Source: Robert and Kathleen Arnold collection)

General Hap Arnold walks the Normandy beachhead with U.S. First Army Commander General Omar Bradley on June 12, 1944— D-Day plus six.
(Source: Robert and Kathleen Arnold collection)

General Hap Arnold sits at his desk in the Pentagon, circa 1944.
(Source: Author's collection)

Hap Arnold poses with a North American Aviation P-51B Mustang fighter plane. The aircraft went on to be one of the key contributors to the USAAF victory in World War II. (Source: Author's collection)

An official color photograph of General Henry Harley Arnold wearing five-star rank, to which he was promoted on December 21, 1944.
(Source: U.S. Air Force)

USAAF Commanding General Henry Harley Arnold and U.S. Army Chief of Staff George Catlett Marshall paid a visit to the White House on January 5, 1945. Less than three weeks earlier, both men had been promoted to five-star rank as Generals of the Army. These two men first met while stationed in the Philippines forty years earlier and were lifelong friends, close professional allies, and neighbors in Fort Myer, Virginia. The two friends had even managed to take time off for several short fishing trips during World War II.
(Source: Author's collection)

During a stop in Guam as part of his final inspection tour of
the Pacific during World War II, General Hap Arnold dis-
cusses maintenance issues with B-29 crew chief Sergeant
Leo Fliess of the 314th Bombardment Wing on June 13,
1945. General Curtis LeMay, who commanded the XXI
Bomber Command, is seen over Arnold's right shoulder.
(Source: National Archives)

The funeral procession for General Henry Harley Arnold passes the Lincoln Memorial as
it crosses the Potomac River en route from the U.S. Capitol to Arlington Cemetery on
January 19, 1950. Honorary pallbearers included Generals Dwight Eisenhower, Carl
"Tooey" Spaatz, and George Catlett Marshall.
(Source: Robert and Kathleen Arnold collection)

A retired Hap Arnold enjoys an evening by his fireplace at El Rancho Feliz in the Valley of the Moon, Sonoma County, California, in 1946.
(Source: Robert and Kathleen Arnold collection)

the Superfortress, the crash of the XB-29 was a potential setback to the future of strategic airpower. The problems with the XB-29 had to be overcome, and quickly.

The biggest problem was with the engines. The twin-row, super-charged, air-cooled, eighteen-cylinder Wright R3350 Duplex-Cyclone engine that was created in parallel with the Superfortress offered around double the horsepower of the nine-cylinder Wright Cyclone that powered the Flying Fortress, but as it was new, untested technology, it was only after test flights began that engineers saw that the rear row of cylinders tended to overheat, causing engine fires that could burn through the wing spar. This fatal problem had to be addressed, even as the Superfortresses were going into production.

Arnold quickly assigned one of his best men to manage the Superfortress program. As he wrote in his memoirs, "We could not and must not be stopped in our production. I immediately put General K. B. Wolfe of our Materiel Command in charge ... and gave him particular instructions to expedite production in every way possible. By making this a special project, it was possible to assign to it personnel from any part of the Air Force, wherever they might be, and no matter how important the jobs they were filling."

Nothing, Arnold reasoned, could be allowed to hold up the Superfortress program. By June, Wolfe was already setting up operational training units at Smoky Hill Field in Kansas, near where Boeing was building the Superfortresses. With Arnold sidelined by his heart attacks and preoccupied with the Quadrant Conference and the war against Germany, Wolfe became the hands-on USAAF manager of the Superfortress program.

Across the globe, the Combined Bomber Offensive against Germany was beginning to encounter other problems that screamed for Hap Arnold's attention. On August 17, 1943, as he was sitting down for the first day of talks in Quebec, the Eighth Air Force was over Germany in its biggest operation to date.

The Eighth now had two things that it had lacked in January: an adequate bomber force and a plan. The number of heavy bomber groups in the VIII Bomber Command had increased from seven to seventeen, and the number of fighter escort groups in the VIII Fighter Command had grown from three to seven—although maintenance and training issues dragged down the mission availability of total numbers of aircraft.

As for the plan, Richard D'Oyly Hughes and his Enemy Objectives Unit, working with General Fred Anderson, commanding the VIII Bomber Command, had narrowed the target list to the huge Messerschmitt aircraft factory complex at Regensburg, which produced most of the Luftwaffe's Bf 109 fighter-interceptor aircraft, and the ball-bearing factories of Schweinfurt. Bearings were seen by the planners, such as Hughes, who studied the German economy, as a "bottleneck" industry, one which, if damaged or destroyed, would disrupt other industries. Because bearings are essential not only to aircraft but to machinery of all kinds, any interruption in the flow of these components would impact manufacturing throughout numerous production streams.

Hughes and Anderson planned for a "maximum effort" to overwhelm German defenses by hitting both locations simultaneously with a total of nearly four hundred bombers. However, thick ground fog over the bomber bases in England caused delays and doomed a coordinated operation. Colonel Curtis LeMay, commanding the Regensburg contingent, led his force in an instrument takeoff, but General Robert Williams, commander of the bombers targeting Schweinfurt, had his flights delayed for five hours. This meant that the same Luftwaffe interceptors defending Regensburg could refuel and defend Schweinfurt.

Hap Arnold was handed a report on the mission while in meetings in Quebec. He learned the Luftwaffe had shot down sixty Flying Fortresses, and the USAAF had nearly six hundred airmen killed or captured. Loss rates such as this were startling—*and* unsustainable.

This news came on top of the losses experienced on August 1 in another maximum effort, this one attacking the big petrochemical center at Ploesti, Romania, for the first time since HALPRO fourteen months earlier. In this mission, designated Operation Tidal Wave but known to posterity as "Black Sunday," nearly a third of the 162 Eighth and Ninth Air Force B-24 Liberators that reached the target area were lost.

As Arnold pondered more than one hundred losses in just two missions, he decided the situation in Europe demanded his personal attention. Less than two weeks later, he was on his way to Britain.

"For some time I had been receiving reports, letters, and telegrams from overseas, and verbal accounts from returning officers, that made it apparent I was getting out of touch with the Eighth Air Force," he wrote in his memoirs. "I therefore decided to make a personal inspection of its operations, to find out for myself what they needed in the way of equipment and personnel."

He departed Washington on August 31, accompanied by the chief USAAF flight surgeon, General Dave Grant—to keep an eye on Arnold's "ticker"—and by General Haywood "Possum" Hansell of his planning staff, who had commanded a bomber wing with the Eighth Air Force during the first part of 1943.

Hap Arnold's reacquaintance with the Eighth Air Force was inauspicious. "The weather was bad—low clouds and showers," he recalled in his memoirs. "As we approached the field at Prestwick, our destination in Britain, about 50 B-17s and B-24s from America were also coming in to land. Their pilots were new and inexperienced, and we didn't want to interfere with them in the bad weather, so we cruised around in circles out of the B-17 and B-24 area.... I was not satisfied with the way incoming planes were being handled. We lost two bombers and two complete crews out of those planes waiting to land at Prestwick.... Obviously a change in flying control technique was essential." Arnold and his party landed at the big RAF complex at Hendon on the outskirts of London, where they were met by Ira Eaker and General Jacob Devers, then the senior commander of U.S. Army Ground Forces in Europe.

On September 3, Arnold met with the Eighth Air Force aircrews and combat commanders who had been through the cauldrons of Ploesti, Regensburg, and Schweinfurt. He met first with the 2nd Bombardment Wing, whose B-24s had been over Ploesti, and then with the 4th Bombardment Wing, which had flown over Regensburg. Arnold met with the commanders: Colonel Ted Timberlake of the 2nd Bombardment Wing, General Fred Anderson of the VIII Bomber Command, Colonel Curtis LeMay, wing commander of the Regensburg mission, and General Bob Williams, who led the 1st Bombardment Wing to Schweinfurt. Arnold spoke to a large crowd of veteran combat crews and watched aircraft from a 140-plane strike force return after bombing Luftwaffe fields in northern France.

What made the biggest impression on him that day was seeing the battle damage German anti-aircraft fire and the 20mm cannons of Luftwaffe interceptors had inflicted on American aircraft. As he wrote in his diary, he "saw a B-17 badly shot up, being repaired; one tail flipper gone, right wing with hole big as a bushel basket, holes in fuselage from stem to stern, control rod to right aileron shot off, one engine blown from wing, but it came home with but two men wounded."

Arnold wrote in his diary that the bomber groups were "doing a grand job. Losses, which look very large, have not so far affected morale. Remarkable the way the youngsters [air crewmen half Arnold's age] are … matured and experienced men in a very short time, operational accidents are very few. Pilots, copilots have done the impossible in landing planes without rudders, one flipper, ailerons shot away, holes in wing and fuselage large enough to put a wheelbarrow through, and yet they are brought home."

The next day of his British tour found Hap Arnold meeting with the crews and fighter pilots of the VIII Fighter Command at Duxford, home of the 78th Fighter Group, where he discussed their need for more external fuel tanks. The 108-gallon tanks gave the P-47 Thunderbolt fighters the combat radius to accompany Eighth Air Force bombers about 475 miles from British airspace. Regensburg and Schweinfurt were, however, beyond the reach of the P-47. Arnold also saw the P-51 Mustang fighters, which were then only beginning to arrive in the theater. They had the range to escort the bombers nearly five hundred miles without auxiliary tanks, and the 108-gallon tanks extended the Mustang's radius to 850 miles.

Arnold and Eaker also called on Arthur Harris of RAF Bomber Command at his headquarters. Arnold raised the issue of a single joint commander for the Combined Bomber Offensive, an idea that Harris opposed.

"His chief objection was that the Royal Air Force would probably not be put in command," Arnold recalled in his memoirs.

> In that he was right, for we were building up rapidly in strength, and numbers alone should give the United States Air Force the command. They therefore would lose control of their night bombing. Bomber Command now had virtual autonomy in its operations, with little interference

from higher levels of the RAF, an arrangement that permitted Harris to go directly to the Prime Minister and give him full details. If they did not have control, the RAF would lose prestige with the British people. [In retrospect] I am convinced it was not such a good suggestion after all. It would have caused many needless complications.

In London, Hap Arnold met the press. As he noted in his diary, "Maybe I can stay clear of trouble."

"The time table of victory [is] first, supremacy in the air and then a crushing invasion by land and by sea," Arnold told the reporters. The *New York Times* reported that Arnold's number one priority was heavy bombers. Unmentioned was the Superfortress—still secret—but this was the heavy bomber Arnold had in mind.

Two days later, on September 6, the Eighth Air Force launched 407 bombers, most of them dispatched to Stuttgart, home of Daimler-Benz, manufacturers of the aircraft engines used in Messerschmitt Bf 109s. That night, as Arnold dined with General Devers and Ira Eaker, as well as Arthur Harris and Peter Portal, he had no details about the mission. The discussion centered on areas of responsibility, shared—not always harmoniously—by the USAAF and the RAF in the European and Mediterranean Theaters.

The next day, Arnold learned the bad news. Cloud cover over the primary targets in Stuttgart had compelled the bomber crews to divert to secondary targets and targets of opportunity. Forty-five of the bombers were shot down, a loss rate of 17 percent of the aircraft reaching the target area, a quarter of the total force.

"Certain features of the operation never did find their way into the reports sent up through channels," he laments in his memoirs. "The fact is, despite all the optimistic talk at the dinner table that night, the mission had been a complete failure … not one [bomber] saw its assigned target."

After talks with RAF Air Marshal Trafford Leigh-Mallory, who had been picked to command the Allied Expeditionary Air Force (AEAF) for the planned 1944 cross-channel invasion, Arnold departed Britain.

After twenty-seven hours and three stops along the North Atlantic Ferry Route, Arnold landed in Washington to face difficult challenges. He praised the courage of his combat aircrews but lamented their insufficient training. Arnold relieved of command two generals charged with stateside bomber training: Major General James Chaney of the First Air Force and Major General Davenport Johnson of the Second Air Force. In a September 10 memo to Johnson, Arnold wrote, "It is awfully hard in cases like this not to allow the personal element to enter into it…. As you know, you are all friends of mine [Chaney had been a year behind Arnold at West Point], and I like you all, and in addition, I am not naturally at heart an SOB. I am trying my damndest to get this war over in the shortest space of time so that we can all go back to a normal way of living. I was not picking on you when I relieved you from command. I was trying my damndest to get the maximum efficiency out of an organization."

On October 14, 1943, the Eighth Air Force launched more than 350 bombers to take out the German ball-bearing factories at Schweinfurt. The Flying Fortresses of 1st and 3rd Bombardment Divisions would attack abreast from the north, and the Liberators of the 2nd Bombardment Division would circle around the city and strike from the south.

The mission ran into trouble almost immediately when much of the Liberator force failed get into formation because of thick cloud cover over England. The 2nd Bombardment Division planes that did get airborne were too few for the Schweinfurt mission and were diverted to a secondary target in northern Germany.

The Flying Fortresses reached the target as planned, the two divisions arriving minutes apart. The Luftwaffe, however, was ready. Of the 291 Flying Fortresses that had taken off that morning, sixty failed to return. Another seventeen were damaged so badly they had to be written off. The 305th Bombardment Group alone lost thirteen of its sixteen aircraft in a matter of minutes. It went down in the annals of the Eighth Air Force as "Black Thursday."

Still, as Arnold noted in a memo to Secretary of War Henry Stimson, "All five of the works at Schweinfurt were either completely or almost completely wiped out. Our attack was the most perfect example in history of accurate distribution of bombs over a target. It was an attack that will not have to be repeated for a very long time, if at all."

The U.S. Strategic Bombing Survey studied the effects of strategic bombing in quantifiable detail immediately after the war. In its report, *The German Anti-Friction Bearings Industry*, it is noted that the attack was the most important of the raids made on Schweinfurt, causing "the most damage and the greatest interference with production, and it led directly to a reorganization of the bearing industry."

The Eighth Air Force had nevertheless suffered heavy losses. "No such savage air battles had been seen since the war began," Arnold wrote in his memoirs.

> Our losses were rising to an all-time high, but so were those of the Luftwaffe, and our bombers were not being turned back from their targets. Could we keep it up? The London papers asked the question editorially. To this day, I don't know for certain if we could have. No one does. We had the planes and replacement crews by then to

maintain the loss-rate of 25 percent which I had originally determined must be faced; but obviously there were other factors. To obscure the argument forever, in mid-October the weather shut down foggily on southeast Germany for most of the remainder of the year.

In his memoirs, Arnold refers to Schweinfurt as "the high-water mark of our daylight bombardment without fighter escort."

What these missions brought into focus was that in order to continue daylight strategic bomber missions into the heart of the Reich, the Eighth Air Force needed escort fighters with longer legs than the P-47s and P-38s. They needed the P-51 Mustang. In August, fewer than one hundred had gone overseas. By January 1944, the number would be climbing toward one thousand. The strategic mission could not continue without them—and they were finally on the way.

CHAPTER 15

ALLIED WAR STRATEGY AT THE CROSSROADS

O
n November 11, 1943, less than a month after Black Thursday, Hap Arnold was on his way overseas once again, this time to a series of high-level summit conferences, and for his first visit to the Mediterranean Theater since the Allies landed in Italy.

During the fast-paced, five-week journey, he accompanied President Roosevelt to his only wartime conference with Churchill and Chiang Kai-shek, code-named Sextant, and to the first of two "Big Three" conferences between Roosevelt, Churchill, and Stalin, code-named Eureka. Because the Soviet Union was not then at war with Japan, Stalin refused to attend the meeting with Chiang in Cairo, so the Anglo-American leaders flew to meet Stalin in Tehran.

For Roosevelt and Churchill, the objective now with conferences was not so much planning strategy, but managing the momentum of previously initiated strategy. In the European Theater of Operations, it was the momentum building toward Operation Overlord, the long-awaited cross-channel invasion. Because of the "Germany first" doctrine, this was the most important initiative of all.

In the Mediterranean Theater of Operations, the focus was on Italy, a campaign that was moving slowly because of determined German resistance and tough terrain. In the Pacific and in the China-Burma-India Theaters, Japan's imperial expansion had finally been halted, though the Allies were only just beginning the difficult chore of reversing the Japanese tide.

To further the strategic air campaign against Germany, and to complement the Eighth Air Force in England, Arnold created another strategic air force, the Fifteenth, which would be based in Italy now that the U.S. Army had captured territory in which bases could be located. The mission of the Fifteenth would be to undertake a full program of strategic missions against southern Germany, Austria, and points east, such as Ploesti.

As Arnold submitted his plan for the Fifteenth to the Joint Chiefs of Staff on October 9, his idea was to use the heavy bomber groups then assigned to the Ninth Air Force to form the nucleus of the Fifteenth. The Ninth would become an all-tactical bomber organization and move to England to support the cross-channel invasion, which was now designated as Operation Overlord. Here, it would be augmented by the tactical groups then part of the Eighth. This would leave the Eighth and Fifteenth with a solely strategic mission. This plan was approved on October 22, with the Fifteenth Air Force formally activated under the command of General Jimmy Doolittle on November 1.

Though it would not be officially created until early 1944, the Joint Chiefs of Staff had already agreed to Arnold's proposal for the creation of a new organization called the U.S. Strategic Air Forces in Europe (USSTAF) that would be the coordinator of the Eighth and Fifteenth.

It was against this backdrop that Hap Arnold set sail—literally—for Sextant and Eureka. Unlike during his previous wartime transatlantic trips, the commanding general of the USAAF did not fly, but rather traveled by ship aboard the 45,000-ton, 887-foot battleship USS *Iowa* for the Sextant and Eureka conferences. The boredom of the long voyage was broken by gin rummy, the Joint Chiefs of Staff betting on the Army-Navy football game, and Roosevelt's insistence that his companions join him each night for movies. The Navy treated its guests to the spectacle of gunnery practice, in which the *Iowa* barely missed being hit by a torpedo. Many aboard naturally feared a German U-boat attack, but to the embarrassment of the admirals aboard, it had been fired accidentally by an American destroyer that was part of the escorting flotilla. It would have been a spectacle indeed had President Roosevelt and the Joint Chiefs of Staff been sunk by friendly fire!

The ships passed the Rock of Gibraltar on November 19, and the delegation transferred to aircraft upon reaching Algeria. Flying over the terrain en route to Cairo, where the British had battled Germany's Afrika Korps for three years, Arnold observed in his diary, "Our trip covered a 1,500 mile battlefield, desert country that stretches the imagination to find a reason for fighting for it.... Wrecked tanks, trucks and armored cars, some black from burning, others with camouflage paint, many partially covered with sand, all making a shadow that identified them in the desert; thousands of them here and there over that 1,500 mile stretch of desert. Airdromes occupied in turn by RAF, [Luftwaffe], AAF with wrecks of German planes sprawled out flat on the ground like animals whose legs have given way and could no longer support the weight."

The three planes carrying the Washington delegation touched down in Cairo late on November 21. Here, the reception committee included Averell Harriman, who was now the U.S. ambassador to the Soviet Union, as well as General Chennault, who had arrived from China ahead of Chiang. Arriving at about the same time were the British members of the Combined Chiefs of Staff, Air Marshal Peter Portal, Field Marshal Alan Brooke, and Admiral Andrew Cunningham, who had commanded the Royal Navy since Dudley Pound passed away a month earlier. General Eisenhower and his staff flew in to join them on November 25.

Roosevelt and Churchill sat down with Chiang Kai-shek and his entourage on November 23. In his diary, Arnold calls it a "historic meeting," but in his memoirs, it is merely a "meeting." His dislike for Chiang, his supplicants, and his narrow-mindedness is palpable in both. Reflecting upon Sextant in his memoirs, he wrote, "Sometimes I wondered why we were saving China, for the dissensions among their warlords [Chiang's bickering generals] gave us few clues."

However, saving China *was* the immediate goal of the actions in the China-Burma-India Theater, and the supply routes into China were an important topic of conversation, although Chiang's parochial and intransigent position was essentially unchanged since Arnold had met with him in Chungking. An agreement was reached on the tonnage that Arnold committed the USAAF to deliver across the Hump. He noted in his diary that this was unilaterally rewritten by the Chinese two days after Sextant adjourned, committing him to "2,000 tons [monthly] more than I could possibly carry." He rewrote the rewrite and sent it back. Chiang did not quibble.

In retrospect, the Cairo Communiqué (or Cairo Declaration) that concluded the meeting could have been written without the conference, but it did serve to summarize the aims of the United States, Britain, and China with regard to the war against Japan. "The Three Great Allies expressed their resolve to bring unrelenting pressure against their brutal enemies by sea, land, and air," read the document.

The communiqué concluded with a reaffirmation of that controversial declaration of the Casablanca Conference, stating that the "three Allies ... will continue to persevere in the serious and prolonged operations necessary to procure the unconditional surrender of Japan."

Though Arnold made no mention of it in his diary for security reasons, an important element of the discussions of waging war against the Japanese from China included the still-unrealized strategic air campaign against Japan itself, and the B-29 Superfortress, which would make this a reality.

Assuming that the B-29s would be operational by the spring of 1944, the biggest obstacle to these strategic bombing missions was the tremendous distances involved. To put this predicament into perspective, Schweinfurt, which was the signature challenge for the Eighth, was 450 miles from England, while Japan was three thousand miles from the nearest Allied base that could be supplied by sea.

When eying a map of the Pacific, the planners could see that the ideal bases for the bombers would be on Guam and the Mariana Islands (such as Saipan and Tinian). They were about 1,500 miles from Tokyo and could be supplied easily by large cargo ships. But these potential bases were held by the Japanese and unlikely to be recaptured until late in 1944. Therefore, the only potential near-term basing scenario would be deep inside China.

The American commanders in China, Stilwell and Chennault, contributed ideas about *where* in China the bombers could be based, and from this, K. B. Wolfe developed a plan, approved by Arnold in October 1943 and code-named Operation Matterhorn. On November 20, Arnold activated the XX Bomber Command, with Wolfe as commander, to operate the Superfortress fleet against Japan from fields at Chengtu (now transliterated as Chengdu) beginning in June 1944.

"The operations from China against Japan were not simple," Arnold says in his memoirs. "After hauling their own gasoline and bombs from India, the B-29s would have to go back to India and refuel, taking on as much gasoline as they could, and return to China, where they would bomb up and take off for Japan. The distance from the Assam region to the Chengtu area was about 1,200 miles; from China to the nearest point of bombing in Japan, about 1,600 miles. So, when the airplanes finally got back to their bases in India, they had covered a distance of about 5,600 miles, and had carried some 3,500 gallons of gasoline into China."

President Roosevelt signed off on the plan at Cairo. It was now up to Wolfe to deliver the Superfortresses and up to Chiang to build airfields of adequate size for the huge bombers.

Roosevelt, Churchill, and the Combined Chiefs of Staff departed from Cairo on November 27 for their meeting with Stalin in Tehran. Iran had been picked as a conference site because of its proximity to the Soviet Union and Stalin's wariness of traveling too far from home while his armies were still locked in fierce combat with the Germans across a vast front.

In 1943, Iran was an occupied country, having been invaded in August 1941 by Britain and the Soviet Union and subdued in three weeks. The catalyst for the invasion was the pro-German leanings of Iran's monarch, Reza Shah Pahlavi, and the underlying strategy involved keeping Iranian oil out of Axis hands and securing a supply route into the Soviet Union that could be used for American lend-lease shipments.

Roosevelt, Churchill, Stalin, and some of their advisors met briefly on November 28 for an unscheduled preliminary meeting, which Arnold and Marshall missed. They were touring the country-side in a borrowed car and were not notified until after the meeting had started.

The principal Big Three portion of the Eureka Conference came during the following two days. The leading agenda item, as it had been when Churchill and Harriman had met with Stalin on previous occasions, was the Soviet leader's impatience with his Anglo-American allies for not yet having opened a "second front" against the Germans. By this, he meant the cross-channel invasion of northern France, not the invasion of Italy that they had conducted two months earlier. For their part, Roosevelt and Churchill assured him that they were working toward this goal for the spring of 1944.

Arnold had come to Tehran with a generally dismissive attitude toward Josef Stalin, referring to him in his diaries as "Red Joe." However, as he had the opportunity to speak with Stalin at length—through an interpreter—he came to be greatly impressed with the Soviet leader's command of facts and details. In his postwar memoirs, Arnold describes his conversations, recalling that "I talked with Stalin quite a bit … about our airplanes; about our methods of operations; our heavy bombers; about the ability of the Russians to fly our airplanes, and how, before they could fly our heavy bombers, they would have to receive special instruction about all the gadgets in the cockpit. Stalin surprised me with his knowledge of our planes. He knew details of their performance, their characteristics, their armament, and their armor much better than many of the senior officers in our own Air Force."

Although Arnold noted that "neither [Stalin] nor his generals seemed able to comprehend the necessity for strategic bombing," Stalin had obviously been following the Eighth Air Force campaign against the Reich with great interest. He went so far as to inquire about obtaining some American four-engine bombers for his own air force.

"He asked me for improved airplanes and he asked me for heavy bombers," Arnold wrote. "I told him if he wanted heavy bombers he would have to send his engineers and maintenance and combat crews to the United States to go through our schools, or we could send the necessary personnel to instruct his men in Russia. He thought over these two suggestions for a while and finally agreed that something like that must be arranged."

It never was.

Arnold reminded Stalin that the USAAF had been trying without success to obtain Soviet cooperation for "shuttle bombing" missions. Under this concept, Eighth Air Force bombers taking off from England could bomb targets deeper inside of the Reich if they could land and be refueled in the Soviet Union. As Arnold points out, the Soviets did agree at Tehran to allow shuttle missions, but they did not begin until June 1944, and they were terminated in September.

"For a while, the Russians were glad to have us," Arnold recalled in his memoirs.

> They permitted their people to come around and talk with our soldiers and officers, see what we were doing, and how we were doing it. It created a cordial relationship. But when our radios and our magazines—*Life*, *Time*, the *Saturday Evening Post*, *Collier's*, *Look*, *PM*, and such periodicals—started coming into our various squad rooms, dayrooms, and clubs, and their people had an opportunity to see the kind of life we lived in the United States, apparently the Russian leaders didn't like it. Orders were given that there would be no more fraternization between the Russians and the Americans at the shuttle bombing bases. Almost as quickly as it had started, all contact with the Americans stopped.

"Looking back on the Teheran Conference, I think everyone who had carefully thought out our over-all strategy for beating the Germans must have been in accord with Stalin's idea of how to win the war," Arnold wrote in his memoirs. "In simple words, as taken from my notes, this was: 'Hit Germany hard. Synchronize the operations of Allied troops on the two fronts, east and west. Then hit the Germans from both sides where it hurts most. Hit her where the distance to Berlin is shortest. Don't waste time, men or equipment on secondary fronts.' The prescription matched the planning of the Joint Chiefs of Staff in the United States, wherein we adopted the principle set by the President, of beating Germany first and then turning to Japan."

However, when it came to fighting Japan, Stalin was immovable. Roosevelt and Churchill tried at length to cajole him into a commitment to enter the war against Japan, but he flatly refused. As Arnold observed, "Regarding Japan, my impression was that Stalin had made up his mind and was not going to change it. Under no circumstances would he be drawn into a two-front war."

Though he was as disparaging about the Soviets in general as he was about the British in general, Arnold was quite taken with their "fearless, brilliant" leader. In his diary, he also betrayed a sense of wonder—absent in his accounts of other summit conferences—about his having been at what he perceived as a crossroads of history.

The next overnight stop for Arnold, Marshall, and the other American chiefs was Jerusalem, a crossroads of the ancient world, where they were to be lavishly entertained at the plush King David Hotel by the British Chiefs of Staff, who wished to reciprocate for the gracious manner in which they had been received in America during the Arcadia Conference two years earlier.

In his diary, Arnold wrote at length about visiting the holy sites, including those of Christ's Passion and of Christ's curing the crippled man that is described in John 5:8 ("Stand up, pick up your mat and walk!"). Calling the day "one of the most interesting of my career as far as travel is concerned," Arnold was duly impressed with all he saw, with the exception of the deteriorating condition of the Church of the Holy Sepulcher, which he described as looking "more like a construction job than a Cathedral."

On December 2, the Anglo-American caravan returned to Cairo, with Arnold accepting a ride from Peter Portal in the Avro York he used as his executive transport. Arnold wrote in his diary that the York was fitted out more luxuriously than *Argonaut II*, the Flying Fortress Arnold had taken to Jerusalem, and had a better galley— though it was much noisier.

During this second Cairo Conference, Arnold had intensive talks with General Eisenhower, the American Joint Chiefs of Staff, and the Anglo-American Combined Chiefs of Staff to discuss planning for Operation Overlord and preparing a report for the president and the prime minister. The conference led to a reorganization of the Allied command. On December 7, Eisenhower was formally confirmed as the supreme Allied commander in Europe, leading Supreme Headquarters, Allied Expeditionary Force (SHAEF). Allied command in the Mediterranean Theater went to British General Henry Maitland "Jumbo" Wilson. Air Chief Marshal Sir Arthur Tedder became Eisenhower's deputy supreme Allied commander, in charge of air operations for Overlord. Another RAF man, Trafford Leigh-Mallory, was named to command the joint Allied Expeditionary Air Force, which was to be the umbrella for all of the American and British tactical air operations in connection with Overlord. This included the USAAF Ninth Air Force, now relocated to England.

Meanwhile, in one line of his diary for December 4, Arnold noted a cable informing him that he now "owned a ranch" in California's Sonoma County. His wife Bee had found it while visiting her friend, Antonia Bartholomew, whose husband, Frank "Bart" Bartholomew, was a United Press war correspondent and would later become president and then chairman of this worldwide news-gathering agency. Frank and Antonia maintained a country house in the Sonoma Valley, also known as the "Valley of the Moon" after the Jack London novel of the same name, near where they would resurrect the Buena Vista Winery, the oldest in California.

Hap and Bee had long wanted a country place in California where he could retire when the war was over. Most of the properties in the area were too expensive for the Arnolds because they were vast agricultural tracts. But while visiting Antonia, Bee found a property that was just under forty-two acres with an old, ramshackle one-bedroom farmhouse, fruit trees, and some livestock. She made a small down payment and sent the telegram that reached Hap in Cairo.

On December 8, as the Combined Chiefs adjourned, Hap Arnold flew to Italy, with a brief stop in Sicily, where he had some important news for his longtime friend, General Tooey Spaatz, now commanding the Twelfth Air Force. It had previously been decided that the new U.S. Strategic Air Forces in Europe (USSTAF) would be headquartered in England, with its staff drawn from the existing bureaucracy of the Eighth Air Force. As suggested in Arnold's diary, it was at this point that it was confirmed that Spaatz would command the USSTAF—as Arnold had recommended, and Eisenhower had agreed—effective on the first of January, 1944.

With Spaatz moving to the USSTAF, Arnold reshuffled his other commanders. He moved Ira Eaker from the Eighth Air Force to lead the joint Mediterranean Air Command, which became the Mediterranean Allied Air Forces (MAAF), and sent Doolittle to England to command the Eighth. To command the Fifteenth, he brought in General Nate Twining, who then commanded all American air forces in the Southwest Pacific, including the Thirteenth Air Force. General John Cannon replaced Spaatz at the Twelfth Air Force, and General Hubert Harmon, Twining's deputy, took command of the Thirteenth.

Except for Eaker's strong objections to his own reassignment—especially without the personal notification from Arnold that he felt was deserved—the whole process went smoothly. Though Eaker was bitter about the incident, and would remain so for many years, he wired Arnold on December 24, confirming that he would comply with orders. Eisenhower himself sent a memo the following day in which he told Eaker that it would have been a misuse of resources to have retained "both you and Spaatz in England [considering that we] do not have enough top men to concentrate them [in one place]."

Accompanied by Spaatz, Arnold visited the sprawling complex of airfields being built for the Fifteenth Air Force between Bari and Foggia, on the heel of the Italian boot, northeast of Naples.

At Foggia on December 8, Arnold was met by his son Hank, who was temporarily detached from his duties as an artillery officer with the 45th Infantry Division to serve as his father's aide for the next few days. Together, they visited the Foggia-Bari area and traveled to Naples. Here, they looked at pre-invasion damage done by Allied bombers and post-invasion damage done by German bombers.

Arnold held meetings with Spaatz, Doolittle, and Cannon, then called on General Mark Clark, commander of the U.S. Fifth Army, the umbrella organization for all American ground operations in Italy, as well as British General Harold Alexander, commander of the Allied 15th Army Group, the command umbrella above the American Fifth and British Eighth Armies in Italy.

In 1918, Hap Arnold had gone to Europe hoping to see the battle-fronts of World War I from the air, but instead, he viewed the front from the eye level of an infantry soldier. In December 1943, he found himself within earshot of the front lines of World War II for the first time. He also made his first visit to a field hospital.

"Modern battle: jeeps and mud, trucks and tanks, more mud, trucks and road jams, bridges and culverts blown out by bombs and demolitions of the Germans," he wrote in his diary for December 11 of his visit to the 34th Infantry Division at Caserta, about twenty miles north of Naples.

> Bomb holes, mine holes, railroad ties cut in two by German heavy ploughs pulled by locomotives. Villages and towns demolished, partly demolished. Destruction and devastation everywhere, mud and more mud. Trees cut down by explosives to block the road. Hospitals, field and evacuation, ambulances, operating room, removing bomb and shell splinters from the soldier's head, pulling a mangled hand together, tying a body together after a shell fragment tore loose a hip and almost all of a buttock, wounds in the abdomen, holes in back and abdomen the size of a football, blood, transfusions.... Hands, legs, shoulders separately and together in plaster casts to rebuild broken and shattered bodies. Nurses doing their part, working overtime, smiling. Patients gritting their teeth and saying: "I'm feeling fine."

Stepping out of the hospital, he watched artillery

> barking at the Germans on a hill just beyond. Aircraft fighting overhead. Whistling shells going overhead with

their loud bangs as they explode. Bombs and shells burst-
ing on the German positions a scant 1,800 yards away.
Men crouching behind walls in the mud, tents under
bushes and trees. Wet feet, shoes muddy and wet, never
dry; trench feet. More whistling shells and their deafening
explosives and our guns barking. [Antiaircraft] guns opening up [on] Fw 190s and [Bf] 109s overhead. Spitfires
coming into the fight, bridges out, infantrymen crouching
behind any kind of cover. German observers watching our
movement up the road from the hill beyond. A tank blown
to bits from running over a mine, five bodies lying in small
pieces on the ground. Civilians, men and women, clinging
to desolated and despoiled houses, and mud, mud, mud.
The Germans over on the hill watching us, perhaps won-
dering who could be so foolish to come up there.

Later in the day, Arnold held a press conference at which he
called Germany "groggy" after the weight of the Combined Bomber
Offensive, although he knew that the offensive was barely under
way. The Associated Press reported that Arnold "predicted today, in
a tour of the Italian front that Germany would be unable to offer
much resistance to the Allies' assault from the west when it came."

The *New York Times* asked him about USAAF strategic operations in the Mediterranean and reported his reply as confirming that
"the airfields now available in southern Italy and other Mediterranean bases are enough for the total bombing of southern Germany
and the Balkans."

Though the spin, clearly designed for morale purposes, was
positive—and hopeful—Arnold knew that the strategic campaign
was still on the uphill side of the curve. The Schweinfurt missions
were not isolated among the total scope of operations in illustrating

the difficulty that the USAAF still faced in their portion of the Combined Bomber Offensive.

Arnold left a rainy Naples for a stopover in Tunis and another meeting with Eisenhower and Tedder; then he flew on to Marrakech and Dakar before crossing the Atlantic to Belém, Brazil. The leg of his return home between Brazil and Puerto Rico found Arnold on the flight deck "taking my turn at the wheel."

He landed in Washington at about half past four o'clock on the afternoon of December 15, having covered more than twenty-two thousand miles in five weeks. By his diary notes, he does not seem to have been as exhausted as he had been by his previous extensive trip to the Middle East and Asia at the beginning of the year. Indeed, he did not suffer another heart attack. Nor did he, as he had on his September trip to Britain, make a point of mentioning in his diary that he was accompanied by USAAF chief flight surgeon, General Dave Grant.

The USAAF was now a massive organization, including 2,372,292 personnel and 64,232 aircraft by the end of 1943. Most important for Arnold was that he now had 3,528 Flying Fortresses and 3,490 B-24 Liberators, not to mention 3,181 medium bombers (B-25s and B-26s), 5,100 P-47 Thunderbolts, and 1,165 P-51 Mustangs.

Now operating 10,456 transport aircraft, the USAAF maintained an infrastructure of bases and depots on six continents. The Air Transport Command, meanwhile, was now the largest "airline" the world had yet seen, flying a busy passenger and freight schedule that crossed the Atlantic and the Pacific and routinely circumnavigated the globe. Most of its routes were clear of Axis interference.

On December 17, 1943, Orville Wright traveled to Washington, D.C., to celebrate the fortieth anniversary of his first heavier-than-air flight and to present the Collier Trophy for the "outstanding contri-bution to aviation during the past year." The recipient was Henry Harley Arnold, whom Wright himself had taught to fly at Huffman Prairie, Ohio, thirty-two years before. Hap Arnold's "outstanding contribution to aviation during the past year" was building the USAAF into the largest air force in the world.

CHAPTER 16

BIG WEEKS
AND LONG DAYS

s 1944 began, the Anglo-American Allies were preparing in earnest for the climactic moment of their "Germany first" strategy: Operation Overlord. Backed by the massive production capacity of the "Arsenal of Democracy," arms and personnel were flowing into Britain, and the countdown clock was ticking toward the intended D-Day of May 1 (later postponed to June 6). The pieces were being moved together for the largest amphibious operation in history—all the pieces, that is, but one.

A year earlier, at Casablanca, the airmen of the USAAF and the RAF had been handed a great opportunity to prove the war-winning promise of strategic airpower. With the Combined Chiefs of Staff approval of the Combined Bomber Offensive came the immense responsibility of fulfilling that promise. Defeating the Luftwaffe and achieving air superiority over occupied Europe was considered an indispensable prerequisite to Overlord's success.

Operation Pointblank had been initiated in June 1943 to accomplish this task, but more than half a year later, it had not yet succeeded. On December 3, in fact, the RAF's Air Chief Marshal Portal had told the Combined Chiefs of Staff in a memo that Operation Pointblank was "a full three months behind schedule."

The entire Anglo-American strategy hinged on Operation Overlord, Overlord hinged on Operation Pointblank, and Pointblank hinged on the ability of the USAAF to make precision, daylight raids on specific targets within the German aircraft industry.

"This is my personal directive to you," Hap Arnold wrote in a New Year's Day memo to Jimmy Doolittle at the Eighth Air Force. "Destroy the enemy air forces, in its factories on the ground and in the air."

With January, there came new opportunities for the USAAF with the rising inventory of Flying Fortresses and Liberators, and especially with the attainment of a critical mass of long range P-51 Mustang escort fighters. With this steadily increasing capability, there also came a steadily increasing impatience on the part of Hap Arnold that it should be used soon and decisively.

"As you know I have been much concerned over the small number of bombers dispatched to destroy an important target," Arnold told Spaatz in a January 24 memo. "Why, with the great number of airplanes available ... can't we, some day and not too far distant, send out a big number—and I mean a big number—of bombers to hit something in the nature of an aircraft factory and lay it flat?"

There was such a plan on the table. Tooey Spaatz and his deputy commander for operations, General Fred Anderson, the former commander of the VIII Bomber Command, had been working with the Enemy Objectives Unit in London, where Dick Hughes and

Charlie Kindleberger understood the minute nuances of the German economy and had refined a secret plan for what was designated Operation Argument. This was to be a weeklong maximum effort against the German aircraft industry and the Luftwaffe that would involve coordinated operations by the Eighth and Fifteenth Air Forces, both under Spaatz's USSTAF command.

This plan was on the table, but, as with all precision bombing plans to date, it was dependent on bombardiers being able to see the target precisely. The USSTAF desperately needed a break in the weather. As Arnold himself had written, "In mid-October the weather shut down foggily on southeast Germany for most of the remainder of the year."

Watching the skies for a change in the weather, Spaatz waited through January and into February, with the Eighth flying missions to northern Germany and France, and the Fifteenth confining its operations to the Mediterranean.

"We have a superiority of at least five to one now against Germany and yet, in spite of all our hopes, anticipations, dreams and plans, we have as yet not been able to capitalize to the extent which we should," Arnold complained in a January 14 memo to Spaatz. "We may not be able to force capitulation of the Germans by air attacks, but on the other hand, with this tremendous striking power, it would seem to me that we should get much better and much more decisive results than we are getting now. I am not criticizing, because frankly I don't know the answer and what I am now doing is letting my thoughts run wild with the hope that out of this you may get a glimmer, a light, a new thought, or something which will help us to bring this war to a close sooner."

At last, Hap Arnold's wild running thoughts beheld that glimmer. He turned to that amazing weatherman whom he had first met a decade earlier when he was stationed at March Field. The theories of the maverick Dr. Irving Krick of the California Institute of Technology were considered unorthodox, but they seemed to work. His "weather typing" method involved a detailed analysis of past weather patterns. Arnold contacted him and sent him to help Spaatz and Anderson. Krick arrived at USSTAF headquarters asking for past weather maps, which he knew had been made in northern Europe since the end of the nineteenth century. By studying these, Hap Arnold's weatherman spotted patterns that led up to periods of clear weather across most of Germany. On February 18, 1944, Krick predicted that German skies would be clear from February 20 to 22, and perhaps longer.

On Sunday, February 20, the skies were clear, and Spaatz launched a maximum effort with more than one thousand Eighth Air Force heavy bombers and 835 fighter escorts. Aircraft factories from Rostock in the north to Gotha and Leipzig in the heart of the Reich were struck and struck effectively. RAF Bomber Command, meanwhile, had sent 921 bombers over Leipzig the night before. Back at Bushy Park, the USSTAF men braced themselves for more than two hundred losses, which would have been in keeping with the percentages lost on Black Thursday and the first Schweinfurt mission, but instead, only twenty-one were lost.

The good weather prevailed on Monday and Tuesday, and returned on Thursday and Friday. On Tuesday, the Eighth Air Force bombers were joined by a Fifteenth Air Force armada flying 550 miles from Foggia to bomb Regensburg. On Thursday, 231 Flying Fortresses of the Eighth Air Force's 1st Division bombed Schwein-furt, with only eleven losses, while 238 2nd Division Liberators hit Gotha.

On Friday, the final day of what came to be known as "Big Week," the 3rd Division of the Eighth coordinated with the Fifteenth in another strike against Regensburg, while other Eighth Air Force bombers targeted Fürth and Augsburg, the headquarters factory of Messerschmitt, Germany's largest maker of fighter aircraft.

In six days, the USSTAF force dropped roughly twenty million pounds of bombs on targets that included 90 percent of the aircraft factory complexes in Germany. During Big Week, the Eighth flew around 3,500 bomber sorties, and nearly that in fighter sorties, while the Fifteenth added more than five hundred bomber missions. RAF Bomber Command, meanwhile, flew more than 2,350 nighttime missions against the same targets during Big Week. The overall loss rate for the USSTAF bomber force was less than 6 percent, compared to a feared 20 percent. Only around two dozen American fighters were lost, compared to around five hundred for the Luftwaffe.

Operation Pointblank was no longer behind schedule. The effect on the Luftwaffe could be seen by the bomber crews themselves. With each passing day, they encountered less robust opposition from the German interceptors.

German fighter plane production, heavily damaged during Big Week, recovered. It actually increased later in 1944, but it did so at great economic cost and under steadily escalating assault from the USSTAF and the RAF. Indeed, the cost was so great that the recovery proved unsustainable. Within a year, the German aircraft industry had collapsed.

As Hap Arnold wrote in his report to Secretary of War Henry Stimson a year later on February 27, 1945, "The week of 20–26 February 1944, may well be classed by future historians as marking a decisive battle of history, one as decisive and of greater importance than Gettysburg."

As the USSTAF seemed to have at last turned a corner over Europe, Hap Arnold was able to turn his attention to the complexities of the strategic air campaign against Hitler's Axis partner. In the nearly two years after Doolittle's mission impossible, and nearly a year after Arnold had recoiled at the news of the XB-29 crash in Seattle, the USAAF had not yet mounted strategic operations against Japan. At the Sextant Conference, he had promised Roosevelt that Operation Matterhorn would begin in June 1944, and he was determined to make good on that commitment.

K. B. Wolfe moved his XX Bomber Command headquarters overseas to Kharagpur, India, on February 12, 1944, but the forward operating fields in China were still under construction.

"These runways were built with Chinese labor, and, literally, by hand," Arnold wrote in his memoirs. "Stones were placed by hand in their proper positions, with smaller stones on top. All stone used was delivered in baskets carried on the shoulders of thousands of coolies. Water to wet down the stones was carried in buckets by other thousands of coolies, and then the runway was rolled by a great roller, pulled by several hundred Chinese. It was a long, tedious process, but the airports were finally completed."

This was not the least of Arnold's worries when he turned his attention to the air war against Japan. Even if the fields were ready, the airplanes were not. In order for the June deadline to be met, the airplanes had to be overseas by the middle of April, and almost none were ready. Because the Superfortress had been ordered into production before it was fully flight-tested, aircraft had to be modified after manufacturing, and they were piling up at the modification centers.

"On March 8, 1944, I took a trip to Kansas to see how the B-29 units were progressing in so far as training, organization, and equipment were concerned," he wrote. "I was appalled at what I found. There were shortages in all kinds and classes of equipment. The engines were not fitted with the latest gadgets; the planes were not ready to go. It would be impossible for them to be anywhere near

China by the 15th of April unless some drastic measures were taken."

With K. B. Wolfe now overseas, Arnold assigned General Bennett Meyers to take over what came to be called the "Battle of Kansas."

As he wrote in his memoirs, Meyers was "a go-getter, a pusher, a driver; he got things done. When he was given a task, he did it. In this particular instance, I told Meyers he had to get those airplanes out on time, and the crews must be ready to go with them.... Meyers had less than two or three weeks in which to finish the job if the planes were to get to China on [April 15]. Everybody pitched in and the first of the B-29's headed for China landed in India on April 2."

Two days later, Arnold formed the last of the USAAF's numbered air forces, the Twentieth, as the umbrella organization for the operations of the XX Bomber Command, as well as the new XXI Bomber Command, which had been formed on March 1 at Smoky Hill Field in Kansas. The XXI Bomber Command was earmarked for operations from Guam and the Marianas after they were captured by American forces later in 1944. On April 6, Arnold selected General Haywood Hansell, his deputy chief for planning, who had designed the coming strategic air campaign against Japan, as chief of staff of the Twentieth Air Force.

In order to be sure that the all-Superfortress air force would be used solely for strategic operations, Arnold took the unprecedented step of personally assuming command of the Twentieth Air Force, to keep it under direct JCS control, and not under the umbrella of any theater command. In a later conversation with Tooey Spaatz and Ira Eaker, which Arnold cites in his memoirs, he explained that

> both General MacArthur and Admiral Nimitz wanted the Twentieth Air Force, but that it could not be under either one because we were operating beyond the battle area

controlled by either of them—far beyond. Without a single over-all commander in the Pacific, MacArthur and Nimitz each visualized the operation of the Twentieth Air Force as being for the benefit of his particular campaign plans. Therefore, I must continue to hold on to the Twentieth Air Force myself until such time as there was a unified command out there. As there never was unified command in the Pacific, I retained command of the Twentieth Air Force until VJ Day.

The first Superfortress, piloted by Colonel Leonard "Jake" Harmon, arriving to take command of the 40th Bombardment Group, reached India on April 2. By April 15, Arnold's deadline, there were thirty-two B-29s on hand, and by May 8, there were 130. However, the news was not entirely good. Five of this initial batch of B-29s were lost to engine failure, and four more were badly damaged. The engines continued to overheat, especially as they made their way eastward across North Africa, pausing in Cairo, which sweltered at 120 degrees Fahrenheit. It was scarcely any cooler in India, and the weather was only heating up.

To address the problems, which were supposed to have been solved already, engine baffles and crossover tubes to pump more oil into the rear cylinders had to be designed and flown out to India to be retrofitted in the aircraft.

Dogged by the strain of long hours and sleepless nights, on May 10, 1944, Arnold suffered his third wartime heart attack, coincidentally on the first anniversary of his previous coronary.

Arnold was sent to the USAAF convalescent hospital at the Biltmore in Coral Gables, Florida, where he was initially confined to bed rest and isolated from the day-to-day problems that had laid him low. He was spared some hand-wringing over the preparation for the first Superfortress missions and the postponement of Operation Overlord from May to June. His life was spared, too, which was not the case with Boeing president Philip Johnson, who dropped dead of a stroke on the Superfortress assembly line in Wichita on September 14.

The XX Bomber Command flew its first mission on June 5, with seventy-seven Superfortresses flying from India to bomb Bangkok. During World War II, Thailand had allied itself with Japan, and its capital was an important link in the Japanese supply line into Burma and beyond.

In June 1944, however, everything was overshadowed by a single battle. On June 6, as Operation Overlord went forward, roughly 160,000 Allied troops crossed the English Channel, supported by seven thousand ships and boats, and landed on the coast of Normandy. They established a beachhead from which the Germans were unable to dislodge them. Within ten days, there were half a million troops ashore, and within three weeks there were two million.

Overhead, the Eighth Air Force contributed 1,361 four-engine heavy bombers to support the landings on June 6. By now, the USSTAF boasted fifty-nine bombardment groups and more than 2,800 four-engine bombers, four times the number of a year earlier. Meanwhile, the combined efforts of the fighter commands of the Eighth and Ninth Air Forces flew nearly four thousand fighter sorties on D-Day alone. These came after seventeen thousand heavy bomber sorties and fifteen thousand fighter sorties during May. Concurrently, over the objections of his Anglo-American air officers, Eisenhower had transferred operational control of the four-engine heavy bomber assets from the Combined Bomber Offensive to SHAEF. During the weeks leading up to Overlord, the primary air mission was no longer strategic, but tactical. The idea was to "isolate the battlefield" by destroying the transportation network leading to northern France as well as the infrastructure supporting Luftwaffe operations there. The plan worked. The battlefield had been isolated. Overhead, the fruits of Operation Argument and the Combined

Bomber Offensive were also evident. The once-powerful Luftwaffe was virtually absent from the skies over Normandy. The air superiority over the invasion beaches, which had long been considered the vital prerequisite to Operation Overlord, had been achieved.

Two days after D-Day, Hap Arnold and General George Marshall boarded a C-54 in Washington. They were bound for Europe to meet with their officers on the ground and to see the Normandy invasion beaches for themselves. They were met in England by General Larry Kuter, who had observed the Normandy landings from the air. He provided them with his firsthand account as they traveled by train to their official reception in London.

Here, they were greeted by the British Chiefs of Staff, Air Marshal Portal, Field Marshal Brooke, and Admiral Cunningham, as well as by Tooey Spaatz, who took Marshal and Arnold to their quarters, a large sixteenth-century manor house that was the home of civil engineer and gentleman cattle farmer J. W. Gibson. Arnold noted in his diary that he was "so tired [I] went to sleep in car when talking to [Spaatz]; two and a half hours sleep [in 24] does not go very well any more."

In a later diary entry from this visit, Arnold noted that Gibson promised to make a gift of a prize bull for Arnold's ranch in California. The animal was never sent.

After meetings at Eisenhower's headquarters and with the Combined Chiefs of Staff, Arnold noted that the Luftwaffe appeared to be greatly reduced in numbers, that it "does not have the will to fight," and that it had "lost its morale." In his memoirs, Arnold elaborates more on the agenda at the staff meetings, writing that they discussed the effectiveness of the Combined Bomber Offensive's "round-the-clock" bombing of Germany, as well as "the progress of the war in France, Italy, Burma, the Southwest Pacific, the Pacific, China, and in Russia."

He observes with satisfaction that "one of the subjects brought up was the traffic over the Hump into China. I was glad to be able to report that the Air Transport Command had carried over 11,000 tons during the preceding month. It looked as though we might reach 16,000 tons for July."

After an overnight trip to southern England aboard Winston Churchill's private train, Arnold, Kuter, Marshall, Eisenhower, Admiral Ernest King, and their respective staff officers departed from Portsmouth Harbour for Normandy early on June 12.

"As we left the harbor we passed (30 knots) literally hundreds of ships of all kinds, escorted and proceeding singly," Arnold wrote in his diary. "Such a mass one never saw before, uninterrupted and unimpeded. As we approached the coast of France there were literally hundreds anchored offshore. What a field day for the [Luftwaffe] if there is a [Luftwaffe]."

As Arnold points out, a major air assault against the invasion fleet would have been devastating to the Allies, but it never came. It was a pivotal missed opportunity for Hermann Göring's Luftwaffe.

"Trucks being driven from LSTs [ships carrying vehicles to the shoreline] over beach and up road," Arnold wrote, jotting notes of his impressions of the Normandy beachhead in his diary.

The ever present sound of explosions: bombs, mines being set off by Engineers. Airplanes on the cliff top taking back wounded to [England]. A regular madhouse but a very orderly one in which some 15,000 troops a day go from ship to shore and some 1,500 to 3,000 tons of supplies a day are landed. But where is the [Luftwaffe]? After a tour of the harbor a DUCK [DUKW amphibious truck] comes alongside. We leave subchaser and start toward beach. The tide is low and we lift the top off an obstruction.

Fortunately there were no mines; we slid off and continued through obstacles to beach. Passed by the wrecks and
ships unloading, then out we climbed.

On the beach, the reception committee was headed by General
Omar Bradley, commander of the United States First Army, and
General Elwood "Pete" Quesada, commander of the Ninth Air Force's
IX Tactical Air Command. After their beachhead tour and a visit to
Bradley's headquarters, Arnold and Kuter went with Quesada to his
headquarters at Grandcamp-les-Baines and to see the airfields under
construction. Amazed by the speed at which this was being done,
Arnold jotted in his diary that he had seen "four landing strips, one
used now, one used by tonight, two to be available in 48 hours, one
additional in another 72 hours. Hundreds of US planes but not one
of the [Luftwaffe]. Four thousand planes, US and RAF in air today."

When invited to return to England with Marshall and the rest of
the party the way they had come, Arnold and Kuter pondered spending four hours on a destroyer and seven on train, and they decided
to fly aboard an ATC C-47. It took them about an hour to get back.
Arnold was in his bathtub at Gibson's house while Marshall was still
bobbing in the English Channel.

That night, Hap Arnold relaxed at J. W. Gibson's country estate,
thinking of an England no longer at the mercy of the Luftwaffe, of
the extraordinarily successful Allied beachhead in France, and of
total Allied air superiority.

He had a rude awakening.

There was an air-raid alarm, but, as he wrote in his memoirs,

[W]e couldn't figure out its meaning. At 5:30 in the morning,
there was a long series of explosions following one another
in quick succession, most of them several miles from the
Gibson house, but a few very close by. The charges were

quite heavy and we couldn't figure out what they were. Bombs? Rockets? Something with delayed fuses? What were they? I ran out of the house to see. A pilotless plane was flying through the air, circling right above the Gibson house. It just missed the house. It came down out of the clouds in a dive, leveled off, made a low turn, then crashed into the ground and exploded about a mile and a half away!

Three years after the London Blitz, Arnold had lived through the first night of a new blitz. As he quickly ascertained, southern England was now being targeted by a fresh weapon from the Luftwaffe arsenal. It was a jet-propelled, twenty-seven-foot, two-ton pilotless airplane. It was the first operational cruise missile.

This strange new weapon went by many names. Built by the German firm of Fieseler, it was officially designated as Fi 103. Adolf Hitler named it Vergeltungswaffe 1 (Vengeance Weapon 1), or V-1. The British people who would now have to live under its threat for the next three months called it a "Buzz Bomb" or a "Doodlebug." In his diary, Hap Arnold prophetically called it a "drone."

Arnold had long-standing firsthand knowledge of pilotless drone aircraft, as in the First World War, he had helped develop a primitive cruise missile called "the Bug" with engineer Charles Kettering.

"By mid-1918, the development of the Bug had proceeded so favorably that we decided to tell General Pershing and the Commanding General of the Air Service in France what we were doing," Arnold recalled in his memoirs. "We were sure we would be ready to send some of the pilotless bombs overseas within a few months.... It was planned to launch thousands every day against German strong points, concentration areas, munition plants, etc.— which would certainly have caused great consternation in the ranks of the German High Command at least." He now found himself on the receiving end of the "consternation in the ranks."

"The Bug was twenty-five years ahead of its time," Arnold wrote accurately. "For all practical purposes—as a nuisance weapon—it compared very favorably with the German V-1. It was cheap, easy to manufacture, and its portable launching track would have permitted its use anywhere.... [It] is interesting to think how this little Bug might have changed the whole face of history if it had been allowed to develop without interruption during the years between the two wars. It was not perfect in 1918, of course, and as new gadgets and scientific improvements came out they continued to be incorporated into the Bug until the economy wave of the mid-twenties caused it to be shelved."

Though the Kettering Bug was a piston-engined biplane, it had a lot in common with the jet-propelled Doodlebug. Both "drones" were cheap, launched on a rail, and lacked the sophisticated guidance that might have made them more than just a nuisance weapon. The gyroscopic guidance of the V-1 was so primitive that it could not be sent against a specific target. Most crashed harmlessly into fields and forests.

After their rude awakening, Arnold and Marshall went out to inspect some of the craters that had been made by this first salvo of Buzz Bombs and to pick through the fragments of metal and wiring that were left in Gibson's fields and forests. Arnold ordered remnants to be gathered up at each of the impact sites and sent to Wright Field for examination by USAAF engineers. One Buzz Bomb was found intact, and within three months, reverse-engineered copies, developed by Republic Aviation and Ford as the JB-2, were being tested back in the United States.

He also sent a handful of V-1 fragments home to Bee, with a letter describing the experience of being attacked by Hitler's wonder-weapon. At the time, however, the event most prominent in Bee's mind was the June 10 wedding of their second son, which Hap had missed by being overseas.

Lieutenant Bruce Arnold, a U.S. Army antiaircraft artilleryman in training at Fort Irwin in the California desert, had just married Barbara Douglas, one of the most eligible young ladies in Southern California *and* the daughter of Hap's long-time friend, plane-maker Donald Douglas. Hap and Bee had socialized with Don and Charlotte Douglas when Hap was posted to March Field before the war, but while Bruce had known Barbara's brothers, Will and Don Jr., he had never met her while he was in California.

As their son, Robert Arnold, tells it, his mother was quite popular on the social circuit, always out "playing golf, playing tennis," with "all the big money guys in LA, whether it was the banking people or the land development people, [who] wanted to marry my mother. She had a million of these guys chasing her, but she wasn't interested in any of them."

On a trip back east, Charlotte and Barbara visited West Point. Bruce saw her from afar, and it was the proverbial "love at first sight." Robert still has the dance card from their first West Point soiree, having found it in his mother's safe deposit box. Bruce had signed it "Cary Grant," "me," "me again," and so on, as they danced together six times. At the end, he penciled in, "Hope you make it again sometime."

She did. Robert says of his parents, "They were astonishingly happy people," and their marriage was a perfect match.

On June 13, the morning after the V-1 attacks, Hap Arnold was taken by Jimmy Doolittle and Fred Anderson to see various Eighth Air Force units, including the 91st Bombardment Group at Bassingbourn, which had been badly mauled in the second Schweinfurt mission. It had flown for all five days of the Big Week operations as well as missions in support of Overlord. Arnold also called on the 355th Fighter Group at Steeple Morden and the 344th Bombardment Group (Medium) flying B-26s out of Stansted.

On June 14, Arnold was received at Buckingham Palace by King George VI, whom he had met in 1941 on his first trip to Britain as America's top airman.

"Three years before, when I had been at Buckingham Palace after a German bombardment, the windows of the Palace had been blown out and the draft in the halls had made it a cheerless place," Arnold wrote in his memoirs. "The King had talked with me anxiously about how long it would be before we would be able to get air and other assistance to England to change the character of the war, to swing the tide in favor of the Allies. In 1944, the tide had now swung, and the King's attitude was different. And not only his. Over all the people in England had come a transformation."

Apparently, the V-1s had not dampened the monarch's spirits.

That evening, the King attended a dinner at 10 Downing Street that Winston Churchill hosted for the Combined Chiefs of Staff— Arnold, King, and Marshall on the American side, and Portal, Cunningham, and Brooke on the British side. Also present were South African Field Marshal Jan Smuts, whom Arnold had met at the Sextant Conference, and Churchill's socialist deputy in his coalition government, Clement Attlee.

Arnold wrote that the drinking, toasting, and talking went past midnight, with both the King and prime minister in "good form."

At about one o'clock, the King turned to Arnold and asked, "Doesn't anyone ever go to bed around here? How long do we sit up and wait?"

"Well, your Majesty," Arnold replied. "You are the one to set the pace."

When the King repeated the question to Churchill, his prime minister replied, "It is early yet; we still have a lot to talk about."

In his diary, Arnold reports that he said his goodbyes at half past two o'clock in the morning. He does not say when His Majesty departed. Churchill was still holding court as the USAAF chief made for the door.

Late on June 17, Arnold and Marshall, as well as Larry Kuter, departed from England in a C-54, flying westward under fighter escort before circling south to Algiers. From there, they proceeded east to Naples. Arnold noted in his diary that he had seen the lava flows from the most recent eruption of Mount Vesuvius, three months earlier.

When they landed, Arnold noted their being met "officially" by Field Marshal Henry Maitland "Jumbo" Wilson, commander of Allied forces in the Mediterranean and General Jacob Devers, now the commander of U.S. Army forces in the Mediterranean. He adds that he was met "personally" by his son Hank. The next day, George Marshall went to visit the grave of his stepson, Lieutenant Alan Brown, who had been killed by a sniper three weeks earlier.

Devers took Marshall and Arnold on a flyover of the Anzio beachhead. In January 1944, a month after Arnold's last visit to Italy, Allied forces had conducted a major amphibious assault at Anzio, thirty-five miles south of Rome. Bottled up in the beachhead area for four months by German defenders, the Allies finally managed a bloody breakout at the end of May and swiftly captured Rome. News of the fall of Rome on June 5, the first Axis capital to be captured, was overshadowed—like most war news that week—by Operation Overlord, which came the next day.

With Hank serving as their guide, Arnold and Marshall toured the Anzio area, visiting forward airfields, talking with men from a USAAF photoreconnaissance squadron, and visiting a field hospital, where the wounded soldiers seemed pleased to be noticed by the top brass.

From here, they flew on to Rome, where Arnold was anxious to see the damage wrought—and not wrought—by USAAF bombers.

As the air war had come to the Italian capital, there were domestic political concerns over the possible damage and destruction to priceless ancient art and architectural treasures, especially within Rome and Vatican City.

"One of the hottest potatoes I had had to handle during the war was the mission of our bombers in support of the Allied troops moving up through Italy," Arnold wrote in his memoirs.

> We had finally come to the conclusion that if our bombers could cut the railroads running north and south in Italy, all supplies to [General Field Marshal Albert] Kesselring's [German armies in Italy] would be stopped. Then had arisen the question of bombing the marshaling yard in Rome. Through the President and the Secretary of War, influences from all sides were brought to bear to prevent me from bombing Rome. I told them I was confident we could hit the railroad yard, destroy it, and thus cut that last link between north and south Italy without badly damaging a single church. If we destroyed that yard it would be impossible for Kesselring's army to receive any supplies except by road, and I was convinced that our light bombers and fighters could take care of the road traffic. Finally, very reluctantly, we were given the necessary authority.

In his diary, Arnold noted that he found the city of Rome "remarkably free from damage from bombs," but not so the railroad marshaling yards on the edge of town.

"What a mess!" Arnold wrote. "Most done by B-26s; over 800 railroad cars thrown around, turned upside down, burned, tossed on top of one another, over a stretch of the entire yard. Certainly it would take weeks to open up one track through. The station and the warehouses completely destroyed. It was a delightful mess from my viewpoint. None of the apartments bordering the yards were injured in any way."

Arnold and his party drove north to Viterbo, inspecting the German escape route from Rome. He observes in his diary that the wreckage of German vehicles was strewn "along the road for over 40 miles and gave pictorial evidence of the desperate straits the Germans were in as they fled northward."

His optimism would be tempered by continuing difficult battles that were still ahead during the coming winter.

After a few more hours spent with his son on June 19, Arnold departed the following day for the United States, traveling via the newly constructed USAAF field in the Azores, and then across the North Atlantic.

Arriving in Newfoundland, he and George Marshall stopped for a rainy morning of river fishing. "Had a wonderful change, even if the fishing was rotten," he wrote in his diary. They had caught five, including an Atlantic salmon, which doesn't seem so bad for two hours.

In his diary, Arnold noted that there were recent newspapers aboard the C-54 that took them to Washington, and that the June 16 headlines were of particular interest. On June 15, forty-seven Superfortresses had bombed the Imperial Iron and Steel Works in Yawata. It was the first Twentieth Air Force strike against Japan and the first American air attack on the Japanese home islands since Doolittle's more than two years before.

CHAPTER 17

AT THE APOGEE OF EXPANSION

Hap Arnold returned to his desk at the Pentagon in an optimistic frame of mind. He had stood on the streets of a former Axis capital city, and he had stood on the soil of northern France as hundreds of his USAAF aircraft thundered through the skies above. He had received the news that his Superfortresses had finally bombed Japan—and that they had done so again and again.

By the end of August, the American ground offensive in northern France, supported by massive Ninth Air Force tactical airpower, had captured more territory faster than any American Army in history. Allied troops landed in southern France on August 15; among the units coming ashore was Hank Arnold's 45th Infantry Division. The Allies liberated Paris on August 25.

★ ★ ★ ★ ★

The news from Europe was so encouraging that Arnold and Marshall went trout fishing in the Sierra Nevadas of California. There was great trepidation in Washington at the idea of having Hap Arnold and George Marshall on horseback in the wilderness, but, as Arnold happily reports in his memoirs, "for ten days [in August], the Chief of Staff and the Chief of the Air Forces operated from the High Sierras, directing the war in all parts of the world by radio."

One of Arnold's first stops after his return to the "outside world" was at the Massachusetts Institute of Technology, visiting the Radiation Laboratory (the "Radlab") where they developed cloud-penetrating radar that allowed USAAF bombers to conduct bombing raids on enemy targets that were blanketed by overcast. The first version, designated H2X and based on the earlier British H2S system, was used by Eighth Air Force Flying Fortresses in February 1944 and had steadily improved. In cooperation with Western Electric and Bell Laboratories, the Radlab was developing the much-advanced AN/APQ-13 ground-scanning radar that would be deployed aboard Superfortresses in the Pacific.

From Cambridge, Arnold traveled to Lake Kezar, Maine, where he and Bee celebrated their thirty-first wedding anniversary on September 10. Early the following morning, accompanied by Larry Kuter, Hap traveled to Quebec as part of the Combined Chiefs of Staff contingent for the Octagon Conference. This would be the first face-to-face meeting of President Roosevelt and Prime Minister Churchill in nine months—and the first since Operation Overlord.

The Anglo-American Allies had now almost advanced to within sight of Germany. There was hopeful talk in the media of the war with Germany being over by Christmas, which was unrealistic, but illustrative of the optimism that prevailed in September 1944.

Those who had held most steadfastly to the "Germany first" dogma for nearly three years were now thinking about Japan. Hap Arnold perhaps best summarized this swing of attitude when he wrote in his diary on September 14 that "in the conference yesterday there was no doubt as to the Prime Minister desiring for political reasons to be in at the kill when we hit Japan. He wanted to be there with his main Fleet and some 500 to 1,000 [heavy bombers]. There was also no doubt as to the President's being in accord."

"The British could not hold up their heads if such was not done," insisted Roosevelt.

In conversation with Arnold the day before, Peter Portal mentioned sending an RAF bomber force to the Pacific to participate in the strategic air offensive, but Arnold wondered where the RAF's Avro Lancasters could be based given that their range was so much less than that of the USAAF Superfortresses.

When Arnold reiterated his comment that there was no place to put an RAF bomber force, Churchill quipped, "With all your wealth of airdromes you would not deny me a mere pittance of a few!"

In fact, there would be no bases within the practical range of RAF bombers for the better part of a year.

Another issue that now reared its ominous head was the realization that the Anglo-American Allies and the Soviet Union were not exactly on the same page with regard to the postwar circumstances of Poland. In August, as the Red Army approached Warsaw, there was a mass uprising against the German occupiers. The Poles expected to coordinate their rebellion with the arrival of the Soviets. The Red Army, however, halted its advance outside the city and did not intervene as the Germans ruthlessly put down the revolt, which was still ongoing during the Octagon Conference.

It was the point of view of many at the time, and of many postwar historians, that the Soviet reaction was aimed at allowing the

Germans to destroy Polish elements that could potentially oppose the later long-term Soviet occupation of Poland. The British and Americans were powerless to do more than airdrop supplies to the beleaguered Poles.

"For some time it has been apparent that if some help was not given to Polish patriots they would be exterminated in Warsaw," Arnold wrote in his diary on September 11 in Quebec.

> Last time the RAF sent in planes with supplies they lost some 48 ... and the Germans got most of the supplies dropped. Now the British are trying to force the Russians to assist in the enterprise. The Russians would just as soon have all of the Warsaw Poles exterminated.... Hence they reportedly stood by and watched while the debacle was happening in Warsaw. Now when public opinion is aroused at the lack of help, the Russians come back with.... "That is our war theater and you must not interfere. We will do the job. If you now feel that you want to help the Poles, give us your plan and we will look it over."

Arnold adds a comment prophetic of postwar geopolitics and relations with the Soviets, writing that he "went to bed and dreamed of alligators lurking in the shadows, awaiting such victims as came their way."

For the United States, the three months following Octagon were characterized by continued good fortune—albeit not without substantial cost—on the world's battlefronts. American armies continued to advance in France and Italy under an umbrella of tactical airpower that kept enemy fighters at bay and harassed the enemy's rear echelons.

The Combined Bomber Offensive, meanwhile, was moving through its target priorities. The Third Reich's economy was collapsing from the damage done to its petrochemical industry and the destruction of its transportation network. Without rail transportation, German industry, which had dispersed its factories under the pressures of Allied bombing, began to fall apart. The Strategic Bombing Survey credited this stage of the air campaign as "the most important single cause of Germany's ultimate economic collapse."

Back in October 1943, Black Thursday over Schweinfurt had been a maximum effort of fewer than three hundred heavy bombers. A year later, the Eighth Air Force alone was sending out missions of 750 to 1,000 bombers on a routine basis. On October 6, the Eighth launched nearly 1,200 bombers, and on October 14, 1944, the first anniversary of Black Thursday, 1,100 heavy bombers targeted Germany's industrial heartland, escorted by fifteen fighter groups. The Luftwaffe response was feeble. Thanks to mushrooming numbers of P-51 Mustangs, which now roamed across European skies with virtual impunity, the Allies maintained air superiority wherever they chose to concentrate the weight of their power.

As Arnold wrote,

> November 1944 found our air units roving at will over all Germany, and the Luftwaffe's air and ground defenses helpless to do anything about it. On one auspicious day, General Doolittle's Eighth Air Force sent P-51s and P-47s on a strafing and bombing mission over the heart of Germany that covered a round-trip flight from England of over 1,100 miles. On this mission our airmen destroyed 27 German aircraft, including one German jet-propelled Me 262 in the air, and destroyed 64 planes, among which were 30 jet-propelled planes, on the various airfields over which they passed. Every time they saw an engine, a train,

an oil car, a marshaling yard, they dove down to smash it. That day's report showed the destruction of 131 locomotives, 24 railroad cars, 42 oil cars, none of which would ever run again. On their way home, the fighters wiped out factories, warehouses, and airplane hangars. As a result of the day's work, in which 400 of our fighters participated, we lost eight airplanes.

In October, in the Pacific, Douglas MacArthur made good on his promise to return to the Philippines. In fact, the operation, originally planned for December, was ahead of schedule; and as Allied troops advanced, so did the engineers, building a great archipelago of tactical airfields.

In the Battle of Leyte Gulf, fought offshore from the Philippines, the United States Navy dealt the Imperial Japanese Navy a permanently crippling blow, sinking more than two dozen major warships, including four aircraft carriers and three battleships.

The Marines had landed in the Marianas and had captured Guam, Saipan, and Tinian, where Arnold intended to base his XXI Bomber Command for the final strategic air offensive against Japan. Parenthetically, Hap Arnold's son-in-law, Lieutenant Commander Ernie Snowden, a pilot and the commander of Air Group 16 (AG-16) aboard the USS *Lexington*, had earned a Silver Star during the battle for the Marianas in June 1944.

By the end of August, General Curtis LeMay, formerly a division commander with the Eighth Air Force, took over the XX Bomber Command in China, and new Superfortress-length runways allowed the advance echelon of the XXI Bomber Command, General Emmett "Rosey" O'Donnell's 73rd Bombardment Wing, to start arriving in the Marianas.

General Haywood Hansell, picked by Arnold to command the XXI Bomber Command, arrived on October 12. He had been an obvious choice. He had developed the strategic plan for the Twentieth Air Force, had served as its chief of staff, and had essentially run the show when Arnold was incapacitated by his May heart attack. General Lauris Norstad succeeded Hansell as chief of staff of the Twentieth Air Force.

On November 24, with Hansell in command, the XXI Bomber Command flew its first mission; Rosie O'Donnell led 111 Superfortresses against Tokyo. Five days later, Hap Arnold spoke to a meeting of Kansas City Veterans of Foreign Wars. His remarks caught the attention of the *New York Times*, which reported him as having said, "We're going to bomb Japanese industry into a state of paralysis— just as we're doing in Germany."

By the end of 1944, the USAAF had reached the apogee of its power. By Arnold's own reckoning, "During the year 1944 the US Army Air Forces dropped over a million tons of bombs on the enemy, fired over 225,000 rounds of ammunition, destroyed over 18,200 enemy aircraft, and sank over 950,000 tons of shipping in the Pacific alone. This was accomplished by ten separate air forces in combat, plus two B-29 commands operating from the Twentieth Air Force. Flying hours meant little, for in the continental United States we flew over 37 million hours and used over five billion gallons of gasoline."

During 1944, Eighth Air Force bomber groups had gone from twenty-six to forty; the number of fighter groups from seventeen to thirty-three, most of them now equipped with Mustangs. In the Mediterranean Theater, the total numbers of bomber and fighter groups went from fewer than thirty to thirty-eight. Within General

Kenney's Far East Air Forces in the SWPA, the numbers increased from twenty-seven to thirty.

The total number of USAAF aircraft had risen from 10,329 on the eve of Pearl Harbor to 72,726 at the end of 1944. In just one year, the numbers of Flying Fortresses had grown from 3,528 to 4,419, while the inventory of Liberators had come from 3,490 to 5,678. A year earlier, there had been just seventy-nine Superfortresses, none of them operational. At the end of 1944, there were 942, and they were rolling out of the factories at a rate of more than one hundred each month. Like the Superfortress, the P-51 Mustang fighter was a revolutionary warplane that was virtually absent at the start of the year, but which had proven itself to be a game-changer during 1944. At the close of the year, the inventory stood at 3,914, with the factories adding around three hundred each month.

Arnold was especially proud of his Air Transport Command, recalling in his memoirs that it "had developed into the largest outfit of its kind the world had ever seen or would see again for a long time. During 1944, we carried 1,200,000 passengers and 400,000 tons of cargo and freight. ATC was operating approximately 3,000 airplanes when it attained that record. In just one month of 1944, in returning evacuees to the United States, more than 24 million air-patient miles were flown."

The personnel strength of USAAF had now grown to 2,372,292. After building up the USAAF with great urgency over the previous years, Hap Arnold saw that his force was now actually as large as it needed to be. In his memoirs, he recalled,

> In the fall of 1944, it had become apparent that our output of pilots, gunners, bombardiers, navigators, mechanics, and all other qualified personnel had reached a point where our production was far in excess of our demands. In fact, we were replacing losses in our overseas combat

units faster than they occurred.... Our plans for meeting
estimated losses up to 25 percent per month had worked
out very satisfactorily. There were few months when we
actually needed such replacements, but when we started
rolling, the 25 percent margin came in handy as a reserve
for many unforeseen situations, and enabled us to build
up our programmed strength much more quickly than
we could otherwise have done.

In the meantime, the other services had also grown in personnel
strength. From 1939 to 1944, the Army (exclusive of the USAAF)
had grown from 166,384 to 5,622,453; the Navy from 125,202 to
2,981,365; and the Marine Corps from 19,432 to 475,604. Since the
start of 1943, the largest navy in the world had launched four battleships, twenty-three aircraft carriers, eighty-seven escort carriers,
twenty-four cruisers, 655 destroyers and destroyer escorts, and more
than twenty million tons of transport ships.

Against the backdrop of the armed forces having grown to a size
unprecedented in American history (or, in the case of the USAAF
and U.S. Navy, *world* history), the subject of increased rank for the
service leaders had been a topic of serious discussion all year long,
and it was finally acted upon at the end of 1944.

Among the officers of the Combined Chiefs of Staff, Arnold, Marshall, and King, as well as Admiral William Leahy, Roosevelt's chief of
staff, who functioned as chairman of the Joint Chiefs of Staff (the
formal post of chairman of the Joint Chiefs of Staff was created in
1949), held four-star rank. Their opposite numbers in the British high
command, Air Marshal Charles "Peter" Portal, Field Marshal Alan
Brooke, and Fleet Admiral Andrew Cunningham held the equivalent
of five-star rank. Talk of elevating the rank of the American officers
dated back to the Arcadia Conference, but no action had yet been taken.

"In my own case, rank never meant an awful lot to me," Arnold wrote in his memoirs.

> I was senior air officer in southern California [1931-1936] where I was pretty nearly always doing business with Admirals—and I was a Major.... When I went to England, as Chief of the Air Corps, I had two stars, but I found myself doing business with Air Chief Marshals, Field Marshals, and Fleet Admirals.... Marshall was in charge of an army of about eight million men [including the USAAF]. Usually, he was spokesman at our conferences.... I know for a fact that General Marshall never agitated for the five-star rank for himself or for any of the other [American] members of the Combined Chiefs of Staff.

By most accounts, Marshall was particularly apprehensive of being given the title of field marshal because of the awkwardness of being called "Marshal Marshall."

However, several events in 1944 propelled the introduction of five-star rank in the United States. First, in early January, President Roosevelt suggested that Leahy should have five stars. Leahy countered that each member of the JCS should be promoted if he was promoted. Secretary of War Stimson had agreed that Army generals should have the rank if admirals were promoted, but nothing was done. This was partly out of deference to the popular General John J. Pershing, commander of American forces in World War I, who had been promoted in 1919 to "General of the Armies," a five-star equivalent. Promoting anyone to outrank the retired, but still living, Pershing was deemed inappropriate.

The final straw came in September 1944, when the British promoted General Bernard Montgomery, commander of the 21st Army

Group, to field marshal. As such, he now outranked his boss, General Dwight Eisenhower, the supreme Allied commander in Europe, who wore four stars.

President Roosevelt asked Congress to approve five-star rank, although the authorization bill was not passed until December 12. As a concession to Pershing, the Army rank would be called "General of the Army"—not field marshal—allowing Pershing's "General of the *Armies*" title to remain as a higher rank. The authorization called for five-star rank to be extended to the three principal theater commanders—MacArthur, Nimitz, and Eisenhower—as well as Admirals Leahy and King, and Generals Marshal and Arnold.

The promotions were scheduled one day apart in order of seniority, alternating between Army and Navy officers. The promotion list read as follows:

- Fleet Admiral William D. Leahy: December 15, 1944
- General of the Army George C. Marshall: December 16, 1944
- Fleet Admiral Ernest J. King: December 17, 1944
- General of the Army Douglas MacArthur: December 18, 1944
- Fleet Admiral Chester W. Nimitz: December 19, 1944
- General of the Army Dwight D. Eisenhower: December 20, 1944
- General of the Army Henry H. Arnold: December 21, 1944

CHAPTER 18

OUT OF DARKNESS, THE LIGHT OF DAWN

The sense that the end of the war was tangibly near ended on December 16, 1944, when the Germans launched a major offensive against American forces in the forests of the Ardennes in Belgium. Four German field armies punched through the Allied front in a heavily wooded, and therefore lightly defended, salient between the 12th and 21st Allied Army Groups. Unchecked—overcast skies neutralized the ability of Allied airpower to intervene—they raced forward, creating a fifty-mile "bulge" in the front line, which led the media to dub this the Battle of the Bulge.

Though the Germans failed to recapture the Belgian port of Antwerp, or push the Bulge deeper than fifty miles, they cost the U.S. Army nearly ninety thousand casualties, including more than twenty thousand captured. The front line was not restored for a month. It was the worst American setback since Bataan, and the largest and bloodiest battle for the United States Army in the European Theater.

Worst of all was the damage done to American morale. Not only had the war not ended by Christmas, as some optimists in the home-front media had been speculating, the war effort and the troops on the line were in worse shape on Christmas than they had been on Thanksgiving. Unrealistically sanguine speculation gave way to unrealistically pessimistic conjecture.

There were rumors of German secret weapons, which were fanned by the reality of German missile attacks. Just as the V-1 blitz had ended when the Allies overran their launch sites, the Germans upped the ante with their V-2 ballistic missiles. Though its guidance system was as unreliable as that of the V-1, the V-2 was more terrible for the fact that it traveled at supersonic speed, therefore arriving at its target without warning, and with unstoppable vengeance. It also created unfounded fears of a whole new arsenal of secret weapons that might soon be emanating from the dark and sinister workshops of the Third Reich. However, if Germany's factories were dark, it wasn't from metaphorical evil but because the USSTAF had turned out the lights.

While the USSTAF operated from easily supplied facilities and well-maintained bases, the air war in the Pacific depended on the long runways handmade on remote Chinese plateaus and hacked from thick and ancient Pacific island jungles. Curtis LeMay and Haywood "Possum" Hansell were operating the most modern bomb-ers in the world from some of the world's most primitive air bases.

Of the seven missions flown against the home islands of Japan through the end of 1944, only the first had mustered more than one hundred aircraft, and weather prevented the desired bombing accuracy.

Hansell, both in his memoirs and in his later conversations with me, readily admitted the poor results of these initial missions, which he blamed on a variety of factors, including shortcomings in training, continued mechanical problems with the Superfortress, an inefficient depot and supply system, and second-guessing from General Kenney of the Far East Air Forces (FEAF), who commanded all the other numbered air forces in the Pacific—the Fifth, Seventh, and Thirteenth—under the FEAF umbrella.

"The only decent operation that we flew during this series of high-altitude attacks was the last one I ran," Hansell told me.

> It was a 62-plane raid against the Kawasaki aircraft factory at Akashi on January 19. For once we obliterated an engine and aircraft factory! The bombing was not as good as it should have been by standards established in the European Theater, but we had so many bombs that we were able to simply obliterate the place. The Japanese never even tried to rebuild it. That is what we wanted to do with the rest of the factories, but weather and ineptitude on our part kept us from doing so. This was my last mission. The next day, the 20th of January 1945, General LeMay took over from me.

Hap Arnold had been growing increasingly impatient with the strategic campaign against Japan. By most accounts, his mounting displeasure with XXI Bomber Command operations was directed at Hansell personally, so he decided early in January 1945 to bring LeMay in to take over the XXI.

"When I had gone into China [on August 29], it was with the basic understanding that the XX Bomber Command would get out of there as soon as the better bases in the Marianas became operable and capable of supporting large numbers of B-29s," LeMay told me. "China had proved to be a horrible, almost impossible, logistical situation, and we knew it."

General Norstad personally delivered the message to both Hansell and LeMay, on Arnold's behalf, on January 7 while LeMay was visiting the Marianas.

"I think the major factor in the decision to move General LeMay to the Marianas had to do with General Arnold's dissatisfaction with my rate of operations," Hansell recalled.

> I wasn't satisfied with it either. I knew it would improve over time, but he was very impatient. He was also aware that if the XX Bomber Command were moved to Saipan there would then be two commanders—General LeMay and myself—when we only needed one. General Arnold had asked me to stay on as vice-commander to General LeMay, but I didn't think that was a good idea. It wasn't that I didn't have confidence in General LeMay—in fact I had every confidence in him. I simply felt that he didn't need a second-in-command, especially one who was in effect being relieved from first-in-command. It is a difficult thing and probably a bad idea, to take the commander of an outfit and keep him on in a subordinate position, so I asked Arnold that I be relieved, and I was.

Driving Arnold's urgency to act quickly and decisively was his renewed fear that the strategic campaign against Japan might fall behind schedule—just as Operation Pointblank had in Europe. Recalling the media criticism of the costly strategic campaign against Germany in 1943, he wanted to move quickly to demonstrate the effectiveness of the campaign against Japan by replacing the methodical Hansell with the uncompromising, results-oriented LeMay.

Arnold was convinced that this strategic campaign was the only effective way to defeat Japan. As he wrote in his memoirs, "Before we got the Marianas, the columnists, commentators, and newspaper reporters had all talked about the Naval capture of the Islands. The Navy would take the Islands and use them as a base. No one had mentioned using them as bases for the B-29s, yet it was the B-29s and the B-29s only that could put tons and tons of bombs on Japan. The fleet couldn't do it; the Naval Air couldn't do it; the Army couldn't do it. The B-29s could."

Having taken the unprecedented step of retaining personal command of the Twentieth Air Force, Arnold wanted to see it through to the climax. He goes on to say, "To end the war as quickly as possible, it was essential that we use such power as was available to carry out our major objective, which was to mass the maximum number of heavy bombers possible for the destruction of interior Germany, and in due course mass the maximum number of Superfortresses for the destruction of Japan."

For Hap Arnold, it was a situation of extreme personal anguish to sack Hansell, who had drafted the strategic air plan, built up the force, and been the shadow commander of the Twentieth Air Force since its birth. As these events were playing out in the Pacific, Arnold suffered his fourth—and most severe—wartime heart attack on January 17, 1945. Arnold wrote of his succumbing to forces beyond his control, "I did not know how ill I was, but I knew I was a very sick man."

The fishing trips with George Marshall notwithstanding, Arnold was suffering mightily under the strain of leadership in humanity's greatest war. This is not to mention the cumulative damage done by three earlier heart attacks in the space of fifteen months.

He reacted as he had to those earlier heart attacks—by denial. He simply crawled into bed, hoping for the best. With Bee out of town on the West Coast, he went generally undisturbed until those in his office expressed concern and summoned Dr. Dave Grant, the chief USAAF flight surgeon.

"I passed out of the picture with a heart attack, and went to the hospital at [Coral Gables]," he wrote. Unlike the previous heart attacks, which he sidestepped or ignored in his memoirs, this time, he looked in the mirror and took stock of his own mortality. "The sudden realization that a man isn't as good physically as he had thought himself to be comes as a distinct shock."

Also weighing heavily on Arnold's mind at the time was the slow death of his friend and colleague, Sir John Dill, who had passed away in Washington from aplastic anemia two months before.

More than a week of around-the-clock care was prescribed, and this was followed by weeks of convalescence. As before, there was no move made to relieve him from duty as the war—at least against Germany—seemed to be nearing its conclusion.

"As the days and weeks passed, I had time to think of many things that had happened during the war, things that were still happening, and things that had yet to happen before we completed our victory," he confides in his memoirs. "My experience during the war indicated that it is very easy to see the mistakes the other fellow makes, but far more difficult to give him credit for the good things he does, and see his side of the picture."

"Listen to the other fellow's story," Marshall had cautioned Arnold in September 1942 after the tempestuous JCS meeting on the eve of his first Pacific tour. "Don't get mad, and let the other fellow tell his story first." He was still absorbing this counsel.

The thing that troubled Arnold most was being sidelined for the upcoming "Big Three" Argonaut Conference, which was scheduled for February at the Black Sea resort of Yalta in the Soviet Crimea.

"The worst part of my predicament, as I saw it then, was that the Yalta-Malta Conference was coming up within a few days [the Malta Conference began on January 30] and I had expected to be present," he wrote.

"I knew it [Yalta] would be an important meeting. Subjects would be discussed that would materially affect our future [USAAF] operations, and perhaps influence the peacetime setup of commercial aviation," Arnold lamented. "I wanted to be present to exercise my influence when the Russians, the British, and the Americans talked about these matters, but I had to send a substitute. General Kuter went in my place and, incidentally, did a wonderful job."

However, in a memo to his boss, Kuter explained to Arnold just how much the USAAF chief was missed. In previous conferences, Arnold's opinions about airpower's role had been heard and respected, but in his absence, the USAAF perspective was largely ignored by the generals, admirals, and statesmen at every level. Kuter complained that "without you, we are just tolerated from bottom to top."

At Yalta, the Big Three laid out plans for the postwar occupation of Germany, and Roosevelt, tired and in ill health, acquiesced, over Churchill's objections, to allow Stalin a sphere of influence in Eastern Europe. A dominant topic was Poland. Stalin refused to restore the sections of Poland that the Soviet Union had seized under his pact with Hitler in 1939, so it was decided that some sections of eastern Germany would be transferred to Poland to compensate. Stalin was reminded of his promise to join the Anglo-American Allies in the war against Japan after Germany's defeat, and he assured them he would do so ninety days after Germany surrendered.

★　★　★　★　★

By March, German resistance began to crumble, as the Western Allies and the Soviets felt the soil of Germany beneath their combat boots. On March 7, the Americans seized the Ludendorff Bridge at Remagen, the only bridge across the Rhine that the Germans had failed to destroy in advance of the Allied offensive. With this, the last serious natural barrier on the Western Front was no more, and Allied troops streamed across Germany's great river.

The USSTAF found clear skies for precision bombing. On February 22, 1945, during the first anniversary of Big Week, the Eighth Air Force launched a maximum effort of 1,359 heavy bombers supported by a force of more than eight hundred fighters. The Luftwaffe was, by now, so badly damaged by losses and shortages that some bomber missions encountered no interceptors at all.

Göring's air arm, however, had one last card up its sleeve. On March 18, the Luftwaffe fielded a squadron of revolutionary new aircraft, Me 262 jet fighters, against the Eighth. The German jets downed twenty-five U.S. bombers over Berlin, surprising the bomber crews and the escorting fighter pilots with their blistering speed.

By this time, both the USAAF and RAF were testing jet fighters— the Lockheed P-80 and the Gloster Meteor, respectively—but Göring was throwing his jets into combat first. More attacks came. Twice in April, the Luftwaffe put nearly sixty Me 262s against the Eighth, but by then, American fighter pilots were figuring out how to fight the jets, and twenty-seven went down in a single battle. The Luftwaffe was first into the new age of jet fighters, but they were too late.

During the winter of 1945, the USAAF was essentially leaderless. As he had done before, Hap Arnold attempted to turn his suite at the Biltmore into an extension of his office at the Pentagon and to manage his far-flung global empire from Coral Gables. However, given the severity of his 1945 heart attack, his doctors had conspired to limit his activities, his phone calls, and his official visitors. Even his family—much to Bee's dismay— had been kept away during the early days of his convalescence.

As before, there was speculation about forced retirement, and this was seriously discussed by George Marshall and the assistant secretary of war for air, Bob Lovett. On the one hand, they were concerned about his being absent at such a critical time, and they worried about whether he would have the strength, when he returned, to effectively lead the USAAF during the final dash to victory in Europe and the climactic campaign against Japan.

On the other hand, they knew that there was no substitute for the man himself. As Kuter pointed out in his memo at the time of Yalta, Arnold commanded respect from the Joint and Combined Chiefs of Staff more than any other airman.

Major General John Huston, who edited Arnold's wartime diaries, wrote that "the question of who spoke for Army aviation in his absence was exacerbated by Arnold's practice of ensuring that all of his senior staff experience active combat command, something that the vicissitudes of both world wars had denied him. This policy led Arnold to make frequent changes among his immediate high-level subordinates. Consequently, there was no recognizable deputy with tenure, sufficient rank, experience in the Pentagon, and credibility within the executive and legislative branches to speak authoritatively for the AAF."

Marshall and Lovett's worries were somewhat ameliorated by the fact that Arnold recalled Ira Eaker from the Mediterranean— despite Eaker's displeasure at being withdrawn from a combat command on the eve of the war's climactic moment—and made him his deputy at the Pentagon.

A rested and recovered Arnold left Florida on March 21. Ten days later, he set out for another extended overseas inspection tour. Huston notes of the trip,

Lovett and others continued to be uneasy about the AAF chief's illness and projected absence when major European, Far Eastern, and postwar issues remained to be decided.... Lovett and Marshall wanted to retain the 'workaholic' airman in Washington, where his considerable influence was important; at the same time, they were aware of the possible advantages to Arnold's health of sending him abroad. There, under close medical supervision away from the telephone, extended meetings, and a mountain of paperwork, he might continue a recuperative, relaxed, yet constructive routine.... His physical presence overseas in a combat theater would contradict the rumors of his incapacitation.

Arnold did compromise by modifying his planned trip to cover only Europe rather than the USAAF's global commitments.

The impact of the fourth heart attack on Arnold's mood and outlook is repeatedly underscored in his diary. While his previous coronary bouts go unmentioned in his diaries and memoirs, or are dismissed only as "a bit of trouble with my 'ticker,'" he was now making frequent mention of his need to rest and take care of himself physically. His midday naps are dutifully recorded in his diary, and the scheduled stops on the tour included Bermuda and Cannes in southern France, where the USAAF had established rest and recreation centers for its combat-exhausted airmen.

Accompanied by a small entourage that included flight surgeon Dr. Gilbert Marquardt, Arnold departed from Washington on March 31. Contrary to what was suggested by his promised regimen of rest stops, Arnold and his companions spent only one night in Bermuda before taking off for Europe.

Late in the afternoon of April 2, the party checked into the Hotel Ritz at the Place Vendôme in Paris, where Arnold was given the suite that had allegedly been occupied by Hermann Göring on his visits to Paris. "My bedroom is tremendous, my bathroom is large," Arnold wrote in his diary. "The bathtub is extra large, it is made of porcelain; Göring must have sat down with a thud for the porcelain is cracked."

That night, Arnold was joined at dinner by Tooey Spaatz (whom Arnold calls "Tuey" in his diaries) and Colonel J. Henry "Hank" Pool, Bee's brother, who served as an assistant to Spaatz on the USSTAF staff. Like Pool, Arnold's two brothers joined the service as officers during the war even though they were over fifty and didn't have to. Clifford, who was a doctor, served in the Medical Corps, while Tom, the engineer, joined the Corps of Engineers. Also sitting in at the Paris dinner was George S. Patton, the colorful commanding general of the U.S. Third Army and a lively conversationalist.

The following day, accompanied by Spaatz and Pool, as well as by Dr. Marquardt, Arnold boarded a B-25 for the short flight to Reims for a visit to General Eisenhower at SHAEF.

"Ike was very enthusiastic about what the air [forces] had done in the war in Europe, and the support it had given to his Armies," Arnold recalled with satisfaction, going on to mention that a big part of the USAAF job in Europe now was logistics. "Our troops were moving forward so rapidly that [the USAAF] had gone into the supply business in Europe in the same big way as over the Hump in China. For instance, on one day the C-47s of the IX Troop Carrier Command delivered 250,000 gallons of gasoline to troops in advance positions. Next day, they carried 500,000 gallons to the various motor transport and armored units as they were moving up toward the Rhine."

After lunch, Arnold sounded Eisenhower out on "the postwar situation, what he thought about future national defense, the organization for national security, and so on." Heading Arnold's list in his notes was Eisenhower's advocacy of an independent air force within "a Department of National Defense with three equal parts:

ground, sea, and air.... Air, ground, and naval forces of a size required to do the job; not a size based upon money."

By this time, with George Marshall having given the idea his blessing as early as 1941, and with Eisenhower on board, there was no serious opposition within the Army for Arnold's dream of transitioning the USAAF into a fully independent Air Force after the war.

Having based himself in the "Göring Suite" at the Ritz, Arnold made a series of side trips to Germany and Luxembourg, often accompanied by General Hoyt Vandenberg, commander of the Ninth Air Force. He visited American troops and met with leaders from Patton to General Omar Bradley, now commander of the 12th Army Group. He also viewed the damage done to Germany by his USSTAF. The latter was of special interest to him, because it was the culmination of his two-decade advocacy of destroying an enemy's ability to wage war by destroying his means of production and transportation. The Strategic Bombing Survey (SBS) was already at work inside Germany, but Arnold had a keen interest in seeing for himself.

Established in late 1944 under the direct control of Secretary of War Henry Stimson, the SBS produced more than three hundred volumes of bombing reports, going into minute detail. Like the Enemy Objectives Unit in London, which planned the targeting, the SBS was staffed by large numbers of civilian economists and was headed by banking executive Franklin Woolman D'Olier, with Henry C. Alexander of Morgan Guaranty Trust as his vice-chairman. Among its members were Paul Nitze, George Ball, and the economist John Kenneth Galbraith, who would go on to influential postwar careers in the public policy arena.

"We [flew] over Frankfurt and found a large city with railroad yards and airports a shambles, runways pockmarked and unusable, the balance of the airport filled with bomb craters," Arnold recalled in one passage in his memoirs that is typical of his observations.

"The airport [near Frankfurt, where they landed] was fifteen miles from the front line, but our transports came in and out completely unmolested by the Luftwaffe. There just wasn't any German Air Force any more. We climbed into a car and started traveling down the Autobahn, passing German Air Force barracks, cars, and machine shops damaged or destroyed by our bombings. In the woods, miles away from the airport, were airplanes, more airplanes, and still more airplanes, all in good, serviceable condition; bombs, gasoline tanks, and repair hangars, concealed from above by the trees."

Like Eisenhower, whose impressions of the German autobahn inspired his advocacy of the Interstate Highway System after he became president, Arnold speaks glowingly of the German super-highway, calling it a "wonderful road," and noting that he and his companions were able to cruise with ease at 60 mph.

While he was making this day trip to Germany, Arnold added another member to his entourage. As had happened on previous visits, young Hank Arnold was given leave to accompany his five-star general father for the several days that he was in the theater. From his duties as an artillery battalion commander in the 45th Infantry Division, which had captured the German city of Aschaffenburg just two days earlier, Hank was now flying to Paris where he would be sleeping between high-thread-count sheets at the Ritz. In fact, as his father recalled in his diary, Hank wound up in the suite that had once been reserved for the use of SS chief Heinrich Himmler.

On April 10, Hap said goodbye to Hank, tipped "more or less 200 minions" at the Ritz, and headed south to Cannes, where he checked into a commandeered villa used by Tooey Spaatz.

In his diary, he describes the house as "a grand one right on the shore of the bay looking across to Cannes; big, roomy, with all fur-nishings specially designed and made for villa; specially-shaped lights, furniture of the modernistic type. One tile platform after another dropping down to water, an outdoor bar between wings of house, must have cost $150,000 [more than tenfold this estimate in today's dollars] in for house and furnishings.... Owned by a British lady of wealth who married a Pittsburg[h] man; she now lives in Palm Beach. The bar has a modernistic picture of half-nude men and women of the Tahiti type in rear."

Here, for the next twelve days, Arnold had the opportunity to at least appear to be getting the rest for which he had promised Marshall and Lovett that he would find the time. Though artillery could still be heard in the distance, he wrote of having breakfast al fresco under clear blue skies, and of Spaatz's daughter, who worked for the Red Cross in Cannes, coming to the villa "with two other Red Cross girls and three aviators to swim and enjoy the sunshine."

He also noted having the opportunity for a drive in the countryside toward Marseilles, which reminded him of the area around Santa Barbara, California, although he spends several pages describing the vast numbers of never-used defensive fortifications built by the Germans.

While at Cannes, appearing to rest, Arnold devoted a great deal of time to sketching out plans for more reshuffling of his commanders. In addition to Eaker, he put together a tentative list of others whom he planned to bring back to the Pentagon. He noted in his diary that Fred Anderson would take charge of personnel and administration; Vandenberg would head operations; and Curtis LeMay, who was commanding the strategic effort in the Pacific, would return to take charge of USAAF logistics. He picked Jimmy Doolittle to go to the Pacific to head the XX Bomber Command. In fact, among these, only Anderson would actually move into the post that Arnold had indicated in his notes from Cannes. Doolittle *was* sent go to the Pacific, but only briefly, and in his existing job as head of the Eighth.

On Friday the thirteenth, Arnold was awakened at half past seven o'clock by Dr. Marquardt with the news that Franklin Roosevelt had died. Given Roosevelt's longevity in office—he was now in his fourth term—there were people in their late thirties who had never voted in a presidential election in which he was not a candidate.

Sitting down with Tooey Spaatz and Jimmy Doolittle, Arnold decided that the "proper procedure of events" would be for Arnold to send a message of condolence to Mrs. Roosevelt, and that it might be a good idea to send an officer from the European Theater to Washington each week to brief Harry Truman, who had just been sworn in as president.

Arnold already knew Truman; they were acquainted mainly as two men who saw eye-to-eye on budget overruns and waste. Arnold was already known for cutting orders for materiel and downsizing the requirements of the nearly victorious USAAF. As a U.S. senator from Missouri, Truman had risen to national prominence as chairman of the Special Committee to Investigate the National Defense Program. The "Truman Committee," whose mandate was the investigation of waste and profiteering by war contractors, is said to have saved the government around $15 billion. Truman's prominence had led Roosevelt to pick him as his fourth-term running mate in 1944.

After Roosevelt's death, Arnold wrote that Spaatz wanted him "to return to Washington and … to get the Air Force back in the sun again." However, while others worried that Arnold needed to have Truman's ear immediately, Arnold himself was "of the opinion that I would only make an invalid of myself if I returned before Eaker and the men whom I am getting from Spaatz. I realize that there is much spade work to be done right now with a new President and war in Germany coming to a close. I cannot see my way clear to deliberately ruin myself again physically when there is so little chance of permanent change in Air Force activities."

On April 26, though, after he had left Cannes for Italy, and two days before he departed from Europe, Arnold received a "very pessimistic letter from Lovett; since my departure AAF has been ignored in all high-level conferences; he wants me to come back home at once."

Arnold's remaining days at Cannes were spent visiting USAAF officers and men who were in the various rest and recuperation facilities operated by the USAAF in the area, and in a series of meetings with his European Theater generals and numbered air force commanders, including Spaatz commuting from SHAEF in Reims, Fred Anderson of USSTAF, Doolittle of the Eighth, John Cannon of the Twelfth, Nate Twining of the Fifteenth, and Hoyt Vandenberg of the Ninth.

On April 19, Arnold had what, even in his own diary, he termed a "heated" discussion with Ira Eaker about joining him at the Pentagon. When Eaker protested about going to Washington, Arnold shot back, "Who in the hell ever did ask to go to Washington? Do you think I asked to go there and stay there for 10 years? Someone has to run the AAF. We can't all be in command of [Air Forces] around the world!" Arnold goes on to say that Spaatz "stepped in and calmed us down."

On April 22, Arnold flew to Italy, where he moved into a villa in Florence for three nights. While here, he called on General Mark Clark, commander of the 15th Army Group in Italy, and visited Bologna. At Clark's headquarters, he learned that after two difficult winters in the easily defended terrain of central Italy, the Allies were moving quickly north toward Austria. German resistance had collapsed, and it was expected that the Allied armies in Italy would reach the border of the Third Reich by early May.

In his memoirs, he noted that "General Clark received a message on the 25th of April that Genoa had been captured, with about

54,000 prisoners. The Germans had no gasoline; tanks and trucks had been abandoned, and trucks were being pulled by horses and oxen. The Brenner Pass was out, all communication had been severed, and the enlisted men of the German Army were surrendering in large numbers. The war in Italy was finished."

In Bologna, Arnold "saw an excellent example of our precision bombing. The railroad yards, the bridges, the airport, and the huge supply dump had all been destroyed, but little harm had been done to the city itself. The University, the oldest in the world, was only slightly damaged and could be easily repaired."

On April 26, Arnold continued on to Caserta, where he met with Britain's Harold Alexander, now a field marshal and supreme commander of the Allied forces in the Mediterranean Theater. Arnold wrote that Alexander, like Clark and his staff,

> was sure the war in Italy was about over, and believed we could be in Austria in two weeks if the high command wanted us to. He didn't think the Germans would continue fighting much longer. He thought Himmler would be the one to make the overtures for the surrender. In his opinion, Hitler had brain trouble and was hiding out somewhere—probably at some island in the Baltic. The report would come out that Hitler had been killed in the defense of Berlin, and in about five years, if conditions were right, he would suddenly reappear from the dead and become a hero to his people and a new threat to the world. I could not agree with Alexander, for after what I had heard and what I had seen of Germany, I didn't believe there was anything left in Hitler's "thousand year Reich" to provide a threat for a long, long time.

Hitler committed suicide four days later.

From Caserta, Arnold flew on to Bari, visited Twining at Fifteenth Air Force headquarters, and was told that "they had run out of targets for heavy bombing in southern Germany, Austria, and the Balkans. It looked as if the job of the Fifteenth Air Force [like that of the Eighth] was about finished. Before long we could take them [both Air Forces] out of the European Theater and send them to the Pacific."

On April 28, as he left Italy for the last time, heading for West Africa and the South Atlantic route home, Arnold noted that the "time has come when all supplies to Europe but gasoline should stop. There are enough in depots and in the pipeline; sent message to Eaker telling him so."

Arnold stayed in Brazil for a week, including four nights in Rio de Janeiro, traveling with Dr. Marquardt and Colonel Hank Pool. The official purpose was to inspect the Air Transport Command facility at Recife, which was the western anchor of the South Atlantic air route. He found the "whole set-up greatly improved" since his last visit in February 1943.

In Rio, Arnold had the opportunity for a chat about South American aviation with Brazilian president Getúlio Dornelles Vargas, and he toured Força Aérea Brasileira facilities with Joaquim Pedro Salgado Filho, the minister of aeronautics. At a dinner on the evening of May 3, hosted by Salgado, Arnold met the war minister, General Eurico Gaspar Dutra, and reconnected with Brigadier Eduardo Gomes, whom he had met previously. A topic of conversation was the Brazilian 1st GAVCA (1st Fighter Group), commanded by Lieutenant Colonel Nero Moura. They were fighting alongside the Americans in Italy, attached to the 350th Fighter Group of the Twelfth Air Force. As Arnold explained, he had visited them ten days earlier and had been impressed. In his memoirs, he made mention of their "splendid record."

He also had time for a little sightseeing in Rio, some long naps, and a little shopping. "Bought ten mangoes at a market yesterday, they cost me 25 cents," he reminisced. "Probably could have got them cheaper but I didn't argue. They were big ones."

CHAPTER 19

BUT THEIR WAR GOES ON

"**F**ellow Americans," General Henry Harley Arnold said, his pre-recorded voice emanating from radios around the world on May 7, 1945, "this is a day of rejoicing. A battle—a bloody and bitter battle, has been won. The men who won it—your sons, brothers and husbands—have triumphed over a host of relentless, desperate and powerful enemies. They have earned the deepest and most enduring gratitude of every civilized human being, in whatever country, for all time to come."

For Hap Arnold, according to his diary, May 4 had been "about the toughest day I have had yet. The climb up the long flight of stairs to make the disc for broadcast was the final test."

He passed the test, and three days later, the world passed through a momentous milestone as the Third Reich surrendered. On May 7, Field Marshal Wilhelm Keitel, the chief of Oberkommando der Wehrmacht, the German high command, traveled to Eisenhower's headquarters in Reims—where Arnold had lunched with Eisenhower a month earlier—to sign the unconditional surrender. The following day, a similar formal ceremony took place in Berlin, which the Soviet Red Army had captured a few days before.

Secretary of War for Air Bob Lovett had contacted Arnold in Brazil when it seemed that the capitulation was imminent. All of the service chiefs were being asked to record messages for immediate broadcast when the news came through.

By the time of the Berlin ceremonies, the disc that Arnold had climbed the long flight of Rio de Janeiro stairs to record had been broadcast, and Arnold was back in the United States after his 17,900-mile, thirty-nine-day European-Brazilian tour.

Back on December 6, 1943—a day shy of the second anniversary of Pearl Harbor, and well ahead of the great events of 1944 that defined the course of the war's final stages—the Combined Chiefs of Staff were dining at Ambassador Alexander Kirk's residence within sight of the pyramids in Cairo. After dinner, General George Marshall decided to take a poll, asking everyone when they predicted that Germany would be defeated. They all agreed that it would be in 1945. Marshall and Sir John Dill optimistically predicted February. The top naval commanders were the most cautious, with the Royal Navy's Admiral Andrew Cunningham picking September and the U.S. Navy's Admiral Ernest King going with October. The airmen came closer. Hap Arnold said March–April, and Peter Portal prognosticated May–June.

"The US Army Air Force is proud of what it has done toward making this day possible," Arnold continued in his recorded message.

> To provide airpower needed for victory over the Axis partners in Europe, the Army Air Force had to travel a long way over an arduous road.... For many months now, scarcely a day has passed without our B-29s making their appearance over the Japanese homeland. The men in those airplanes know what their job is. The Japanese industry will have to be battered to the same chaos that engulfed Germany's military machine. That is a campaign barely begun. Daily, our air crews return to their work at the risk of death and capture by the Japanese. They have read the details of the Death March of Bataan as closely as you have. They know what and whom they are up against, and yet, they return to their targets, day after day, night after night, simply because they know that it must be done.

Knowing that the job against the Axis was not finished, Arnold asked his listeners to remember the men in the B-29s and reminded them that "although a great battle has been won, their war, and your war, goes on!"

Arnold's reminder of the job left undone echoed the views of his fellow service commanders, especially Admiral King, whose Navy now dominated the Pacific. Meanwhile, General Marshall was preparing to transfer the U.S. First Army from Europe, just as Arnold was preparing for the enormous task of relocating the Eighth Air

Force to that theater. To coordinate the efforts of the Eighth and the Twentieth, Arnold planned to create the United States Strategic Air Forces in the Pacific (USASTAF), which was analogous to the USSTAF in Europe.

The primary mission of the USASTAF, also analogous to that of the USSTAF, was the systematic destruction of Japanese industry and internal transportation in advance of the coming invasion of Japan. Designated as Operation Downfall, this was to be a two-phase operation. The first, Operation Olympic, would be the capture of the southern main island of Kyushu in November 1945. Occupying Kyushu would provide bases close to the larger main island of Honshu, where, under Operation Coronet, the Allies would land in the vicinity of Tokyo early in 1946. A secondary mission of the Twentieth Air Force, already in motion, would be to soften up defenses on Kyushu.

It was Arnold's plan that the USASTAF would be headed by Tooey Spaatz, now promoted to four-star general, who had commanded the USSTAF. As the Twentieth flew from the Marianas, the Eighth was to operate its B-17s and B-24s from bases on Okinawa, which were less than 350 miles from Kyushu, and less than one thousand miles from Tokyo. Meanwhile, bases and depots would also be built on Okinawa for the use of the fighters and tactical bombers of General George Kenney's Far East Air Forces (the Fifth, Seventh, and Thirteenth).

The fierce battle to capture Okinawa began on April 1 as a joint U.S. Army/U.S. Marine Corps operation and was still ongoing as Germany surrendered. It was shaping up as the bloodiest battle in the Pacific thus far and was considered as an ominous foretaste of the difficulties that would come in the invasion of Japan's home islands.

Meanwhile, Twentieth Air Force operations with B-29 Superfortresses had reached their stride. When Curtis LeMay had taken over from Possum Hansell in January, he had inherited many of the same problems—from lack of ordnance to lack of facilities to lack of training—that had hampered Hansell and that Arnold was insistent that LeMay correct.

LeMay started by centralizing his maintenance system to compensate for the small number of experienced B-29 crew chiefs. Because LeMay thought the Navy, which controlled logistics in the Pacific, was too slow, he set up an aerial supply route to the Air Materiel Command depot in Sacramento using C-54 transports. He also set up a training program, which involved air attacks against Japanese garrisons isolated on islands that had been bypassed when U.S. Navy cut their supply lines.

"As could have been predicted, our major problem was the lack of practical experience in the new crews that were coming in all the time," LeMay recalled to this author.

> The situation was, however, somewhat better than it had been two years before in Europe. A lot of our pilots who went to England had gone right out of flying school into an airplane, without the proper training. For instance, the people I took to England had only 200 hours of flying time. Half of my class went with me to England, and the other half went into the Training Command, because we had to build it to teach the millions of people who were going to make up the huge air force we were planning for. Those who stayed in the Training Command, and later got into the B-29 program, they flew the B-29 out to combat as soon as it came out of the factory instead of practicing with it.

LeMay, like Hansell, began running missions against Japan as he had over Germany, flying at high altitude, an environment for

which the pressurized Superfortress was technically suited. However, by the end of February, after he had launched only two missions against Japan with more than one hundred B-29s, LeMay
realized that he wasn't getting the results that he wanted, so he
revamped his plan.

"I made up my mind to make some major changes in the way
we were using the B-29s because it was now clear that we couldn't
possibly succeed by basing our strategy on our experience from
Europe. That system wasn't working," LeMay explained.

> As I looked over the reconnaissance photos, I noticed that
> there wasn't any low altitude flak such as we'd encoun-
> tered in Europe. It looked reasonable to me that we could
> fly a successful mission with less fuel and a larger bomb
> load by going in low, particularly if we went in at night.
> After sizing up the situation and knowing that I had to do
> something radical, I finally arrived at the decision to use
> low-level attacks against Japanese urban industrial areas
> using incendiaries. Even poorly trained radar operators
> could find cities that were on or near the coast, and going
> in at between 5,000 and 8,000 feet instead of 25,000 feet
> would ensure that all the bombs would fall in the target
> area. This method solved the weather problem
> because ... we would go in under the weather when we
> were ready.

On March 9, LeMay was ready, ready with sufficient Superfortresses to initiate his own variation on the USSTAF Big Week of a
year earlier. On that night, he sent 325 Superfortresses low over
Tokyo. Through March 18, he followed up with four more maximum
efforts averaging 295 bombers against Kobe, Osaka, and Nagoya
(twice). This exercise had the result of delivering the same level of

destruction to Japanese urban areas that the Combined Bomber Offensive had to Germany, and the incendiaries were particularly effective because of the extensive use of wood in Japanese construction.

Over the ensuing month, LeMay followed up with smaller attacks, alternating between incendiaries and high explosives, forcing Japan to undertake a costly dispersal of its industry.

Hap Arnold drastically reduced the number of hours that he spent at the Pentagon. Out were the twelve-hour days, in was a midday nap for an hour or two. However, only three weeks after he returned from Brazil, he was out to the Pacific to get a firsthand look at the B-29 operations taking place in the Marianas, to discuss operations with Admiral Chester Nimitz and General Douglas MacArthur, and to underscore the major role he saw for the USAAF in the climactic operations against Japan.

Under a Joint Chiefs of Staff directive, the Pacific Theater had been reorganized in April 1945 with the upcoming operations on the Japanese home islands in mind. Nimitz, as commander in chief, Pacific (CINCPAC), would command all of the U.S. Navy and Marine Corps assets, while MacArthur was designated as the commander in chief, Army forces in the Pacific (CINCAFPAC) and would control all U.S. Army forces in the Pacific (AFPAC).

Winging westward in the C-54 dubbed *Argonaut IV*, Arnold's first stop was at Suisun Field, fifty miles from San Francisco. He was briefed on the United Nations conference then ongoing in that city, but he did not go into San Francisco. Instead, he picked up a car and headed north to Sonoma County. Here, he planned to visit the small patch of rural property in the Valley of the Moon that he and Bee had purchased at the end of 1943, and where they planned to retire.

Instead of strategic airpower and intrigues between heads of state, Arnold's diary entries are filled with discussions of pigs, chickens, a cow, two calves, and finding a blacksmith to shoe the gray mare named "Duke" that he had purchased along with the ranch. Pronouncing his fruit trees to be "doing OK," he made arrangements for the purchase of hay, the construction of a chicken house, and the erection of a fence to keep the deer at bay.

On June 9, Arnold arrived at Hickam Field in Hawaii, adjacent to Pearl Harbor, which was now the hub of the largest navy in history. The next day, he was briefed on the progress of the Pacific war by General Robert Richardson and Admiral John Towers, a former naval aviator who was now the deputy Pacific Ocean Areas commander under Nimitz, and whom Arnold had known personally for many years. Towers explained that the carrier force had lost 750 planes in two months, a third of them to kamikaze attacks against aircraft carriers, but the Navy had also flown 4,300 sorties and had destroyed 2,400 Japanese aircraft.

Arnold gave his own report on the B-29 operations and heard Towers's perspective on why the Navy, not Arnold and the USAAF, should have jurisdiction over the B-29s. Arnold then made his famous observation about the Navy and B-29s: "At first, the Navy opposed our B-29 operations, and opposed them violently; then they tolerated them, and then the whole Navy was [backing] them, but they wanted control of all the Superforts."

Once again, he was glad that he had personally, with the authority of his five stars and his seat on the Joint Chiefs of Staff, retained *direct* control of the Twentieth Air Force.

Accompanied by General Barney Giles, the senior USAAF man in the Pacific Operations Areas, Arnold headed westward, with refueling stops in Kwajalein and Eniwetok, along an increasingly well-traveled air corridor. Arnold's "airline," the Air Transport Command, was flying a routine schedule of thirty-four daily flights between Hawaii and Guam. In his diary, Arnold noted plans to expand this number to sixty-four. Of the eastbound flights, many, if not most, were medevac flights.

Having crossed the International Date Line, Arnold reached Saipan on the afternoon of June 13, where he met with LeMay and his staff. Arnold had decided to send LeMay to Washington to brief the Joint Chiefs of Staff on the strategic air campaign. Arnold wanted this to be done in advance of a June 18 JCS meeting at which details of Operation Olympic, the November invasion of Kyushu, would be discussed with President Truman.

From Saipan, Arnold continued to Guam, 120 miles to the south. Arnold noted in his diary that the "Navy's attitude on a strategic bomber headquarters is intolerable. They would not countenance either JCS or the War Department telling them how to organize fleet units."

But when he met with Nimitz to discuss his plan for a USASTAF headquarters on Guam, he was stunned to find the admiral

> agreeable to every one of the propositions I made to him. He wanted the Strategic Command here at Guam; he wanted Spaatz to command it; he was agreeable to having the Eighth and Twentieth Air Forces in the Strategic Command; he could see no conflict between headquarters that could not be overcome and was certain the advantages attained could outweigh the disadvantages.... He agrees to a set-up that will give [the USAAF] everything needed by Strategic Air Force.... welcomes a representative from Spaatz Headquarters to sit with their people to determine priorities, shipping, etc., will have changes made to eliminate procedures that interfere with our operations. In fact in general he agreed to everything that I asked.

However, in a memo to MacArthur that Arnold saw at the latter's headquarters in Manila four days later, Nimitz showed himself to be very possessive of his own turf. In this letter, he insisted that Kenney's Far East Air Forces, which was under MacArthur's operational command, should restrict itself to land targets, not venture more than ten miles over water, and not attack shipping. These targets, he insisted, belonged to naval airpower.

On June 15, having inspected the 314th and 315th Bombardment Wings of the Twentieth Air Force, newly arrived on Guam, Arnold flew to Tinian, near Saipan, where the veteran 58th Wing was operating. Here, he was on hand to mark the first anniversary of the first Superfortress raid on Japan. By now, LeMay had already departed for Washington in a B-29 to brief the JCS.

Arnold next headed north, flying 745 miles to Iwo Jima, which had been captured by the Marines at a cost of ninety thousand casualties three months earlier. "We have made three landing fields on Iwo," he noted in his diary. "We use them for three Groups of [P-51 Mustang bomber escort] fighters and to save crippled B-29s. So far 1,299 crippled planes or planes out of gas have landed here. Of the 528 B-29s that went over to bomb Osaka today, forty-three had to land at Iwo."

Departing Iwo Jima at midnight, Arnold flew 1,560 miles south to Manila, recalling that he had passed through this city on his first overseas deployment, nearly thirty-eight years earlier. Having landed at Nichols Field, he was taken by jeep to Fort William McKinley, where he had twice been posted as a young infantry officer. Here, he was greeted personally by George Kenney.

Commenting on the appearance of Fort William McKinley after more than three years of Japanese occupation, he wrote in his diary that "most of the houses [were] burned and destroyed, our house among those gone, only a few remain.... Post Exchange destroyed, all by Japs; parade ground growing up with grass, almost a jungle. It is very hard to pick out landmarks."

Before he left the Philippines, Arnold visited other places he remembered from his two tours there, including the quarters at Fort Stotsenburg where he and Bee had stayed while he was on maneuvers in the area in 1915. He even managed to get up to Mabalacat and to take a look at the stone building where he lived while working with the 20th Infantry on the mapping project in 1908. Here, he had a chance to reflect back upon seeing the numerous Japanese "photographers" who had seemed to be taking a close interest in the Philippines.

On June 17, Arnold was driven through the heavily battle-damaged Manila to meet with MacArthur at his headquarters. MacArthur, he was pleased to learn, fully supported an Air Force that was separate from the Army. Arnold noted that MacArthur was "willing to organize Army Air in Pacific along those lines now."

In his notes, Arnold describes a MacArthur extremely distrustful of the Navy, writing that he "resents Navy holding back on turning over Islands and supply system...feels that Navy is building up a postwar organization and laying plans, completing facilities for such an organization now...[and] he recognizes the necessity for Army having its own supply system all the way through from the United States." Arnold recorded that MacArthur "gets excited and walks the floor, raises his voice. I thought I was one of the few who did it."

As for the final endgame in the Pacific, MacArthur believed that airpower would play a role in ending the war, and he liked Arnold's promise of two hundred thousand tons of bombs monthly "to destroy targets in invasion area and 80,000 tons on invasion day." However, he admitted that he did not "fully understand" the doctrine of strategic airpower, and he told Arnold that "in the final analysis, doughboys will have to march into Tokyo" before the war could be won.

Arnold departed Manila on June 20, accompanied by Kenney, who flew in a separate aircraft. They headed north, 840 miles to Okinawa, where American doughboys were in the final stages of securing this 877-square-mile stepping-stone to the final Battle of Japan. Watching, from the air, the explosions on the southern tip of island where the Japanese were making their last stand was the closest that Arnold got to the actual fighting during his Pacific tour.

He stepped onto the red dirt of Okinawa just two days after the death by Japanese artillery of General Simon Bolivar Buckner Jr., an old friend of Arnold's who had commanded the Tenth Army. The Tenth was the ground force for Okinawa operations, consisting of three Army and three Marine Corps divisions—an early joint operation of the type that became a key doctrine of the American armed forces late in the century and that flew in the face of the mutual distrust and bickering between the services illustrated by the ongoing MacArthur-Nimitz tiff. Arnold was met at Tenth Army headquarters by Marine Major General Roy Geiger, who had assumed command upon Buckner's death, and by General "Vinegar Joe" Stilwell, late of the China-Burma-India Theater, who had just arrived to take over command from Geiger. Having been briefed on the progress of the battle, Arnold asked about the timetable for building airfields. In the midst of conversation, Arnold was approached by a young first lieutenant in Marine Corps fatigues.

"Hiya, Pop," the man said without saluting.

Everyone in the headquarters turned to see Lieutenant Bruce Arnold, U.S. Army, with a Marine Corps insignia over his left pocket.

A short time earlier, Bruce had gotten a call that "the Big Eagle had landed."

He said that he did not know who the "Big Eagle" was.

Somebody in the battalion said, "That's your father, you stupe, and you're supposed to go to Tenth Army headquarters to meet him."

"He thought that was the funniest damn thing he had ever seen," Bruce remembered of his father's reaction to the Marine uniform.

> He was absolutely intrigued by the fact that I wasn't in an Army uniform.... He just couldn't get over that. In the background, was all the Tenth Army [brass] seething, absolutely seething. And I was so naive and stupid, I didn't realize that I was really putting myself into rather a delicate spot [by being out of uniform and failing to salute a five-star general]. Everybody certainly was pleasant enough to me while we had lunch, and so forth, but as soon as we put Daddy on the airplane and he flew off into the blue. The coldness around there would have frozen all hell.

The antiaircraft platoon that Bruce led was attached to the 2nd Marine Division, which was, in turn, under the umbrella of the Tenth Army. Each platoon of his 834th Antiaircraft Battalion was assigned to a separate Marine battalion.

> Of course, you know the Marines are the best dressed guys in any war. They always seem to have plenty of fatigues and new clothes and the Army is always raggedy.... If you lose your mess kit, too bad, you've got to eat out of your helmet.... The Marines seemed to have a system that after they'd been in combat and were pulled back, they just dropped everything and got issued everything new.... we'd go pick it all up [and] we were wearing Marine fatigues. I really hadn't thought much about it until I arrived at Tenth Army Headquarters to meet my father and I was in this set of Marine fatigues.

Hap Arnold recalled the incident in his memoirs, noting that Bruce created a "terrific sensation among the officers, photographers and everyone else with his entrance." He goes on to describe his visit to Bruce's platoon and noted that he had "an excellent bunch of men with him."

In contrast with his brother Hank, who was overseas for three years and spent several days with their father on several occasions, this was Bruce's only contact with his father during his half-year deployment during the war. The Arnolds concluded their day on Okinawa with dinner with the top brass at Tenth Army headquarters—"which I am sure that [Bruce] did not enjoy"—and Hap held a press conference. As reported in the *New York Times*, he told the journalists that the Twentieth Air Force had made a "very good start" in the strategic campaign against Japan, and he "predicted that Japan would have little industry left by fall."

Threat of a Japanese air raid, which did not materialize, delayed his departure, with Stilwell in tow, until five minutes to eleven o'clock that evening.

His first full day back on Guam was spent communicating with Lauris Norstad, his chief of staff for the Twentieth Air Force, about operational issues, and on June 22, he and Barney Giles conferred with Nimitz, Stilwell, and their respective staff officers. Foremost on Arnold's agenda was the logistics situation. He pointed out that there would be a backlog of a million tons of shipping on Okinawa by September, and he feared that "there would not be sufficient bombs to carry out [the Twentieth Air Force] program for destruction of Japanese industry, pre-invasion bombing and support of invading army [and that] docks would not be completed to permit unloading of supplies [in Okinawa]."

He wrote that in reply, "Nimitz's staff assured me that everything I said had been taken care of; [U.S. Army] Engineers and [U.S. Navy] Seabees were being sent as rapidly as they were available." They also agreed to use British Engineers "if political heads said we must use RAF [and] as Kenney's air units moved forward [to newly built airfields on Okinawa, the] British could use such airdromes as required and not needed by [Superfortresses]. Nimitz said OK if it had to be done." The leadership of the Army, Navy, and USAAF were reluctant to involve the British as the war in the Pacific Theater came to its climax.

Later in the day, Arnold went out to Guam's Northwest Field (now Andersen Air Force Base) to watch a great armada of B-29 Superfortresses return from their missions. In his diary, he wrote of 484 having gone out the night before "to hit aircraft factories in Japan." In *The Army Air Forces in World War II: Combat Chronology 1941–1945*, Kit Carter and Robert Mueller note that 130 Superfortresses bombed aircraft factories at four locations in Japan that night, while 162 attacked the Japanese naval base at Kure.

"Targets were hit and destroyed according to crews I talked to," Arnold wrote. "Those crews who hit targets, even after 15 hours of flying were not tired and their morale was high. Those that aborted, had engine trouble, did not get to target, were tired and morale was low."

In his memoirs, Arnold summarized his Pacific tour by writing that as he departed from the Pacific at the end of June 1945, the major job of the USSAF was "to get our heavy bomb groups into the Pacific area from the European Theater as rapidly as bases were available. It was the lack of bases that provided the bottleneck in that movement."

Having said that, he wrote optimistically that after the discussions he had with Nimitz and MacArthur, "many of the delays in doing this … would be eliminated. However, even under the best of conditions it would be several months before we would get landing fields in Okinawa capable of taking care of the hundreds of B-17s and the B-24s we could throw in there from Europe."

★ ★ ★ ★ ★

Returning across the Pacific by way of Hawaii, Arnold reached Hamilton Field, north of San Francisco, shortly before ten o'clock on June 24, the eve of his fifty-ninth birthday. Bee and their daughter, Lois Snowden, had planned a birthday celebration in Sonoma, but it was canceled in deference to orders from Arnold's commander in chief. The United Nations conference, ongoing since April in San Francisco, was concluding, and President Harry Truman required Arnold's attendance on June 25 at an official dinner at the St. Francis Hotel to celebrate the formal completion of the United Nations Charter.

In fairness to Truman, Arnold himself felt that he should not miss this opportunity to be present on the culmination of the conference. As for the United Nations itself, Arnold agreed that it showed promise in maintaining world peace, but he regarded this with a skepticism steeped in his recollection of the failure of the League of Nations organization to maintain world peace between the world wars.

A small birthday party was held the next day before *Argonaut IV* departed for Washington, D.C., and Hap Arnold prepared to finish the job of winning the war.

CHAPTER 20

THE CLIMAX

N o sooner had Arnold returned from the Pacific than he was packing his bags for Europe to attend the Terminal Conference, the last of the great high-level meetings of World War II. It was to be held in Potsdam, the suburb of the devastated German capital of Berlin where Frederick the Great once had his palace.

Traveling aboard *Argonaut IV*, Arnold departed Washington on July 11 for Paris. As on his previous visits to Europe, his son Hank, now on the staff of the 45th Infantry Division at Reims, was released from normal duties in order to join Arnold's official entourage. On July 13, they flew to Salzburg, from where they were driven, in one of Adolf Hitler's own Mercedes touring cars, to the "Eagle's Nest," Hitler's alpine retreat near Berchtesgaden.

The largely undamaged alpine villages of southern Bavaria, where hotels and tourist accommodations had been taken over by the U.S. Army for rest and recuperation facilities, were in stark contrast to the utter devastation that Arnold and his party beheld upon reaching Berlin on July 15. In his diary, he commented on the looting being done on a massive scale by the Soviet occupation troops, and on their widespread cruelty to German civilians—from mere bullying to gang rapes.

As with previous summit conferences, the Potsdam conclave began with rounds of meetings between Eisenhower and the American Joint Chiefs of Staff and with the Anglo-American Combined Chiefs, as well as meetings at which Ike and the JCS sat down with Truman and Secretary of War Henry Stimson.

As Arnold wrote in his memoirs, "The British accepted our program for the remainder of the war in the Pacific, which meant that operations would remain under the control of the United States, regardless of whether the units were under MacArthur or Admiral Nimitz, or whether they were British or American."

Recalling bets taken at previous conferences with regard to the timing of the German demise, Arnold noted that at dinner on July 16, he bet RAF chief Peter Portal that the war against Japan would end "nearer to December 25 [1945] than to Valentines Day, 1946." He went on to share post-strike aerial photography from the Superfortress raids with his British counterpart.

In a private conversation, Arnold and Portal discussed the future. Over the preceding year, and perhaps longer, there had been a pervasive concern among the Anglo-American military leaders about the intentions of the Soviet Union in the postwar world. Stalin's consolidation of power in Eastern Europe, especially in Poland, had led many to agree with the conclusion that Arnold and Portal reached at Potsdam.

"We both believed our next enemy would be Russia, and a common line of thought emerged from our talk," Arnold wrote in his memoirs. "The Russians understand manpower on the ground, and are confident they have the finest army in the world. They have no fear of any navy because they know no navy can get close enough to harm them. But one thing they fear and don't understand is strategic airpower-long-range bombers. They have never had long-range bombers of their own and they apparently do not know the principles of employing them. Tomorrow, however, things may be different."

That "tomorrow" was an accurate prediction of the arms build-up of the Cold War, which began in earnest as Arnold was writing his memoirs in 1948.

Concerned about security in the Soviet-occupied capital, Arnold was very circumspect in his diary. He made no mention of the fears discussed with Portal or of the successful first atomic bomb test in New Mexico on July 16, of which he was told two days later. In his memoirs, he wrote that "the results of that test proved conclusively that we had in our possession the means to wipe out completely, large areas of an enemy country."

He then adds that a decision now had to be made as to what to do with the weapon:

> With Secretary Stimson and [Assistant Secretary of War and future U.S. High Commissioner for Germany John Jay] McCloy, General Marshall and I discussed the big questions: how soon would we be ready to use the bomb against Japan, and what should the targets be? I told them the best results would be obtained if we turned the matter of targets over to General Spaatz, who had plans ready and waiting out in the Pacific for the arrival of the bomb,

and who knew the cities chosen for the [operational] test. This was accepted as the policy for the selection of targets, so I sent Spaatz a cable.

Robert Arnold tells a story of another diary, known by the family to have existed, but whose whereabouts are now unknown. In it, his grandfather describes a "walk in the park" that he took alone with Stalin and an interpreter. The episode provides an interesting insight into Stalin's perspective on ideological issues.

As the story goes, Hap Arnold understood that in order to work with the Soviets, he should understand their beliefs, so he had made a point before Potsdam of reading the works of Karl Marx and Vladimir Lenin, which are the underpinnings of Communist dogma. Through this, he understood Marx's theory of transitional stages from capitalism to full communism. During their walk, he asked Stalin when he expected "the final triumph of Communism in the Soviet Union?"

"We're not Communists in the Soviet Union," Stalin laughed. "We're Russians." Stalin believed that his soldiers were not fighting for Marxism but on behalf of their motherland, Mother Russia. Robert Arnold says his grandfather found Stalin's quip "a stunning admission that the Soviet Union was not as advertised." Arnold agreed with Churchill's wartime assessment that the key to understanding the Soviet Union was Russia's national interests.

After the successful atomic bomb test on July 16, Truman decided, with Churchill's consent, to let Stalin know about the new weapon. On July 24, according to his memoirs, Truman told the Soviet leader that the Americans "had a new weapon of unusual destructive force. The Russian Premier showed no special interest. All he said was that he was glad to hear it and he hoped we would make good use of it against the Japanese."

When Churchill queried the president on Stalin's reaction, Truman replied, "He never asked a question."

In his history of the war, Churchill observes that "I was sure that [Stalin] had no idea of the significance of what he was being told." Admiral Leahy recalled in his memoirs that Stalin "did not seem to have any conception of what Truman was talking about."

However, Marshal Georgi Zhukov, the Red Army commander in Germany, who was at Potsdam and with Stalin immediately after this conversation, wrote in *his* memoirs that "Stalin, in my presence, told Molotov about his conversation with Truman. The latter reacted immediately: 'Let them. We'll have to talk it over with [the director of the Soviet nuclear weapons program, Igor] Kurchatov and get him to speed things up.' I realized they were talking about research on the atomic bomb."

The Allies had already approved the Potsdam Declaration calling on Japan to surrender unconditionally, disarm, and withdraw to its four home islands from all conquered territory, or face "prompt and utter destruction." It was formally issued on July 26.

In his memoirs, Arnold adds that in the declaration, "we did not mention the atomic bomb."

Nor did he mention it directly in his diary.

The night of July 23 was marked by a celebratory banquet. "The dinner was quite an affair," Arnold noted in his published diary. "President of the US, Prime Minister [Churchill], Marshal Stalin, and their military staffs; three Foreign Secretaries were also present. The toasts were many as per usual; the Prime Minister, Stalin, and the President were all in good form. Stalin announced with no attempt at secrecy, 'now that the War in Europe is over, we have a common enemy in the Pacific, and here's to our next meeting in

Tokyo.' I told Stalin, the Prime Minister and the President that if our B-29s continued their present tempo there would be nothing left of Tokyo in which to have a meeting."

The Allied leaders never met in Tokyo. Potsdam would be their last conference, with Churchill suffering the embarrassment of going home early. He learned on July 26 that his party had been defeated in Britain's first postwar general election. The new prime minister, Clement Attlee, Churchill's partner in the wartime coalition government, arrived in Potsdam in time to be photographed with Truman and Stalin for the obligatory Big Three group photo.

Arnold wrote in his diary of Churchill's departure, "So passes the man who has held the British Empire together, made it work, secured coordinated effort, held off the Germans, united all factions in England. His reward: defeat for office by the radicals [Attlee's left-leaning Labour Party]." He made no mention of the "radicals" in his memoirs. Attlee remained in office until Churchill's return to power in 1951.

Arnold, his staff, and his son Hank departed for Paris on July 27. Two days later, Hank was back in his unit, and his father was trout fishing in the Serpentine River near Stephenville during a one-day stopover in Newfoundland. His diary reports that he caught ten fish, with one being fourteen inches long.

Back in Washington on July 30, Arnold noted in his diary that he had covered 9,697 miles on his final wartime overseas trip. He had spent thirteen of his nineteen days abroad at Potsdam.

Harry Truman, as commander in chief, made the decision to drop an atomic bomb on Japan. He did so based on the casualty estimates for Operation Downfall, the two-phase invasion of the Japanese home islands. Based on the experience of Okinawa, it was assumed that American casualties could range up to a million men.

While many within the USAAF felt that Japan could be defeated by strategic bombing alone, without the necessity of either a ground invasion or a nuclear strike, Hap Arnold never made a definitive statement one way or another.

General John Huston, who edited his wartime diaries, wrote that in his memoirs, "Arnold seems willing to finesse the issue of whether or not he favored the use of the bomb at the time. His failure to address the issue directly is in part explained by his political sensitivity to many issues current when he wrote his autobiography in 1947–48. At that time, the Cold War had continued to intensify, and considerable debate evolved about the history and usage of the bomb. Also Truman, who had made the decision to drop the weapon, was still president, assisted now by Arnold's very close friend and mentor, George Marshall, who was serving as secretary of state."

What Arnold did say in his memoirs was that

> the surrender of Japan was not entirely the result of the two atomic bombs. We had hit some 60 Japanese cities with our regular [high explosive] and incendiary bombs.... Our B-29s had destroyed most of the Japanese industries and, with the laying of mines [by Superfortresses], which prevented the arrival of incoming cargoes of critical items, had made it impossible to carry on a large-scale war. We had destroyed 10,343 enemy airplanes, compared to the 29,900 destroyed in Europe. Accordingly, it always appeared to us that, atomic bomb or no atomic bomb, the Japanese were already on the verge of collapse. Many of the Japanese leaders gave

credit to the Superfortress attacks on interior Japan and
Japanese industrial cities as the greatest single factor in
forcing their surrender.

The cities Hiroshima and Kokura were selected as specific targets for the nuclear attacks on the basis of their military significance
and their having had little damage from the previous conventional
air campaign. This way, the operational effects of the atomic bomb
could be evaluated.

Of course the only aircraft capable of delivering the weapons to
their targets were Twentieth Air Force Superfortresses. On August
6, after the Japanese refused to surrender, the Superfortress *Enola
Gay* dropped an atomic bomb on Hiroshima. Truman told the Japanese, "We are now prepared to obliterate more rapidly and completely every productive enterprise the Japanese have above ground
in any city.... Let there be no mistake; we shall completely destroy
Japan's power to make war. It was to spare the Japanese people from
utter destruction that the ultimatum of July 26 was issued at Potsdam. Their leaders promptly rejected that ultimatum. If they do not
now accept our terms they may expect a rain of ruin from the air,
the like of which has never been seen on this earth."

The second bomb, intended for Kokura, was dropped on Naga-
saki on August 9 when cloud cover obscured the primary target. On
that same day, the Soviet Union declared war and began operations
against Japanese-occupied Manchuria.

"The news of those two [nuclear] attacks came to me over the
private wire which I had during the war, running from my home in
Fort Myer to the White House," Arnold wrote in his memoirs. "I
awaited the reports at home, knowing it might be hours I before I
got them over the regular communication channels. Both times the
private wire brought me the news within a few minutes after the
bomb had been dropped."

Even after the extent of the damage from the nuclear strikes became widely known, the government in Tokyo debated what to do, considering further resistance rather than capitulation in the face of what they had just experienced.

On the night of August 14–15, the Twentieth Air Force launched more than seven hundred Superfortresses in their final combat mission of the war. At noon, Japan time, on August 15, Emperor Hirohito made his first-ever radio broadcast, in which he finally called for an end to the war. With profound understatement, he told his subjects that "the war situation has developed not necessarily to Japan's advantage, while the general trends of the world have all turned against her interest."

From understatement to exaggeration, Hirohito continued, "Should we continue to fight, not only would it result in an ultimate collapse and obliteration of the Japanese nation, but also it would lead to the total extinction of human civilization.... This is the reason why we have ordered the acceptance of the provisions of the Joint Declaration of the Powers.... We have resolved to pave the way for a grand peace for all the generations to come by enduring the unendurable and suffering what is unsufferable."

As Arnold wrote,

> We had a small reception for Air Marshal [Arthur] Harris at our home. Bits and pieces of information had started flowing through official channels during the day, and it was confirmed that the Japanese were about to ask for peace. At the party, General Marshall told Mrs. Arnold to listen over the radio for a special announcement that would be broadcast at seven o'clock. After the guests had gone, we heard the announcement that the Japanese Government had submitted an offer for surrender to the Allies.

That night we had no celebration, just a family dinner—or, at least, that's the way it started. Then Air Force
generals and their wives began dropping in to extend their
greetings and express gratitude that the war was over.
General and Mrs. Hal George, and General and Mrs.
[Howard] Craig came in first—George who had done
such a magnificent job in building up and running the Air
Transport Command, and Craig, who had been one of the
[Operations Division] men so instrumental in planning
and figuring out ways and means of making the "impossible" possible, in the air war.

So the night passed, with Air Officers coming in and
out. Presently someone suggested sending a message of
congratulations to our Commander-in-chief, the President of the United States, so I appointed a committee to
go to the study and prepare it. After some difficulty they
finally agreed on the wording and brought it to me for
approval. I found parts that did not seem to fit the occasion, but after further attempts, and a bit of good brandy,
a greeting was decided upon which seemed to fill the bill,
and I dictated it over my private wire to a clerk at the
other end in the White House. We were afterward told it
was the first message of its kind the President had
received.

On September 2, Douglas MacArthur, whom Truman had named
as supreme commander for the Allied powers (SCAP), accepted the
unconditional surrender of Japan aboard the USS *Missouri* in Tokyo
Bay. Whereas Germany was occupied in sectors by four victorious
Allies—America, Britain, France, and the Soviet Union—Japan was
occupied only by the United States. MacArthur ruled Japan for the
next six years, redefining the role of the emperor and promulgating
a democratic constitution that is still in place.

★ ★ ★ ★ ★

"The abrupt surrender of Japan came more or less as a surprise, for we had figured we would probably have to drop about four atomic bombs, or increase the destructiveness of our B-29 missions by adding the heavy bombers from Europe," Arnold recalled. "With the surrender of Japan, my major mission was to carry out our demobilization as rapidly as possible. Congress and the American public wanted it that way, and we had to make our plans accordingly.... All that mattered was to get the boys home as soon as possible. However, the Army, Navy, and Air leaders were still responsible for maintaining suitable training facilities in the United States, providing ways and means of getting the men home, and insuring that the occupational units overseas remained at least strong enough to perform their duties."

Arnold recalls that another major task, which fell to the USAAF Air Transport Command, was flying wounded and high-priority personnel to the United States from overseas, up to thirty thousand a month across the Pacific alone. Meanwhile, the USAAF had nearly two million of its own personnel overseas, many of whom had been there for three years or more, and who needed to be brought home as soon as possible.

The man who had worked so hard for so long to build the modest U.S. Army Air Corps into the largest and most effective air force in the world was now compelled to disassemble it. Just as the build-up had taken time, so too would the downsizing. The head count at the end of 1945 stood at 2,282,259, which was down 90,033 from the 1944 peak. During 1946, 1,826,744 USAAF personnel were discharged.

When Japan surrendered, the USAAF possessed 63,715 aircraft, of which 41,163 were combat types—down from the peak of 43,248 in May 1945. Arnold imagined that postwar requirements would be for fewer than ten thousand total aircraft, so he was faced with an enormous disposal task.

"The question of what to do with surplus airplanes is one upon which no two people ever seem to agree," he laments in his memoirs.

> I announced at the time we were told to get rid of our planes that there was one way to do it properly. I was not in favor of trying to sell 60,000 airplanes. In the first place, there weren't that many buyers; and in the second place, by the time they were sold, many of them would be so obsolete, or would have so many defective parts, that the buyers would probably get into trouble with them. Furthermore, their sale certainly wouldn't help our aviation industry. To me, the only solution was to create an airplane crematory at some obscure place in the United States. With a big set of shears, cut the wings off, then throw the entire airplane into a press and crush it into a mass of metal. Then throw this mass of metal into a furnace and melt it.

While there was never a mass crematory, most of the aircraft that had helped win the war were scrapped over the next few years. The vast armadas of Flying Fortress and Liberator heavy bombers that headed home from Europe were cut up and scrapped. In the eighteen months following Japan's surrender, the USAAF disposed of 33,680 aircraft, including 10,934 heavy bombers and 8,014 fighters.

Arnold was conscious of the aircraft types the USAAF would need in the postwar world. When the war ended, the USAAF possessed 2,132 Superfortresses. Arnold did not cancel production of the remaining B-29s on the assembly lines but did cancel an order for five thousand B-29C Superfortresses with improved engines. In August 1946, the inventory of Superfortresses stood at 2,150, and there was no talk yet of disposing of *these* aircraft. They were the only delivery system for America's ultimate weapon.

As Arnold downsized the USAAF, he was also reorganizing it. The combat assets and the surviving fleet of combat aircraft were sorted into three combat commands representing the three principal missions of the postwar force. These three, which were all activated on March 21, 1946, after careful organizational planning, were the Air Defense Command (ADC), charged with defending American airspace; the Tactical Air Command (TAC), which would carry out tactical air support operations in time of war; and the Strategic Air Command (SAC), whose role would be long-range bombing of enemy nations in time of war.

USAAF combat assets remaining overseas on occupation duty were reorganized into two regional commands. USSTAF became the U.S. Air Forces in Europe (USAFE), the umbrella organization for all USAAF assets still in Europe, while the Far East Air Force (briefly redesignated as the Pacific Air Command) remained in that role in the Pacific, absorbing the Twentieth Air Force. The Air Transport Command remained, becoming the Military Air Transport Service (MATS) in 1948.

Another issue that rated surprisingly high on Hap Arnold's priority list was hemisphere defense. In his final months in office, he devoted as much attention to the Americas as to the theaters where the war had been fought. During his visit to Brazil in May, he was impressed by the apparent success of the USAAF in positively influencing the development of the Força Aérea Brasileira, and he imagined that the USAAF might do the same elsewhere in Latin America.

"Did we have an obligation to the Western Hemisphere that had priority over our obligation to our European Allies?" Arnold asks rhetorically.

Should we create a military solidarity among all the Americas, with all of us using the same weapons, the same technique and type of training? Or, should we let that go while we continued to build up the facilities required for worldwide war operations? Or should we tie ourselves into a defensive alliance with the European Democracies? To win and maintain the good will of our hemispheric neighbors, we must let them in on our secrets, give them some of our equipment, let them use it and become acquainted with its techniques of operation, and help train their military students. This was antici- pated in the Act of Chapultepec, signed by the American Republics during the InterAmerican Conference on Prob- lems of Peace and War at Mexico City in March 1945.

In this comment, Arnold anticipated a major element of American Cold War military policy, the Military Assistance Program, which began with the Mutual Assistance Act of 1949 and went on to involve more than a dozen countries around the world, especially in Europe as well as Latin America, over the ensuing several decades.

This project was the centerpiece of Arnold's last two overseas trips as commanding general of the USAAF. The first of these took him to Mexico.

"In Brazil, the Air Forces had already started mechanics training schools, supervised the training of Brazilian aviators, and helped in constructing buildings and securing machinery for the manufacture of airplanes and engines. Now we must carry the plan further, and do the same thing for other nations in South America. Why not, I thought, try Mexico?"

Just as the Brazilians had contributed a fighter group to augment USAAF operations in Italy, the Fuerza Aérea Mexicana had fielded its Escuadrón 201, the "Águilas Aztecas" ("Aztec Eagles"), to support the USAAF 58th Fighter Group for several weeks during the campaign in the Philippines earlier in 1945.

Accompanied by Bee and Lois, Arnold traveled to Mexico City in late October 1945, where he met with President Manuel Ávila Comacho and outlined what the USAAF had done in Brazil. Comacho was pleased with the concept and surplus American aircraft, but he admitted that funding a training program was beyond his means.

Meanwhile, Arnold received invitations from the leaders of Colombia, Peru, and Chile to come south to discuss aviation assistance. In January 1946, he was well received in Colombia, but Arnold was unprepared for the 8,600-foot elevation of its capital city.

"The altitude at Bogotá is very high, and is not good for anyone who has a bad heart," Arnold wrote of his visit to Colombia's capital. "I got along all right as long as I watched my step and was careful to rest, but I felt the effects when I got down to Lima, where we were met by our Ambassador [William D.] Pawley and by high-ranking officials of the Peruvian Government. I told Mr. Pawley we would have to slow up a bit in our various operations because of my health, and suggested he might modify our itinerary."

In fact, he had developed a cardiac dysrhythmia, forcing the "modification" to become a cancellation. As Arnold wrote, "My physical condition had become worse, so that we had to call off the part of the trip that would have taken us into Chile and probably across to Argentina and Brazil. We took the plane and headed back to Panama and from there to Miami, where I went into the hospital for a checkup."

It was while he was hospitalized that he learned of the death on January 29, 1946, of Harry Hopkins, who had been battling stomach cancer for some time. Arnold had last seen Hopkins a month earlier when he had visited him in the hospital in New York. Realizing that the dying man needed his rest, Arnold had excused himself, but

Hopkins insisted that he stay and talk. They talked about the memoirs that Hopkins had hoped to finish and his insistence that Arnold write his. Also in Miami, Arnold chanced to cross paths with Winston Churchill, who was vacationing there. The former prime minister shared with him the text of his famous "Iron Curtain Speech" that he was planning to deliver on March 5 in Fulton, Missouri.

In the speech, Churchill pointed out that "an 'iron curtain' has descended across the continent" of Europe, and that the eastern part of that continent was "subject, in one form or another, not only to Soviet influence but to a very high and in some cases increasing measure of control from Moscow." It was a geopolitical reality that concerned both Churchill and Arnold, but the strategic planning to meet this challenge would take place *without* Hap Arnold. While downsizing the USAAF, one of the men Arnold was most eager to dismiss from duty was its only five-star general.

At Potsdam, he had raised the subject to his boss.

"I talked with General Marshall about continuing in harness," he recalled in his memoirs. "Now that the war was about over, I did not believe we could continue to work with 'our necks up in the collars' as we had for the past four years. We should let the next echelon of commanders have their chance. In short, I thought it was about time for us to retire. Marshall agreed with me, but I bet him five dollars he would still be in office six months after Japan capitulated. He took the bet."

Marshall retired as chief of staff on November 18, 1945, and was succeeded by Dwight Eisenhower. However, he was tapped by Harry Truman in January 1947 to come back into government to serve as secretary of state.

Arnold noted that it was early in the fall of 1945 that he firmly made up his mind to "give up my job as Commanding General of the Army Air Forces. I had seen it grow from almost nothing into the mightiest Air Force the world had ever known. I had seen some of the world's finest airplanes developed, tested, and tried out in battle, and I had seen our Air Forces play their part with the RAF and with the Naval Air Force in defeating the German Luftwaffe and the Japanese Air Force."

He goes on to say that

> I was proud to have served as the leader of such an outfit. But I also saw that the future might not be as rosy as the past. There were plans that should be made during this period immediately following World War II which would be very important ten or fifteen years from now. It looked to me as if the time had come when the younger men who would have to carry out those plans, and who would have to continue to build up the Air Force, should be in the driver's seat. It was no place for the old fellows who had served their part and who should not be considered as even probable leaders in any new emergency.

On November 8, 1945, ten days before Marshall retired, Arnold sent his boss, friend, and occasional fishing buddy "not an easy memorandum to write," stating that he wished to retire from active service "at an early date," although he did not set a date. Complimenting Marshall on the support that he had given to the USAAF, Arnold told him, "With your concurrence, I should like to request retirement from the Service. I should like to be separated from the Service and go on terminal leave."

In all his references to his planned retirement, Arnold speaks of turning over the reins of the USAAF to "younger men," although the first generation waiting in the wings were more or less his contemporaries. Certainly, they were men who had held significant levels of command within the service during World War II. To succeed himself as commanding general, he chose Tooey Spaatz, who was, in retrospect, an obvious choice.

Arnold was placed on the retired list effective on June 30, 1946, but he had already handed off the baton of USAAF leadership to Spaatz on February 9.

George Stratemeyer, Arnold's former chief of staff, who ended the war commanding the USAAF assets in the China-Burma-India Theater, was first to head the Air Defense Command; Pete Quesada, who had done so much with tactical airpower in the European Theater, took over the Tactical Air Command; while George Kenney came in from the Far East Air Force to head the Strategic Air Command. On average, they were just four years Arnold's junior, except Quesada, who was 18 years younger.

Back in January 1936, when his family had departed from California for the nation's capital, Hap Arnold had observed that "if I had realized then that I would stay in Washington for ten consecutive years, right up to my retirement, I would almost have dared to turn my overloaded car around and drive straight back to California."

Ten years and two months later, he was able to write that "the President accepted my application for retirement and my wife and I left Washington on March 1, 1946, for Sonoma."

═══ CHAPTER 21 ═══

HIS LEGACY

The legacy of Henry Harley Arnold is manifest in the existence of the United States Air Force itself. He devoted his career to the Herculean task of building the United States Army Air Forces into the immense, war-winning weapon that it became, while having the vision and tenacity to lay the groundwork for an independent air force.

This process culminated in the National Security Act of 1947, signed by President Truman on July 26. It created an entity called the National Military Establishment, which became the Department of Defense in 1949. Most of the act's provisions became effective on September 18, 1947. It was on that date that the independent Air Force, which had been the fervent dream of Hap Arnold and so many others in the decades since Billy Mitchell's time, was born.

On that date, Tooey Spaatz exchanged his khaki cap for a blue one, becoming the first chief of staff of the new Air Force.

On May 7, 1949, three years after he retired, Hap Arnold was given the rank of General of the Air Force, making him the only five-star general in the history of the service, and because of his five-star status in the Army, he is the only officer to have attained that rank in *two* branches of the armed forces.

His legacy is apparent in his having picked and nurtured the remarkable officers who would go on to lead the Air Force for a generation. These included the men who succeeded him as chief of staff, such as Tooey Spaatz, Hoyt Vandenberg, Nathan Twining, and Curtis LeMay.

Beyond this, at the very heart of the identity of the Air Force, the legacy of Henry Harley Arnold is evident in his thorough endorsement of research and development. He recalled how the Army, including the Army Air Service, retrenched after World War I, and he was determined that *his* service should do just the opposite. At his insistence, a forward-thinking perspective on science and technology became an integral part of the identity of the Air Force, which permitted it not only to triumph in the Cold War, but to become and remain the world leader in military aviation technology.

Before Arnold departed Washington, the next generation of warplanes, all of them initially conceived and ordered on his watch, was taking shape. Among jet fighters, the Lockheed P-80 was almost combat-ready when the war ended, and North American Aviation was developing the F-86 Sabre, which would be to aerial combat in the Korean War what the company's P-51 Mustang had been in World War II.

In the pipeline to supersede the remarkable Superfortress was the gigantic Consolidated Vultee B-36 Peacemaker, which had a range of nearly ten thousand miles and a gross weight of more than a quarter million pounds, both specifications more than double those of the mighty Superfortress. During the war, the USAAF was already anticipating its first generation of all-jet bombers. The Douglas XB-43 and North American XB-45 were both ordered in 1944, while the Consolidated XB-46, Boeing XB-47, and Martin XB-48 were ordered early in 1945. All made their first flights in 1947, and the B-47 Stratojet remained an important part of the arsenal until the 1960s.

With the war over, Arnold was anxious not to lose wartime levels of research and development. In his memoirs, he wrote of the great wartime operational and logistical challenges that had come with his job, but adds that

> as Chief of the Army Air Forces, I had yet another job. That was to project myself into the future; to get the best brains available, have them use as a background the latest scientific developments in the air arms of the Germans and the Japanese, the RAF, and determine what steps the United States should take to have the best Air Force in the world twenty years hence. There was no doubt in my mind but that a different pattern must be followed in so far as radar, atomics, [super]sonics, electronics, jet planes, and rockets were concerned. This applied not only to airplanes, to the rockets used from ships and from airplanes, but also to such types of projectiles as the big German V-2 rocket. When we added all such developments together, what did it mean for the future? What kind of Air Force must we have? What kind of equipment ought we to plan for twenty years, or thirty years hence?

To project himself into the future, Arnold had supported and utilized the National Defense Research Committee, a government scientific think tank created in 1940 under orders from the president himself. Roosevelt shared Arnold's belief in the power of technology to shape the future. Evolving into the Office of Scientific Research and Development, the organization undertook highly classified research into a broad range of leading-edge technologies, from radar to computers to nuclear weapons.

Headed by Dr. Vannevar Bush, the director of the Carnegie Institution and former head of the National Advisory Committee for Aeronautics (NACA), the predecessor of NASA, the committee included Karl Compton, the president of MIT; James Bryant Conant, the president of Harvard; and Frank Jewett, the president of the National Academy of Sciences and chairman of the board at Bell Laboratories.

As Arnold recalled in his memoirs, "Few high ranking Army officers seemed aware of the close relationship developing between these specialists and the little Air Corps—a relationship that was to grow to such importance in World War II that civilian scientists would work side by side with staff officers in our overseas operational commands, frequently flying on combat missions to increase their data."

One day early in the war, Arnold invited George Marshall, the chief of staff, to join him at lunch with the members of this committee.

"What on earth are you doing with people like *that?*" Marshall asked.

"Using them," Arnold replied. "Using their brains to help us develop gadgets and devices for our airplanes—gadgets and devices that are far too difficult for the Air Force engineers to develop themselves."

As the war progressed, Arnold decided that he needed his own committee. He got in touch with Dr. Robert Millikan at Caltech, his friend of many years, and asked him to recommend someone to head "a committee of practical scientists" who could point the way to the development of "aircraft in the future."

That man was Dr. Theodore von Kármán, whom Arnold had originally met through Millikan in 1938. A Hungarian-born prodigy who could multiply six-figure numbers in his head at the age of six faster than adults with pencil and paper, von Kármán later wowed his professors and earned a solid reputation in aerodynamics in Germany before coming to the United States in 1930 to accept Millikan's offer of the directorship of the Guggenheim Aeronautical Laboratory at Caltech (GALCIT). Among his protégés at Caltech was Frank Malina, later a founder of NASA's Jet Propulsion Laboratory (JPL).

In 1943, Arnold had asked von Kármán to evaluate the early intelligence that had been received about the German V-2 ballistic missile. The scientist confirmed that the V-2s were theoretically possible. It was also apparent that the Luftwaffe jet aircraft program was well in advance of those in the United States and Britain.

In September 1944, Arnold met with von Kármán to discuss creating his "committee of practical scientists." The meeting had the drama of a Hollywood script, taking place on the windswept runway at New York's La Guardia Airport as Arnold was returning from a European trip. Von Kármán was driven in an Army staff car to meet Arnold's plane at the end of the runway. Here, according to Dr. Dik Daso, curator of modern military aircraft at the National Air and Space Museum, Arnold "dismissed the military driver and then, in total secrecy, discussed his plans for von Kármán and his desires for the exploitation project. Arnold spoke of his concerns about the future of American airpower, and he wondered how jet propulsion, radar, rockets, and other gadgets might affect that future."

In his 1967 book, *The Wind and Beyond*, von Kármán remembered asking Arnold, "What do you wish me to do?"

"I want you to come to the Pentagon and gather a group of scientists who will work out a blueprint for air research for the next 20, 30, perhaps 50 years," Arnold replied. According to von Kármán, he and Arnold thereafter remained in "continual conference" while the committee of practical scientists was assembled. Originally known as the Army Air Forces Consulting Board for Future Research (AAFCBFR), it was redesignated as the Scientific Advisory Group (SAG) on December 1, 1944. As a deputy, von Kármán picked Dr. Hugh Dryden, director of the Aerodynamics Division of the National Bureau of Standards, and later a NASA deputy administrator. He is also the namesake of NASA's important Dryden Flight Research Center at Edwards Air Force Base.

Their work was regarded as top secret, and SAG reported directly to Arnold through von Kármán. In a November 7, 1944, directive to von Kármán, Arnold explained, "I am asking you and your associates to divorce yourselves from the present war in order to investigate all the possibilities and desirabilities for postwar and future war's development as respects the AAF. Upon completion of your studies, please then give me a report or guide for recommended future AAF research and development programs."

As referenced in his memos to Ira Eaker of May 22, 1945, and to Tooey Spaatz on December 6, 1945, Arnold gave von Kármán an open-ended mandate for his aeronautical studies, telling him to let his "imagination run wild."

In the spring of 1945, as Allied armies were beginning to overrun Germany, there was naturally an interest in capturing material related to German scientific development, which was, with regard to some aspects of aeronautics, more advanced than in the United States.

One example is the famous OSS Operation Paperclip, which went into Germany charged with capturing German rocket scientists before they could be scooped up by the Soviets. The OSS netted Werner von Braun and his team, who went on to build artillery rockets for the Army and launch vehicles for the American space program.

Arnold, meanwhile, had his own variation on Paperclip, designated Operation LUSTY (for Luftwaffe Secret Technology), that originated under the aegis of the Air Technical Service Command at Wright Field in Ohio. Beginning in April, LUSTY teams went into Germany, collecting hardware and documents, as well as aeronautical scientists. One team, commanded by Colonel Harold Watson and known as "Watson's Whizzers," had the mission of collecting one example of every type of advanced German plane, especially rocket- and jet-propelled aircraft. When these aircraft were found, they were flown by Watson's men, or by Luftwaffe pilots who had been induced to change sides, to seaports from which they were shipped to the United States.

Many of the aircraft that were rounded up by LUSTY were evaluated by von Kármán, who had gone overseas himself. He also traveled to Potsdam, where he met with Arnold on July 13 during the Terminal Conference. It was here that Arnold ordered him to prepare an interim report as soon as possible. In this summary, entitled *Where We Stand* and submitted on August 22, 1945, he predicted supersonic flight and noted that "defense against present-day aircraft will be perfected by target-seeking missiles."

He went on to accurately predict that "due to improvements in aerodynamics, propulsion, and electronic control, unmanned devices will transport means of destruction to targets at distances up to several thousand miles.... Only aircraft or missiles moving at extreme speeds will be able to penetrate enemy territory protected by such defenses."

When Arnold submitted his *Third Report of the Commanding General of the Army Air Forces to the Secretary of the War* to Henry Stimson on November 12, 1945, he summarized the final accomplishments of the service in the war, but unlike his fellow JCS leaders, he devoted a third of his report to the future that his scientists had shown him. In it, he observes that "during this war the Army, Army Air Forces, and the Navy have made unprecedented use of scientific and industrial resources. Scientific planning must be years in advance of the actual research and development work."

His appetite whetted and the war now finally over, Arnold requested that a document much more detailed than *Where We Stand* be in his hands by December 15. Von Kármán cancelled a planned trip to investigate Japanese aeronautics and submitted the first volume of an eventual twelve-volume report entitled *Science, the Key to Air Supremacy*, on schedule. Dik Daso wrote that von Kármán's "long-range, extremely detailed study was the first of its kind in American military history. Along with *Where We Stand*, it would serve as the blueprint for building the Air Force during the next two decades."

Walter J. Boyne, the former director of the Smithsonian National Air and Space Museum, wrote in the January 2004 issue of *Air Force Magazine*,

> In all the history of aviation there has never been a more productive alliance than that of von Kármán and Gen. Henry H. "Hap" Arnold. The results of their efforts did much to bring the United States Air Force to its current state of unmatched capability and power. Von Kármán could interpret Arnold's visions of the future, which were not always clearly stated. He gave Arnold new ideas and suggestions even as he established a strong liaison between military leaders, scientists, and academics. Arnold in turn gave von Kármán the resources, facilities,

contracts, methodology, and approval on a vastly larger scale than would otherwise have been possible.

Meanwhile, SAG was only one of the far-sighted initiatives whose genesis Arnold crammed into his busy last year and a half at the helm of the USAAF. Another project was undertaken in collaboration with his friend Don Douglas, whose Douglas Aircraft Company had grown into one of the largest plane-makers in the world. The idea was to use the engineering infrastructure at Douglas to jumpstart a permanent research and development institution.

On October 1, 1945, Arnold and Douglas set up Project RAND (Research and Development). Working with them were Arthur Raymond, the chief engineer at Douglas, and his assistant, Franklin Collbohm, as well as Edward Bowles of MIT, who had been a consultant to Secretary of War Stimson. On the USAAF side were General Lauris Norstad, Arnold's assistant chief of staff for plans, and Curtis LeMay. Under a special contract issued to Douglas, RAND began work on March 2, 1946, in an autonomous office located within the Douglas facility in Santa Monica.

Two months later, RAND completed its first report. This amazingly forward-thinking document, entitled *Preliminary Design of an Experimental World-Circling Spaceship*, described the design, performance, and deployment of earth-orbiting satellites—more than a decade ahead of Sputnik. Hap Arnold was gone by this time, and there would be no contract issued for actually building such a "spaceship," but the mere fact that the institution he created was thinking so far ahead is a testament to his vision.

In 1948, Douglas divested Project RAND, and it became the RAND Corporation, destined to be one of the most influential scientific public policy think tanks in the world. It still exists.

Hap Arnold's legacy is grounded in the fact that he created SAG and RAND, and that he set the Air Force on its way, continuing to look ahead into the future, and doing so on the wings of the leading edge of science and technology.

Among airmen, Hap Arnold is considered the father of the United States Air Force. He is the namesake of many of its institutions, including the Arnold Air Society, an honorary organization in Air Force ROTC, as well as of Arnold Hall at the United States Air Force Academy. Arnold Air Force Base in Tennessee is the Air Force's center of development for aerospace systems and home to the Arnold Engineering Development Center, which is considered to be the world's largest flight simulation test facility.

In the twenty-first century, the Air Force characterizes its vision as "providing precise and reliable global vigilance, reach and power for the nation," an evolution of the "global reach, global power" doctrine promulgated by the service in the 1990s. In both instances, the wording could have been taken directly from Hap Arnold's notes. The Air Force's mission is defined as "to fly, fight and win … in air, space and cyberspace." While Hap Arnold might not have anticipated cyberspace, he would have understood its importance. To fly, fight, and win—and to do so *anywhere* within the global reach of the Air Force—was the doctrine that Arnold had articulated in World War II. That forward-looking commitment is Arnold's legacy to today's Air Force.

CHAPTER 22

THE VALLEY OF
THE MOON AND BEYOND

"I'm going out to my ranch in the Valley of the Moon, to sit under an oak tree," Henry Harley Arnold told the attendees at a National Press Club luncheon early in 1946. "From there I'll look across the Valley at the white-faced cattle, and if one of them even moves too fast, I'll look the other way."

After a career of forty-three years, if you include those at West Point, and the frantic pace of the just-ended war years, he was looking forward, most eagerly, to his retirement in Sonoma County.

More than two years had passed since Bee had closed the deal on the 42-acre property, which they had now dubbed "Rancho Feliz," meaning the "Happy Ranch," but the place was not yet ready for them. They wound up living for several months in an apartment that their daughter Lois and her naval aviator husband Ernie had rented, and used sporadically, in San Francisco.

As Robert Arnold notes, the foundation for the Arnolds' new home was not poured until around Thanksgiving 1945. He tells of delays, of angry letters back and forth with the architect, of complaints about postwar materials shortages, of compromises made, and of the tiny kitchen. Robert tells of the construction costs running over budget and of a personal loan from Donald Douglas (which Douglas never asked to be repaid).

Hap and Bee intended this house to be used only as a guesthouse, a place for their children and grandchildren to stay when they came to visit. The plan was for a much larger main house, built on top of the hill overlooking the ranch, and designed in "California Hacienda" style, to replicate their quarters at March Field.

The main house was never built. The smaller house into which they moved in 1946 would be their home for the rest of their lives. For Hap, this would be four years, and for Bee, more than three decades.

"My wife and I could sit in the redwood chairs I had made in my workshop, drink in the quiet beauty of our valley, and watch the half-tame quail feed about our garden," Arnold wrote in his memoirs. "On such calm, sunny afternoons you could almost imagine that the roar of four-engine bombers, the fiery flash of aerial battle, even the wrangles of diplomacy, had never existed."

In those later years, he liked to tell a story of an incident that happened one peaceful afternoon shortly after they moved to Rancho Feliz. His eyes were drawn skyward by the sounds of a pair of AT-6 trainers flying out of Hamilton Field. As he watched them engaged in aerobatics that evolved into a mock dogfight, he saw them *collide*. One came spiraling down, directly at his house!

At this point in his telling of the story, he would remind listeners of an exchange that he had with a Washington reporter shortly before he retired. He had announced that he was giving up flying and the aviation world and going away to the quiet of the country.

"You mean you're through with airplanes?" the incredulous reporter asked.

"Yes!" Arnold replied. "If one dares to fly low over my ranch house, I'll grab a rifle or something and shoot it down!"

The plummeting AT-6, its pilot floating away safely under his parachute, barely missed the Rancho Feliz ranch house, crashed into the east pasture, a few yards away, and exploded. Naturally, the press recalled his previous remark, and there were tongue-in-cheek questions as to whether he had shot down the airplane.

In his memoirs, he recalled that the hole it made was thirty feet across and about six feet deep. Robert Arnold, who planted vineyards on the property with his father many years later, reports that evidence of the crater was still there.

Over the ensuing years, there were no more dramatic events such as this. It was indeed the "Happy Ranch," the peaceful retreat. Their neighbor, Charmian Kittredge London, the widow of Jack London, gave them cuttings from redwood trees on her property, which were then planted at Rancho Feliz. Some of these redwoods are still there. The Arnolds tried their hands at raising chickens and cattle. Hap even registered "Flying A" as his cattle brand, but it turned out that there was not enough land to graze an economically viable herd, and the cattle operation was eventually discontinued.

Having written two articles about airpower for *National Geographic* magazine during the war, he wrote one in retirement that appeared in the December 1948 issue. Entitled "My Life in the Valley of the Moon," the idyllic portrait of the area is credited by some for helping to initiate a postwar land boom in Sonoma County.

☆ ☆ ☆ ☆ ☆

After he moved to California, Hap continued to receive briefings and reports from Air Force headquarters, and he even entertained thoughts—which never went beyond the thinking—of going back on active duty. He flirted with the notion of once again being part of the excitement he had escaped.

Though he had an office set aside for his use at Hamilton Field, about an hour's drive from his ranch, for reasons of health and convenience, his briefing packets were usually delivered to him at home by a courier. Robert Arnold relates an amusing story about a time when the courier decided to bring along a friend of his from Hamilton, a WAF (Women in the Air Force) sergeant. Rather than go up to the ranch, the WAF waited for the courier at the bar of the Swiss Hotel on Sonoma's main square. When the courier dropped off the packet, Arnold wanted to talk, so it was an hour or two before the man returned to Sonoma to collect his friend. By this time, she'd had more than a couple of drinks, and when he picked her up, she left her cap behind on the bar.

The next time that Hap Arnold was in the Swiss Hotel, he was shown the cap and told the story, which he found very funny. Assuming that she would return for the cap, he decided to play a practical joke on the young woman. He pinned one of his metal five-star insignias to the cap, imagining the startled look on her face when she came back.

As it turned out, however, she never did come back, and the cap with the five stars became a conversation piece at the bar. Over time, as the younger Arnolds passed through Sonoma and stopped in to the Swiss Hotel, they, too, started pinning insignia to the cap. Over time, the cap became encrusted with eagles and oak leaves, as well as the stars, and the legend of the artifact grew. As of 2012, when this author lunched with Robert Arnold at the hotel dining room, the cap was still there, although now protected behind glass.

After he was given the rank of General of the Air Force on May 7, 1949, the service sent out a new blue uniform on which he could pin his five-star insignia. Robert Arnold reports that he has seen only one color picture of his grandfather wearing the uniform. It was taken in the main square in Sonoma. When asked where the uniform is now, Robert says simply, "He's wearing it. He was buried in it."

It was in retirement that Arnold was finally able to turn back to his prewar interest in a career as an author. Among the projects that he planned was another boys' fiction series similar to the Bill Bruce books of two decades earlier. This time, the protagonist was to be a young West Point cadet. As the Bill Bruce books were named after his middle son, William Bruce Arnold, these books were to be named after his youngest, David Lee Arnold, who was a member of West Point's class of 1949. He got as far as a first draft of the first book, entitled *David Lee at West Point*, but dropped the project in favor of nonfiction.

He also agreed to write articles on aviation for the *Encyclopedia Britannica*, but his biggest single project during his retirement would be his autobiography. He envisioned it as the first of many books that he hoped to write. It was a time when World War II memoirs by the war's biggest players were highly sought by publishers. Dwight Eisenhower received a contact from Doubleday, and Hap Arnold from Harper and Brothers.

For Arnold, the experience of writing his book, *Global Mission*, was not a pleasant one. Harper was strict on their schedule and nitpicked his work, excluding sections and skewing the narrative in favor of the European Theater at the expense of the Pacific experience—an imbalance with which the author disagreed. This time

Arnold found himself on the wrong side of a "Germany-first" doctrine.

As Robert Arnold explains, *Global Mission* "was not the book he wanted to write. He wanted to write one with more diary-type stories in it."

When the book was published in September 1949, Hap had high hopes for it to be a financial success—knowing that Bee would outlive him and wanting to leave her more than just military survivor's benefits—but it enjoyed only modest sales in its first season in print.

Despite his having made much of his lounging in his redwood chair, forgetting the stress of the outside world, and watching the quail, Arnold did interrupt his self-imposed isolation to remain abreast of world affairs and to comment upon the geopolitical future; these observations found their way into *Global Mission*.

He spoke with pride of the stellar performance of the Air Force during the Berlin Airlift of 1948–1949, which was ongoing as he was writing. "Neither we nor the British helped the civilized world along the road to a permanent peace in 1945 by virtually agreeing that ... the Russians should take over and run most of Germany," he wrote. "We and the other Allied nations were to occupy small areas within Berlin—but only by sufferance. We must rely upon the good nature of Russia for corridors of entry and exit to our areas. Both Great Britain and America, and their leaders, knew what kind of people the Russians were."

Also in the headlines as *Global Mission* was taking shape was the creation of the North Atlantic Treaty Organization (NATO), the international military alliance designed to impede further territorial ambitions by the Soviet Union, which was formed through the signing of the North Atlantic Treaty on April 4, 1949.

"Words do not impress the Russians. They never have," Arnold observed, expressing his skepticism for the potential effectiveness of NATO.

> Hence, the Atlantic Pact, by itself, means little. There must be force and power behind it to show the Russians that the nations in the Alliance mean business. There are several means of putting teeth in the Pact and of arming the nations whose safety and future security may depend upon such an alliance: first, we might send to the various nations the surplus arms and equipment we have on hand or are producing; second, we might send them anything— any kind of equipment they ask for; third, we might do a bit of advance planning and thinking to insure that each of the nations concerned had the kind of equipment it would need as a component part of a joint Allied force. There would then exist a unified command with the proper composition, strength, and equipment to deter any aggressor from war. At the very least, it would cause an aggressor nation to stop and think before making any hostile move.

With respect to planning for the future, he admonished his successors to think creatively and not to be lulled into relying on preparing to fight the wars of the past.

"There is only one question that should be asked about [this station, or that base, or some obsolete technique or pieces of equipment]: 'Do they fit into the modern war picture?' Not the picture of 1918, nor of 1941, but of the war of the future. If they don't, we should be ruthless and throw them out.... The principles of yesterday no longer apply. Air travel, airpower, air transportation of troops and supplies have changed the whole picture. We must think in terms of tomorrow. We must bear in mind that airpower itself can become obsolete."

He wondered aloud about world peace in the formative years of the Cold War. "One thing stands out clearly against the background of my experience: the winning of Peace is much more difficult than the winning of even a global War," he wrote. "One look at the condition of the poor old world today, four years after the supposed ending of World War II, almost makes me gasp. Where is our Peace?"

Against the backdrop of the Cold War, Arnold was pleased that the Air Force could be regarded as America's ace in the hole.

"Russia has no fear of an army; she thinks hers is just as good as, and bigger than, any in the world; she has no fear of a navy, since she cannot see how it can be employed against her; but she does fear our long-range Strategic Air Force, which she cannot as yet match, or as yet understand. In the Strategic Air Force, coupled with our atomic bomb, at this writing we hold the balance of power in the world." The ink had scarcely dried on Arnold's *Global Mission* manuscript, however, when the Soviet Union succeeded in its first nuclear test on August 29, 1949.

Arnold considered the role the Air Force would have in maintaining the global balance of power and yearned to have one of his heirs wearing "Air Force blue." He decided that this heir should be Captain William Bruce Arnold, United States Army. At the time, it was possible for anyone in the Army to transfer straight across into the Air Force, taking his rank and all his allowances and benefits with him.

However, Bruce was of a contrary mind. As he explained to Murray Green in a 1974 conversation, "I had a fairly good start in the Army, and I had fought the war in the Army, [so I figured] it would be best for me to stay in."

Bruce was a missile officer, a seamless progression from his wartime work in antiaircraft operations. He was stationed at a Navy base at Point Mugu, California, south of Santa Barbara, working on temporary duty with the Air Force missile program. The program, which had originated with the Navy, was called "Lark," and encompassed the Fairchild SAM-N-2 and Convair SAM-N-4, which were antiaircraft missiles originally designed to deal with the Japanese kamikaze threat that Bruce had seen firsthand at Okinawa in 1945.

"He really jumped on this," Bruce recalled of his father.

"Now that's what you ought to get into," Hap told his second son. "What you ought to do is to transfer to the Air Corps right away, because the [U.S. Air Force] is going to have the really important missiles."

The discussion reached its climax one weekend when Bruce was visiting his father at Rancho Feliz.

"He did something which he'd never done before," Bruce recalled. "He sat me down on the couch and put a bottle of bourbon on a little table."

"Now," Hap began. "We're going to have this out, because I want to know why you aren't going to join the Air Force.... Can't I have *one* son in the Air Force?"

As Robert recalls, his grandfather told his father that "we're going to sit here and drink this until you agree with me."

In recalling his own thinking on the subject, Bruce speaks of what he calls the

> brotherhood of piloting, where two men sit up [on the flight deck] of an airplane in bad weather, especially in the older days when everything was not done from a scientific point of view—and the bravery it took for them to fly through the night and through the storm to get to where they were going. This set up a bond between them,

and they flew with different men, and pretty soon they
had bonds with maybe 50 men who had bonds with others.... This really is, I think, the pilot/silver-wings syn-
drome, for want of a better word, which really determines
the leadership of the Air Force. There are very, very few
people that can get into that very special, elite society of
pilots unless they wear those wings.... Dad just had the
idea that he could just put out a decree, and say that
wings don't mean anything any more.

According to Robert, Bruce finally looked at Hap, realized how
sick he was, and decided that he couldn't say "no" any longer.

When my Dad said he wanted a son in the Air Force, and
couldn't I at least do that for him, I readily agreed, but I
realized right then that my career in the Air Force was
going to be definitely limited. But I think he also had the
idea that the future Air Force was going to be the brave
new world which wouldn't have all the limitations, perhaps, that the present Air Corps had. It would be conceived of an entirely different concept. So that perhaps
the main mission of the Air Force wouldn't be flying airplanes through flak at 15,000 feet or 25,000 feet to get to
a target.... Perhaps something much more sophisticated.
A pilotless airplane. Who needs wings to sit on the ground
and push buttons.... I think he felt that not only would
the concept change, but the old ties of man to man based
on going up and conquering the blue would also change.

It is eerily prescient that this conversation about the concept
of future "pilotless airplanes" took place in 1948, and that Bruce
spoke of it in 1974. In those years, nobody could predict that in

the twenty-first century, unmanned aerial vehicles (UAV), and indeed unmanned *combat* air systems (UCAS) would be one of the fastest-growing operational components within the Air Force. Interestingly, until 2008, pilots were rotated into the UAV world on temporary duty assignments, then rotated back into the cockpit. In 2008, however, the Air Force began training non-pilots to fly unmanned aerial vehicles as their *permanent* duty assignment—a future that Hap Arnold apparently sensed was coming.

Hap Arnold would live to see *two* of his sons in Air Force blue. When David graduated from West Point in 1949, he also chose his father's service.

By the time that Hap and Bruce sat down for their pivotal conversation, the frailty that the son saw in the father's eyes was real, and serious. Heart trouble, including another heart attack in January 1948 that laid him up for three months, marred his retirement. Pictures of him from the time show the haggard face of a tired eighty-year-old, though Hap had just turned sixty in his retirement year.

His global traveling, which had characterized his last few years at the helm of the USAAF, was a thing of the past. An invitation to come to Britain to be honored by King George VI as a Knight Grand Cross of the Order of the Bath had to be foregone. The medal was delivered to the American embassy in London and sent to Rancho Feliz. He did manage to drive the fifty miles to San Francisco in the autumn of 1949 to do a book signing for *Global Mission*, but that was the extent of his stamina.

The family gathered at the ranch for Christmas that year, knowing that time was short. He seemed to be in especially good spirits, but the end came on January 15, 1950. Henry Harley Arnold passed away in his bed at his beloved ranch house. The Associated Press reported the cause of death as a coronary occlusion, a clotting of the arteries leading to his heart, which resulted in his final heart attack. His physician, Dr. Russell V. Lee, was quoted as saying that he should have retired after his first heart attack in 1944, "but things were hot then and he decided to take his chances with the rest of the soldiers and went back to duty."

Harry Truman sent a plane to bring Hap and Bee on their last trip to Washington. Colonel Hank Arnold came in from the Command and Staff College at Fort Leavenworth to attend the funeral, while Lieutenant David Arnold arrived from March Field, now March Air Force Base. Captain Bruce Arnold came to Washington from his post at a place called Cape Canaveral in Florida.

Hap was given a state funeral, with a rare graveside service on January 19 at the Arlington National Cemetery Memorial Amphitheater. Truman was in attendance, as was Secretary of State Dean Acheson. The honorary pallbearers included Dwight Eisenhower, retired Admiral Ernest King, former Undersecretary of War for Air Bob Lovett, and Secretary of the Air Force Stuart Symington—as well as two of Hap's oldest friends, Tooey Spaatz and George Marshall.

Lovett, later a secretary of defense, spoke at the service, calling Hap Arnold a casualty of World War II, comparing the damage done to his heart during the conflict to wounds suffered in combat. Then, on a cold day in January, Henry Harley Arnold was laid to rest in Section 34 at the Arlington National Cemetery, on the same hill as General John J. Pershing.

Hap's sons returned to their posts and went on with their careers. After the Command and Staff College, Hank went on to a series of staff jobs stateside and overseas. He earned a master's degree from Stanford in 1961, and from 1964 to 1966 he served with the Provisional Military Assistance Advisory Group in Korea (PROVMAAG-K).

He was later posted to the staff of the Sixth Army, headquartered at the Presidio of San Francisco.

David Arnold earned a master's degree from George Washington University in 1956 and served in a variety of Air Force posts, such as the Office of Special Investigations in Berlin and headquarters of the Air Materiel Command at Wright Patterson Air Force Base. During the Vietnam War, David served with Task Force Alpha, processing data from the Operation Igloo White sensors placed along the Ho Chi Minh Trail. His duty station was the supersecret Infiltration Surveillance Center (ISC) at Nakhon Phanom in Thailand, then the largest computer and data processing center in Southeast Asia.

Bruce Arnold pursued his career in missile development, and he was involved in tests at Eglin Air Force Base of the JB-2, the reverse-engineered American missile based on the German V-1s that had fallen near his father back in June 1944. In the early 1950s, he was assigned to Patrick Air Force Base at Cape Canaveral, and later wound up working with General Bernard "Bennie" Schriever as part of his "Schoolhouse Gang," the group that created the first Air Force intercontinental ballistic missile (ICBM), the Atlas. This organization, properly the Western Development Division (WDD) of the Air Research and Development Command (ARDC), was nicknamed for its having been formed in July 1954 at a former school building at 409 East Manchester Road in Inglewood, California.

During Bruce's tenure with Schriever's organization, the Schoolhouse Gang evolved into the Ballistic Missile Division (BMD), developed the Titan and Minuteman ICBMs, and came to account for two of every five dollars spent by the Air Force.

As his son Robert tells, Bruce was slotted to go to the National War College, a must for promotion from colonel to general, but Schriever came to him and said, "I need you with me. I want you to turn down this opportunity. I'll get you another one later."

To this, Bruce replied, "Sir, if you need me, I'll be with you."

However, Schriever retired abruptly in 1966, and Bruce never got that other opportunity. He left the missile trade to serve as supervisor of all the Defense Department's Advanced Research Projects Agency programs in Southeast Asia. As Robert recalls, he was involved in projects "from fixing the problems with the M16 rifle to electronic warfare over North Vietnam." He later served at the headquarters of the Air Force Systems Command (AFSC), ARDC's successor, and ended his career doing legislative liaison work for the Air Force with the United States Senate.

Bruce retired in 1972 and went to work for the Garrett Corporation, an aerospace firm, in their Washington office. In 1986, he and Barbara founded the Chandelle Winery in Sonoma, utilizing grapes that they had planted on the property at Rancho Feliz. The namesake of the winery is the aviation maneuver perfected by French aviators in World War I that was called *monter en chandelle*, or "to climb around a candle." Specifically, it involves a 180-degree change in direction, with an increase in altitude.

Hank Arnold retired from his final service post with the Sixth Army in 1970, while David retired from the Sacramento Air Logistics Center in 1979. All three of Hap Arnold's sons who served in the armed forces retired as full colonels.

Their sister Lois, meanwhile, moved to a home in Sonoma, near that of her mother, after her breakup with Ernie Snowden in the 1950s. She died there on September 26, 1964. Snowden, meanwhile, retired from the Navy as a rear admiral and died on July 8, 1975. They are buried together at the Presidio of San Francisco beneath a common headstone, although Lo is identified by her maiden name.

Bee Arnold continued to live on at Rancho Feliz, and she continued to play a role in Sonoma community affairs. She also had an opportunity for travel in her later years. Her grandson Robert tells of a trip that she and Bruce had made to visit David while he was stationed in Germany, noting that Bee had seen her share of Berlin high society when she was studying there before World War I, and had even danced with Kaiser Wilhelm II.

"There was a certain German aristocrat who fell in love with her at the time," Robert recalls of his mother's prewar sojourn. "Pop [Bruce Arnold] found his letters, a series suspended by various wars, which [the aristocrat] signed 'Willie Boy.' They were all very Victorian, though. The man had survived, and probably fought in, both world wars. Pop talked to Granny about the letters, and asked if she was going to look up 'Willie Boy' while they were in Germany."

"Oh," she answered, "I just don't want to start all that up again."

Eleanor Alexander Pool Arnold died in Sonoma on June 26, 1978, at the age of 91, one day after what would have been her late husband's ninety-second birthday. Bee was buried alongside Hap at Arlington under a separate gravestone. At her request, son John, who had been interred in Ardmore, Pennsylvania, after his death back in 1923, was reburied with his mother. His name appears on the back of her headstone.

Her son Hank died in Sheridan, Wyoming, on May 20, 1990, and David died in Reno, Nevada, on March 11, 1992. Bruce passed away in Washington, D.C., on September 21, 1992. Hank was buried in Wyoming at the Sheridan Municipal (previously Mount Hope) Cemetery, while David and Bruce were both laid to rest at Arlington on the same hill as their parents.

It was after his father's death that Robert Arnold was asked to be part of the design committee for the Air Force Memorial that was being planned at Arlington. He describes the dozen-year effort as a challenge, but remarks that it turned out "better than we ever thought it would.... Best thing I've ever done. I feel good about it."

Originally, the Memorial was to be situated near the Marine Corps Memorial, the Iwo Jima Memorial, on the north side of the cemetery on Arlington Ridge. However, objections to the placing of another service memorial in that area led to a search for a new location on which all parties could agree. In 2001, a new site was authorized near Columbia Pike, on the grounds of Fort Myer and just south of Arlington Cemetery. Designed by architect James Ingo Freed of the firm of Pei Cobb Freed and Partners and dedicated in October 2006, it includes three memorial spires ranging from 201 to 270 feet in height that evoke the image of jet aircraft contrails.

At the base of the memorial are engraved quotes from various Air Force leaders. That of Hap Arnold, describing the role of his service in American life, reads, "Our Air Force belongs to those who come from ranks of labor, management, the farms, the stores, the professions, and colleges and legislative halls.... Airpower will always be the business of every American citizen."

Robert Arnold recalls an unexpected moment that occurred on one of his visits to Washington after the site selection. He had just come from a meeting at the Pentagon with General Michael Ryan, then chief of staff of the Air Force. He had picked up some flowers and had driven to Arlington to place them at the graves of his parents, his grandparents, and his uncles John and David.

> I drove around to that side of the cemetery, parked the car and walked up the hill to where everyone is buried. I had finished placing the flowers for Hap and Bee, and an extra one for John, because Pop would have wanted me to do that, and I was looking around—and *there's* the Memorial site. It's about a quarter of a mile away, just across the Arlington wall. I realized that when the Memorial was completed, *Hap would be looking at it*! Every time there's a ceremony, every time there's a flyby, he'd be *right there*. I just started laughing, asking, "How in the world did *you*

get them to move the Memorial from the other side of the cemetery, all the way over here *so that you could look at it?*" Every time I go there, it makes me smile.

ARNOLD'S TEN PRINCIPLES

ap Arnold wrote in his memoirs that "throughout the war, I tried to have the Air Force operate under certain fundamental principles." He lists them as follows:

1. "The main job of the Air Force is bombardment; large formations of bombardment planes must hit the enemy before the enemy hits us. In short, the best defense is attack."
2. "Our planes must be able to function under all climatic conditions, from the North Pole to the South Pole."

3. "Daylight operations, including daylight bombing, are essential to success, for it is the only way to get precision bombing. We must operate with a precision bombsight—and by daylight—realizing full well that we will have to come to a decisive combat with the enemy Air Force."

4. "We must have highly developed, highly trained crews working together as a team—on the ground for maintenance and in the air for combat."

5. "In order to bring the war home to Germany and Japan, and deprive them of the things that are essential for their war operations, we must carry our strategic precision bombing to key targets, deep in the enemy territory, such as airplane factories, oil refineries, steel mills, aluminum plants, submarine pens, Navy yards, etc."

6. "In addition to our strategic bombing, we must carry out tactical operations in cooperation with ground troops. For that purpose we must have fighters, dive bombers, and light bombers for attacking enemy airfields, communication centers, motor convoys, and troops."

7. "All types of bombing operations must be protected by fighter airplanes. This was proved to be essential in the Battle of Britain, and prior to that our own exercises with bombers and fighters indicated that bombers alone could not elude modern pursuit, no matter how fast the bombers traveled."

8. "Our Air Force must be ready for combined operations with ground forces, and with the Navy."

9. "We must maintain our research and development programs in order to have the latest equipment it was possible to get, as soon as it was possible to get it."

10. "Airpower is not made up of airplanes alone. Airpower is a composite of airplanes, air crews, maintenance crews, air bases, air supply, and sufficient replacements in both planes and crews to maintain a constant fighting strength, regardless of what losses may be inflicted by the enemy. In addition to that, we must have the backing of a large aircraft industry in the United States to provide all kinds of equipment, and a large training establishment that can furnish the personnel when called upon."

APPENDIX 2

THOMAS GRIFFITH ARNOLD'S SERVICE RECORD

Thomas Griffith Arnold, Hap Arnold's grandfather, enlisted in the 43rd Pennsylvania in the wake of the Battle of Gettysburg. This is his Civil War service record. (Source: National Archives)

Form MAGO-41—200M—6-35 Commonwealth of Pennsylvania Department of Military Affairs	RECORD OF BURIAL PLACE OF VETERAN	Montgomery .... County		
NAME Arnold Thomas Griffith (4417)		DATE OF BIRTH	DATE OF DEATH	
VETERAN OF Civil	WAR	SERVED IN ARMY (X) NAVY ( )	MARINE CORPS ( )	
DATES OF SERVICE 7/6/63-8/13/63	ORGANIZATION(S) Co I 43rd Regt. Pa Mil.		RANK Sgt.	
CEMETERY OR PLACE OF INTERMENT	NAME Montgomery			
	LOCATION Norristown, Pa.			
LOCATION OF GRAVE IN CEMETERY SECTION B LOT No. 152	RANGE GRAVE No.3	HEADSTONE Gran. Mon GOVERNMENT ( ) COUNTY ( ) FAMILY ( )		
INFORMATION GIVEN BY DATE 3/10/36		REMARKS		

After being Recorded in the County Veterans' Grave Registration Record This card is to be sent to THE ADJUTANT GENERAL'S OFFICE, Harrisburg, Pennsylvania, for final Record.

MNP

APPENDIX 3

DR. HERBERT ALONZO ARNOLD'S SERVICE RECORD

Dr. Herbert Alonzo Arnold, Hap Arnold's father, served as a U.S. Army surgeon during the Spanish-American War and remained in the Pennsylvania National Guard for many years thereafter. Below is his service record. (Source: National Archives)

NAME OF SOLDIER:	Arnold, Herbert A.				(3-K-5)
NAME OF DEPENDENT:	Widow,				
	Minor,				
SERVICE:	1 Lt + Asst Surg. Squad Pa Vol. Cav				
	Maj + Sgn. Pa. N. gds (B.D.)				

	FILING.	CLASS.	APPLICATION NO.	CERTIFICATE NO.	STATE FROM WHICH FILED.
	Pa June 11	Invalid,	1432.910	1,230,950	Pa.
		Widow,			
		Minor,			

ATTORNEY:	Byington + Wilson
REMARKS:	A 11 C 2-413-425

CHARLES LINDBERGH LETTER TO HAP ARNOLD, 1938

n 1938, legendary aviator Charles Lindbergh wrote to Hap Arnold, explaining the technologically advanced state of the German aviation industry. His letter is reproduced on the following pages. (Source: Robert and Kathleen Arnold collection)

ILLIEC
PENVENAN
CÔTES-DU-NORD

Illiec, November 2 1938

Dear General Arnold,

I have just returned from a three week's visit to
Germany, most of which was spent in trips through various
aircraft factories and aviation establishments. This is
the third consecutive year during which I have had the
opportunity of watching the German aviation development,
and I am more impressed on each visit with the rate of
their progress and the magnitude of their program. Germany
is undoubtedly the most powerful nation in the world in
military aviation and her margin of leadership is increasing with each month that passes. She is developing her
research facilities as rapidly as she is increasing the
rate of her production. The design and performance of
German aircraft are excellent and improving greatly each
year. In a number of fields the Germans are already ahead
of us and they are rapidly cutting down whatever lead we
now hold in many others.

My object in writing to you at this time is to tell
you how essential I believe it is for us to keep in closer
touch with Germany, especially in regard to military
aviation. I realize that you have been kept well informed
through the reports of Colonel Smith and Major Vanaman.

- 2 -

General H.H. Arnold.   3.11.38

I believe they are both exceptionally able officers.
But I wish that you yourself could make a trip to
Germany in the near future to see what is being done in
that country; primarily in aviation but also in other
fields. I believe that such a visit would be of the
utmost value from many standpoints and I am certain that
you would regard the time well spent.

I shall not attempt to outline the aviation developments I saw in Germany for I know that Major Vanaman has
covered all of these in his reports.

I hope that you may find it possible to make this
visit. There is an appalling lack of understanding of
present conditions in Europe and I believe that you could
contribute greatly to a better understanding - certainly
in aviation and probably in many other ways.

With best regards,

Charles A. Lindbergh

Charles A. Lindbergh.

CAL:DH

General H.H. Arnold,
U.S.Army Air Corps,
War Department,
Washington, D.C.,

CHARLES LINDBERGH LETTER TO HAP ARNOLD, 1941

C harles Lindbergh, once America's most famous aviator and a national hero, became controversial on the eve of World War II for his isolationist stance. However, once the war had begun, he was eager to do his part for the war effort. Two weeks after Pearl Harbor, he offered his services to Hap Arnold. Arnold considered him an important confidant. His letter is reproduced on the following pages. (Source: Robert and Kathleen Arnold collection)

Washington
Dec. 20, 1941

Dear Gen. Arnold:

This is a personal note to tell
you that if I can, at any time, be
of assistance to you and to the
Air Corps, there is nothing I would
rather do. I fully realize the
complications created by the political
stand I have taken and by past
incidents connected with that stand.

However, I want you to know that if the opportunity should arise during this crisis, I am ready and anxious to be of service.

Meanwhile I wish you the greatest success. May God strengthen you for the ordeal ahead.

Sincerely

Charles A. Lindbergh

Vineyard Haven
Mass.

ACKNOWLEDGMENTS
AND NOTES
ON PRIMARY SOURCES

The author would especially like to thank Hap Arnold's grandson, Robert Arnold, the son of William Bruce Arnold. He not only generously shared a wealth of personal information about his father and grandfather, but he provided an insightful perspective on their lives and times.

Unless otherwise noted in the text, all the direct quotes attributed to Hap Arnold in this work are taken from his 1949 autobiography, *Global Mission*, or from his diaries, which are in the collection of the U.S. Air Force.

Other primary and secondary material was derived from the significant body of documentation gathered by the researcher and historian Dr. Murray Green (Colonel, U.S. Air Force), whose work is archived at various Air Force installations, especially the Air Force

Academy. Thanks to J. A. (Bill) Saavedra (Colonel, U.S. Air Force, Retired) of the Office of Air Force History for providing material from the Air Force collections.

Statistical data relative to the USAAF, United States Air Force, and predecessor organizations is derived from official sources, including the *Army Air Forces Statistical Digest* (1945 and 1946), the Civil Aeronautics Administration *Statistical Handbook* (1948), the *Air Force Almanac*, published annually by the Air Force Association, and *The Army Air Forces in World War II* by Wesley Frank Craven and James Lea Cate (1948). Operational data is taken from the latter source, as well as *The Army Air Forces in World War II: Combat Chronology 1941–1945*, compiled for the Historical Research Center of Air University by Kit Carter and Robert Mueller.

BIBLIOGRAPHY

Anderton, David. *History of the U.S. Air Force*. New York: Crescent, 1981.

Andrade, John M. *U.S. Military Aircraft Designations and Serials, 1909 to 1979*. Earl Shilton, United Kingdom: Midland Counties Publications, 1997.

Andrews, Allen. *The Air Marshals: The Air War in Western Europe*. New York: Morrow, 1970.

Arnold, Henry Harley. *American Airpower Comes of Age: General Henry H. "Hap" Arnold's World War II Diaries*. Vol. 1. Edited by John W. Huston. Collingdale, PA: Diane Publishing, 2002.

———. *American Airpower Comes of Age: General Henry H. "Hap" Arnold's World War II Diaries*. Vol. 2. Edited by John W. Huston. Collingdale, PA: Diane Publishing, 2002.

———. *Global Mission*. New York: Harper & Brothers, 1949.

Arnold, Henry Harley, and Ira Clarence Eaker. *Army Flyer*. New York: Harper & Brothers, 1942.

———. *This Flying Game*. New York: Funk and Wagnalls, 1936.

———. *Winged Warfare*. New York: Harper & Brothers, 1941.

Biddle, Tami Davis. *Rhetoric and Reality in Air Warfare: The Evolution of British and American Ideas About Strategic Bombing, 1914–1945*. Princeton: Princeton University Press, 2002.

Bland, Larry I., and Sharon R. Ritenour, eds. *The Papers of George Catlett Marshall*. Vol. 2, *"We Cannot Delay," July 1, 1939–December 6, 1941*. Baltimore: Johns Hopkins University Press, 1986.

———, eds. *The Papers of George Catlett Marshall*. Vol. 3, *"The Right Man for the Job," December 7, 1941–May 31, 1943*. Baltimore: Johns Hopkins University Press, 1991.

———, eds. *The Papers of George Catlett Marshall*. Vol. 4, *"Aggressive and Determined Leadership," June 1, 1943–December 31, 1944*. Baltimore: Johns Hopkins University Press, 1996.

Blum, John Morton. *From the Morgenthau Diaries*. Vol. 2, *"Years of Urgency," 1938–1941*. Boston: Houghton Mifflin, 1959.

Brereton, Lewis H. *The Brereton Diaries: The War in the Pacific, Middle East and Europe*. New York: William Morrow, 1946.

Brown, Jerold E. *Where Eagles Land: Planning and Development of U.S. Army Airfields, 1940–1941*. Westport, CT: Greenwood Press, 1990.

Bryant, Arthur. *Triumph in the West: A History of the War Years Based on the Diaries of Field-Marshal Lord Alanbrooke, Chief of the Imperial Staff.* Garden City, NY: Doubleday, 1959.

———. *The Turn of the Tide: A History of the War Years Based on the Diaries of Field-Marshal Lord Alanbrooke, Chief of the Imperial General Staff.* Garden City, NY: Doubleday, 1957.

Buchanan, Jeffrey S., C. McKenna, and H. Raugh. *Institutional Survival: Evolution of the Admissions Process during the United States Military Academy's First Century.* West Point, NY: 1990.

Buell, Thomas B. *Master of Sea Power: A Biography of Fleet Admiral Ernest J. King.* Boston: Little, Brown, 1980.

Bullitt, William C. *For the President, Personal and Secret: Correspondence between Franklin D. Roosevelt and William C. Bullitt.* Edited by Orville H. Bullitt. Boston: Houghton Mifflin, 1972.

Byrd, Martha. *Chennault: Giving Wings to the Tiger.* Tuscaloosa: University of Alabama Press, 1987.

Cannon, John K. *The Contribution of Airpower to the Defeat of Germany.* Wiesbaden, Germany: Headquarters United States Air Forces in Europe, 1945.

Chennault, Claire Lee. *Way of a Fighter: The Memoirs of Claire Lee Chennault, Major General, U.S. Army (Ret.).* Edited by Robert Hotz. New York: G. P. Putnam's Sons, 1949.

Churchill, Winston. *The Second World War.* Vol. 1, *The Gathering Storm.* Boston: Houghton Mifflin, 1948.

———. *The Second World War.* Vol. 2, *Their Finest Hour.* Boston: Houghton Mifflin, 1949.

———. *The Second World War.* Vol. 3, *The Grand Alliance.* Boston: Houghton Mifflin, 1950.

———. *The Second World War*. Vol. 4, *The Hinge of Fate*. Boston: Houghton Mifflin, 1950.

———. *The Second World War*. Vol. 5, *Closing the Ring*. Boston: Houghton Mifflin, 1951.

———. *The Second World War*. Vol. 6, *Triumph and Tragedy*. Boston: Houghton Mifflin, 1953.

Coffey, Thomas M. *Hap: The Story of the U.S. Air Force and the Man Who Built It, General Henry H. "Hap" Arnold*. New York: Viking Press, 1982.

Copp, DeWitt S. *A Few Great Captains: The Men and Events That Shaped the Development of U.S. Airpower*. Garden City, NY: Doubleday, 1980.

———. *Forged in Fire: Strategy and Decisions in the Air War over Europe, 1940–1945*. Garden City, NY: Doubleday, 1982.

Cox, Sebastian, ed. *The Strategic Air War Against Germany, 1935–1945: Report of the British Bombing Survey*. London: Frank Cass, 1998.

Cozzens, James Gould. *A Time of War: Air Force Diaries and Pentagon Memos, 1943–1945*. Edited by Matthew J. Broccoli. Columbia, SC: Broccoli Clark, 1984.

Crane, Conrad. *Bombs, Cities, and Civilians: American Airpower Strategy in World War II*. Lawrence: University of Kansas Press, 1993.

Craven, Wesley Frank, and James Lea Cate, eds. *Army Air Forces in World War II*. Vol. 1, *Plans and Early Operations, January 1939 to August 1942*. Washington, D.C.: Office of Air Force History, 1947.

———, eds. *Army Air Forces in World War II*. Vol. 2, *Europe: TORCH to POINTBLANK, August 1942 to December 1943*. Washington, D.C.: Office of Air Force History, 1948.

———, eds. *Army Air Forces in World War II*. Vol. 3, *Europe: Argument to VE Day, January 1944 to May 1945*. Washington, D.C.: Office of Air Force History, 1951.

Dallek, Robert. *Franklin D. Roosevelt and American Foreign Policy, 1932–1945*. New York: Oxford University Press, 1995.

Daso, Dr. Dik Alan. *Architects of American Air Supremacy: Gen. Hap Arnold and Dr. Theodore von Kármán*. Maxwell AFB, Alabama: Air University Press, 1997.

———. *Hap Arnold and the Evolution of American Airpower*. Washington, D.C.: Smithsonian Institution Press, 2000.

Davis, Richard G. *Carl A. Spaatz and the Air War in Europe*. Washington, D.C.: Smithsonian Institution Press, 1992.

Doolittle, James H. *I Could Never Be So Lucky Again: An Autobiography of General James H. "Jimmy" Doolittle*. With Carroll V. Glines. New York: Bantam Books, 1991.

Douhet, Giulio. *The Command of the Air*. New York: Arno Press, 1942.

DuPre, Flint O. *U. S. Air Force Biographical Dictionary*. New York: Franklin Watts, 1965.

Ehrman, John. *Grand Strategy*. Vol. 5, *August 1943–September 1944*. London: Her Majesty's Stationery Office, 1956.

———. *Grand Strategy*. Vol. 6, *October 1944–August 1945*. London: Her Majesty's Stationery Office, 1956.

Eisenhower, Dwight D. *Crusade in Europe*. New York: Doubleday, 1948.

———. *The Eisenhower Diaries*. Edited by Robert H. Ferrell. New York: W. W. Norton, 1981.

Fogerty, Robert P. *Biographical Data on Air Force General Officers, 1917–1952*. Vol.1, *A through K*. Maxwell AFB, Alabama: U.S. Air Force Historical Division, 1953.

Freeman, Roger A., Alan Crouchman, and Vic Maslen. *Mighty Eighth War Diary*. London: Jane's, 1981.

Futrell, Robert Frank. *Ideas, Concepts, Doctrine: Basic Thinking in the United States Air Force, 1907–1960*. Collingdale, PA: Diane Publishing, 1989.

Gilbert, Martin. *Winston S. Churchill*. Vol. 7, *Road to Victory, 1941–1945*. Boston: Houghton Mifflin, 1986.

Gorn, Michael H. *The Universal Man: Theodore von Kármán's Life in Aeronautics*. Washington, D.C.: Smithsonian Institution Press, 1992.

Green, William. *Famous Bombers of the Second World War*. New York: Doubleday, 1957.

———. *Famous Fighters of the Second World War*. New York: Doubleday, 1957.

———. *Warplanes of the Second World War*. New York: Doubleday, 1964.

Greer, Thomas H. *The Development of Air Doctrine in the Army Air Arm, 1917–1941*. Maxwell AFB, Alabama: Office of Air Force History, 1985.

Griffith, Charles. *The Quest: Haywood Hansell and American Strategic Bombing in World War II*. Maxwell AFB: Air University Press, 1999.

Griffith, Thomas E., Jr. *MacArthur's Airman: General George C. Kenney and the War in the Southwest Pacific*. Lawrence: University Press of Kansas, 1998.

Groman, Alan. "Air Force Planning and the Technology Development Planning Process in the Post–World War II Air Force: The First Decade (1945–1955)." In *Military Planning in the Twentieth Century: The Proceedings of the Eleventh Military History Symposium, 10–12 October 1984*. Edited by Harry R. Borowski. Washington, D.C.: Office of Air Force History, 1986.

Grumelli, Michael L. "Trial of Faith: The Dissent and Court-Martial of Billy Mitchell." Ph.D. diss., Rutgers University, 1991. Ann Arbor, Michigan: University Microfilms, 1991.

Haight, John McVickar, Jr. *American Aid to France, 1938–1940*. New York: Atheneum, 1970.

Hall, H. Duncan. *North American Supply*. London: Her Majesty's Stationery Office, 1955.

Hansell, Haywood S., Jr. *The Air Plan That Defeated Hitler*. Atlanta: Higgins McArthur/Longino and Porter, 1972.

Harris, Arthur Travers. *Bomber Offensive*. London: Pen & Sword Military Classics, 2005. First published 1947 by Collins.

———. *Dispatch on War Operations: 23 February, 1942, to 8 May, 1945*. Edited by Sebastian Cox. London: Routledge, 1995.

Hennessy, Juliette A. *The United States Army Air Arm, April 1861 to April 1917*. Maxwell AFB, Alabama: U.S. Air Force Historical Division, 1958.

Holley, I. B., Jr. *Ideas and Weapons: Exploitation of the Aerial Weapon by the United States during World War I: A Study in the Relationship of Technological Advance, Military Doctrine, and the Development of Weapons*. Washington, D.C.: Office of Air Force History, 1983.

Kelsey, Benjamin. *The Dragon's Teeth: The Creation of United States Airpower for World War II*. Washington, D.C.: Smithsonian Institution Press, 1982.

King, Ernest J., and Walter Muir Whitehill. *Fleet Admiral King: A Naval Record*. New York: W. W. Norton, 1952.

Leahy, William. *I Was There*. New York: Whittlesey House, 1950.

LeMay, Curtis E., and Bill Yenne. *Superfortress: The B-29 and American Airpower in World War II*. Yardley, PA: Westholme, 2006. First published 1988, McGraw Hill.

Levine, Alan J. *The Strategic Bombing of Germany, 1940–1945*. New York: Praeger Publishers, 1992.

Maurer, Maurer. *Air Force Combat Units of World War II*. Maxwell AFB: Office of Air Force History, 1983.

McFarland, Stephen L. *America's Pursuit of Precision Bombing, 1910–1945*. Washington, D.C.: Smithsonian Institution Press, 1995.

Mitchell, William L. *Winged Defense: The Development and Possibilities of Modern Airpower Economic and Military*. New York: G. P. Putnam's Sons, 1925.

Morison, Samuel Eliot. *History of the United States Naval Operations in World War II*. Vol. 2, *Operations in the North African Waters, October 1942–June 1943*. Boston: Little, Brown, 1947.

Morrow, John H. *The Great War in the Air: Military Aviation from 1909 to 1921*. Washington, D.C.: Smithsonian Institution Press, 1983.

Parton, James. *"Air Force Spoken Here"*: *General Ira Eaker and the Command of the Air*. Bethesda, MD: Adler & Adler, 1986.

Patrick, Mason M. *The United States in the Air*. Garden City, NY: Doubleday, Doran, 1928.

Pogue, Forrest C. *George C. Marshall*. Vol. 1, *Education of a General, 1890–1939*. New York: Viking Press, 1963.

———. *George C. Marshall*. Vol. 2, *Ordeal and Hope, 1939–1942*. New York: Viking Press, 1965.

———. *George C. Marshall*. Vol. 3, *Organizer of Victory, 1943–1945*. New York: Viking Press, 1973.

Potter, E. B. *Nimitz*. Annapolis: Naval Institute Press, 1976.

Potter, E. B., and Chester W. Nimitz. *Sea Power: A Naval History*. Englewood Cliffs, NJ: Prentice Hall, 1960.

Price, Alfred. *Battle over the Reich: The Strategic Air Offensive over Germany*. Rev. ed. Hersham, Surrey: Classic Publications, 2005.

Reynolds, Clark G. *Admiral John H. Towers: The Struggle for Naval Air Supremacy*. Annapolis: Naval Institute Press, 1991.

Richards, Denis. *The Fight at Odds*. Vol. 1, *Royal Air Force 1939– 1945*. London: Her Majesty's Stationery Office, 1953.

———. *The Hardest Victory: RAF Bomber Command in the Second World War*. New York: W. W. Norton, 1994.

Schaffer, Ronald. *Wings of Judgment: American Bombing in World War II*. New York: Oxford University Press, 1985.

Seversky, Alexander de. *Victory through Airpower*. New York: Simon and Schuster, 1942.

Sherwood, Robert E. *Roosevelt and Hopkins: An Intimate History*. New York: Harper & Brothers, 1948.

Stilwell, Joseph W. *The Stilwell Papers*. Arranged and edited by Theodore H. White. New York: William Sloane Associates, 1948.

Stimson, Henry L. and McGeorge Bundy. *On Active Service in Peace and War*. New York: Harper & Brothers, 1947.

Sturm, Thomas A. *The USAF Scientific Advisory Board: Its First Twenty Years, 1944–1964*. Washington, D.C.: U.S. Air Force Historical Division Liaison Office, 1967.

Suchenwirth, Richard. *Historical Turning Points in the German Air Force War Effort*. U.S. Air Force Historical Study, no. 189. Maxwell AFB: Office of Air Force History, 1968.

Tate, James P. *The Army and Its Air Corps: Army Policy toward Aviation, 1919–1941*. Maxwell AFB, Alabama: Air University Press, 1998.

Taylor, A. J. P. *Beaverbrook*. New York: Simon and Schuster, 1972.

Tedder, Arthur W. *Air Power in War: The Lees Knowles Lecture, 1947*. London: Hodder and Stoughton, 1948; reprint edition, Westport: Greenwood Press, 1975.

———. *With Prejudice: The War Memoirs of Marshal of the Royal Air Force, Lord Tedder, G.C.B.* London: Cassell and Company, 1966.

Thetford, Owen G. *Aircraft of the RAF since 1918*. 6th ed. London: Putnam, 1976.

Thomas, Lowell, and Edward Jablonski. *Doolittle: A Biography*. Garden City, NY: Doubleday, 1972.

Tillett, Paul. *The Army Flies the Mail*. Tuscaloosa: University of Alabama Press, 1955.

Truman, Harry S. *Memoirs*. Vol. 1, *Year of Decision*. Garden City, NY: Doubleday, 1955.

Tuchman, Barbara W. *Stilwell and the American Experience in China, 1911–1945*. New York: Macmillan, 1970.

United States Strategic Bombing Survey. *The Effects of Strategic Bombing on the German War Economy*. Washington, D.C.: Overall Economic Effects Division, 1945.

USAAF Office of Statistical Control. *Army Air Forces Statistical Digest, World War II*. Washington, D.C.: Director, Statistical Services, USAAF, 1945.

Von Kármán, Theodore. *Science: The Key to Air Supremacy*. Summary volume to *Toward New Horizons: A Report to General of the Army H. H. Arnold, Submitted on Behalf of the Scientific Advisory Group*. Wright Field, Dayton, OH: Air Materiel Command Publications Branch, Intelligence, T-2, 1945.

———. *Where We Stand: First Report to General of the Army H. H. Arnold on Long Range Research Problems of the Air Forces with a Review of German Plans and Developments, 22 August 1945*. Wright-Patterson AFB, OH: Air Force Materiel Command History Office, 1945.

———. *The Wind and Beyond: Theodore von Kármán, Pioneer in Aviation and Pathfinder in Space*. With Lee Edson. Boston: Little, Brown, 1967.

Wagner, Ray. *American Combat Planes*. 3rd enlarged ed. New York: Doubleday, 1982.

Walker, Lois F., and Shelby Z. Wickam. "Part I: Huffman Prairie 1904-1916." *From Huffman Prairie to the Moon: A History of Wright-Patterson AFB*. Wright-Patterson AFB: Office of History, 2750th Air Base Wing, 1986.

Webster, Sir Charles, and Noble Frankland. *The Strategic Air Offensive Against Germany, 1939–1945*. 4 vols. London: Her Majesty's Stationery Office, 1961.

Weigley, Russell F. *The American Way of War: A History of United States Strategy and Policy*. New York: Macmillan, 1973.

Wells, Mark K. *Courage and Warfare: The Allied Aircrew Experience in the Second World War*. London: Frank Cass, 1995.

Wilson, Theodore A. *The First Summit: Roosevelt and Churchill at Placentia Bay, 1941*. Rev. ed. Lawrence: University of Kansas Press, 1991.

Wolk, Herman S. *Planning and Organizing the Postwar Air Force, 1943–1947*. Washington, D.C.: Office of Air Force History, 1984.

———. *Strategic Bombing: The American Experience*. Manhattan: MA/AH Publishing, 1981.

Yenne, Bill. *Aces High: The Heroic Saga of the Two Top-Scoring American Aces of World War II*. New York: Berkley/Caliber, 2009.

———. *Big Week: Six Days That Changed the Course of World War II*. New York: Berkley/Caliber, 2012.

———. *Convair: Into the Sunset*. Greenwich/San Diego: Greenwich/General Dynamics, 1995.

———. *The History of the U.S. Air Force*. New York: Simon and Schuster, 1992. First published 1984.

———. *Lockheed*. New York: Random House, 1987.

———. *McDonnell Douglas: A Tale of Two Giants*. New York: Random House, 1985.

———. *Rockwell: The Heritage of North American*. New York: Random House, 1989.

———. *Secret Weapons of World War II*. New York: Penguin Putnam, 2003.

———. *The Story of the Boeing Company*. San Francisco: AGS Book-Works, 2005. Reprint, Minneapolis: Zenith Press, 2010.

Yenne, Bill and Robert Redding. *Boeing: Planemaker to the World*. New York: Random House, 1989. First published 1983, Crown.

Zhukov, Georgi K. *The Memoirs of Marshal Zhukov*. New York: Delacorte, 1971.

INDEX

Eniwetok, 238
Enola Gay, 254
Escuadrón 201, 260–61
Eureka Conference, 163–71
Europe
   and airpower, 19, 29, 33
   Allied air superiority in, 149, 180, 203
   buildup to World War II in, 61, 63, 65,
      71
   Charles Lindbergh and, 73–74
   isolation of England from, 11
   Operation Overlord and, 149, 180
   Operation Sledgehammer and, 94
   in the postwar era, 248, 259–60, 262
   U.S. military leadership in, 100, 106–
      7, 155–58, 172–75, 188, 209, 220,
      225–26
   U.S. resources in, 155
   victory in, 219, 221, 233, 251
   weather in, 125, 182
   World War I and, 29–32
   World War II and, 71, 92, 100, 128–29,
      180
European Theater of Operations (ETO),
   183, 200, 228, 259, 279
   Operation Overlord and the, 164
   support of Pacific Theater by the, 228,
      233, 245, 257
   U.S. forces in the, 100, 104, 106, 110,
      113, 158, 211–13, 225–26, 264
Executive Order 9082, 86

F

Fairbanks, Alaska, 59, 61–62, 73, 145
Fairchild SAM-N-2, 283
Fairfield Air Depot, 51
Far East Air Forces (FEAF), 87, 205–6,
   213, 234, 240
Farley, Jim, 55
Fechet, James, 47, 51
Federal Reserve System, 128
Fédération Aéronautique Internationale
   (FAI), 20–21
Fi 103s, 191
"Field, the," 18–19
Fieseler Fi 103, 191. *See also* "Buzz
   Bombs," "Doodlebugs," drones, V-1
   missile

Fiji, 114
Filho, Joaquim Pedro Salgado, 228
First Balkan War, 23
First Unitarian Church (Philadelphia),
   26
Florence, Italy, 226
Flying Tigers, 136
Flynn, Errol, 53
Focke Wulf Fw 190, 176
Foggia, Italy, 174, 182
Força Aérea Brasileira, 141, 228, 259
Foreign Legion, the, 76
Fort Apache, 8
Fort Crook, 8
Fort Custer, 8
Fort Donelson, 129
Fort Henry, 129
Fort Irwin, 193
Fort Jay, 10
Fort Leavenworth, 51, 286
Fort McKinley, 27, 240
Fort Myer, 22, 76, 96
Fort Riley, 8
Fort Stotsenburg, 241
Fort Thomas, 26
Fort William McKinley, 9, 27, 240, 254,
   290
Fort Wingate, 8
Foulois, Benjamin ("Benny"), 16, 55, 57,
   60
France
   Allied invasion of, 128–29, 147–48,
      169, 179–190, 199, 202
   appeasement by, 65, 68–69
   use of U.S. supplies by, 69–72, 71, 75
   in World War I, 29, 32–34, 288
   in World War II, 74–75, 145, 156, 181,
      187–89, 256
Frankfurt, 43
Frankfurt, Germany, 222–23
Frederick the Great, 116, 247
Freed, James Ingo, 290
Free French Forces, 123
Freemasonry, 50, 80
French army, 31, 74
Fuerza Aérea Mexicana, the, 260–61
Führer. *See* Hitler, Adolf
Fulton, Missouri, 262